Criticism and
Medieval Poetry

Criticism and Medieval Poetry

2nd edition

A. C. Spearing

Fellow of Queens' College, Cambridge
and University Lecturer in English

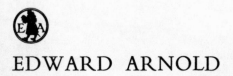

EDWARD ARNOLD

First Edition published 1964 by
Edward Arnold (Publishers) Ltd.,
25 Hill Street, London W1X 8LL

Second Edition first published 1972

Cloth edition ISBN 0 7131 5631 7
Paper edition ISBN 0 7131 5632 5

Printed in Great Britain by Latimer Trend,
Millstrood Road, Whitstable, Kent

Preface

The aims of this book are explained in chapter 1.

A word about the texts quoted: the editions followed are referred to in the notes at the foot of each page, but I have felt free to normalize spelling (removing ȝ and þ, regularizing the use of *u* and *v*, and so on) without comment. I have also altered punctuation where this seemed necessary. Translations are my own, except where otherwise stated. Professor F. R. D. Goodyear has kindly suggested some improvement in my translations from Erasmus and Vives.

Some parts of this book have been published elsewhere in different forms. Chapter 7 has appeared in *Speculum*, and part of chapter 5 in *The Journal of English and Germanic Philology*. I am grateful to the editors of these journals for permission to reprint the relevant passages.

I am grateful to the late Professor C. S. Lewis, Professor Bruce Dickins, and Professor Donald Davie for reading and commenting on various parts of the book, and to Professor Lewis also for much kindly help when I began to study *Piers Plowman* under his direction. To Professor Elizabeth Salter I owe an inestimable debt for her enthusiastic instruction, help, and encouragement since I was first a student at Cambridge. None of those who have helped me are of course responsible for any errors in my writing.

This book was originally published in 1964. For this second edition it has been revised throughout, to take account of the more recent work of others and of my own further thoughts. Chapter 4 is completely new, and so are many paragraphs in other chapters. I am most grateful to the publishers for the efficiency and speed with which they produced the first edition, and for the tolerance they have extended to my shilly-shallying in the matter of preparing a second edition.

Cambridge, September 1971

v

Contents

Suggestions for Reading

The following list includes books and articles which in my opinion are likely to offer the reader help in thinking about the problems of medieval literary criticism and criticism of medieval poetry with which this book is concerned. It also includes a few outstanding examples of modern critical analysis of medieval poetry.

E. Auerbach, *Mimesis*, trans. W. R. Trask (Princeton, 1953); and 'Figura', trans. R. Manheim, in his *Scenes from the Drama of European Literature* (New York, 1959)

L. D. Benson, *Art and Tradition in Sir Gawain and the Green Knight* (New Brunswick, 1965)

J. A. Burrow, *A Reading of Sir Gawain and the Green Knight* (London, 1965); and *Ricardian Poetry* (London, 1971)

Th.-M. Charland, *Artes praedicandi* (Paris and Ottawa, 1936)

H. J. Chaytor, *From Script to Print* (Cambridge, 1945)

Ruth Crosby, 'Oral Delivery in the Middle Ages', *Speculum IX* (1936), 88–110

E. R. Curtius, *European Literature and the Latin Middle Ages*, trans. W. R. Trask (New York, 1953)

E. de Bruyne, *Études d'esthétique médiévale* (Bruges, 1946)

Dorothy Everett, 'Some Reflections on Chaucer's "Art Poetical" ', in her *Essays on Middle English Literature* (Oxford, 1955)

E. Faral, *Les arts poétiques du XIIe et du XIIIe siècle* (Paris, 1924)

G. Henderson, *Gothic* (Harmondsworth, 1967)

R. M. Jordan, *Chaucer and the Shape of Creation* (Cambridge, Mass., 1967)

R. L. Lawrence, 'The Formulaic Theory and its Application to English Alliterative Poetry', in *Essays on Style and Language*, ed. R. Fowler (London, 1966)

A. B. Lord, *The Singer of Tales* (Cambridge, Mass., 1960)

M. McLuhan, *The Gutenberg Galaxy* (London, 1962)

J. J. Murphy, *Three Medieval Rhetorical Arts* (Chicago, 1971)

C. Muscatine, *Chaucer and the French Tradition* (Berkeley, 1956)

E. Panofsky, *Gothic Architecture and Scholasticism* (London, 1957)

M. Parry, 'Studies in the Epic Technique of Oral Verse-Making: I. Homer and Homeric Style', *Harvard Studies in Classical Philology*, XLI (1930), 73–147

R. O. Payne, *The Key of Remembrance* (New Haven, 1963)

D. A. Pearsall, 'Rhetorical "Descriptio" in *Sir Gawain and the Green Knight*', *Modern Language Review*, L (1955), 129–34.

Elizabeth Salter, *Chaucer: The Knight's Tale and the Clerk's Tale* (London, 1962)

E. Vinaver, Introduction to *The Works of Sir Thomas Malory*, 2nd edn. (Oxford, 1967)

1   *Problems for the Critic*

Probably the greatest advance in method made by literary criticism in this century has been the development of techniques for the detailed analysis of literary texture. As a result of this development, which has taken place over the last fifty years or so, we have now reached a position where the approach to literature most commonly taken up by British and American critics has become one that is variously called 'critical analysis' or 'practical criticism' or simply 'close reading.' This approach involves a minute scrutiny of the verbal detail of works of literature, and the scrutiny is designed to bring out certain effects in particular. Among the effects most often commented on are imagery, subtleties of rhythm, variations in tone, onomatopoeic effects and other devices which evoke the world of physical objects and movements, and puns and other forms of wordplay. What is especially sought after in literature is 'concreteness' of texture—the evocation or re-creation in words of sensory perceptions and bodily movements. This approach to literature is based on the assumption, whether or not this is stated, that the distinctive qualities of a complete literary work will be present and detectable locally in its verbal detail, so that this detail can be used to support more general statements about the work. Anyone who has done even a little reading in literary criticism written since the nineteen-twenties will know roughly what is meant by 'close reading,' and so perhaps it will be better not to attempt to describe the method any further, but simply to give a few examples of it in operation, taken from the works of some influential twentieth-century critics. The first example is taken from an essay by Dr F. R. Leavis; he is commenting on some lines from *Macbeth*:

> All our service,
> In every point twice done, and then done double,
> Were poor and single business to contend
> Against those honours deep and broad wherewith
> Your majesty loads our house.

This is an ordinary piece of mature Shakespeare. That is, without exemplifying the more remarkable Shakespearean complexity, it has the life and body which are the pervasive manifestation of Shakespeare's genius in his verse. The effect of concreteness—of being, we might say, 'realized' and not merely verbal—depends above all on the implicit metaphor introduced with 'deep and broad.' Those adjectives, plainly, describe a river, and, whether we tell ourselves so or not, the presence of a river makes itself felt in the effect of the passage, giving a physical quality to 'contend,' in the third line, that it would not otherwise have had. Prompted by 'honours' Shakespeare has, in the apprehensive rapidity of his mind, picked up the conventional trope of the king's being the 'fount of honour,' and, characteristically, in his rapid motion, brought it to life—its life, which is a matter of its organic relation to the context, being manifested in the very absence of explicitness. It is this absence of explicitness in the metaphor—of full realization, one might put it—that conditions the hardly noticeable shift to the metaphor of 'loads' in the next line: the common effect of being borne down by overwhelming profusion covers the shift.[1]

The second example is an analysis by Professor William Empson of a stanza from George Herbert's poem *Pilgrimage*:

> That led me to the wild of Passion, which
> > Some call the wold:
> A wasted place, but sometimes rich.
> Here I was robbed of all my gold,
> Save one good Angel, which a friend had tied
> > Close to my side.

Angel, of course, is a pun on the name of a coin; *wild* and *wold* seem, as Herbert pronounced them, to have been puns on 'willed' and 'would.' The most striking thing about the verse is its tone, prosaic, arid, without momentum, whose contrast with the feeling and experience conveyed gives a prophetic importance to this flat writing; there is the same even-voiced understatement in the language of the Gospels. This is made possible because, in the apparent story, he adopts the manner of a traveller, long afterwards, mentioning where he has been and what happened to him, as if only to pass the time. Several pretty devices carry this out,

[1] F. R. Leavis, *Education and the University*, rev. edn. (London, 1948), p. 77.

particularly in the word *good*, by which the traveller means, as in
'my good sword,' 'a thoroughly useful piece of gold,' while the
mystic, actually meaning 'holy,' uses it as a distinguishing mark:
'I mean the good angel, not the bad one, of the two that accompany
a man.' *Passion*, in the apparent story a proper name which
insists on the allegory, has a wide range of meanings, such as an
irritated lack of patience, the loves of the flesh, and the ambitions
at Court which he had abandoned; nor is it easy to map out
its underground connections, by opposites, with the *Passion* of
Christ. . . .[2]

Finally, a third example is taken from a reading of Keats's *Ode on a
Grecian Urn* by the American critic, Professor Cleanth Brooks:

> Who are these coming to the sacrifice?
>   To what green altar, O mysterious priest,
> Lead'st thou that heifer lowing at the skies,
>   And all her silken flanks with garlands drest?
> What little town by river or sea shore,
>   Or mountain-built with peaceful citadel,
>   Is emptied of this folk, this pious morn?
> And, little town, thy streets for evermore
>   Will silent be; and not a soul to tell
>   Why thou art desolate, can e'er return.

We are not told to what god's altar the procession moves, nor
the occasion of the sacrifice. Moreover, the little town from
which the celebrants come is unknown; and the poet rather goes
out of his way to leave us the widest possible option in locating it.
It may be a mountain town, or a river town, or a tiny seaport. . . .
The poet is willing to leave much to our imaginations; and yet
the stanza in its organization of imagery and rhythm does describe
the town clearly enough; it is small, it is quiet, its people are
knit together as an organic whole, and on a 'pious morn' such
as this, its whole population has turned out to take part in the
ritual.

The stanza has been justly admired. Its magic of effect defies
reduction to any formula. Yet, without pretending to 'account'
for the effect in any mechanical fashion, one can point to some of

[2] William Empson, *Seven Types of Ambiguity*, 3rd edn. (London, 1953), pp.
129–30. The analysis continues for a further two paragraphs, but enough has
been quoted to illustrate its method.

the elements active in securing the effect: there is the suggestive-
ness of the word 'green' in 'green altar'—something natural,
spontaneous, living; there is the suggestion that the little town is
caught in a curve of the seashore, or nestled in a fold of the moun-
tains—at any rate, is something secluded and something naturally
related to its terrain; there is the effect of the phrase 'peaceful
citadel,' a phrase which involves a clash between the ideas of
war and peace and resolves it in the sense of stability and independence without imperialistic ambition—the sense of stable
repose.[3]

It must be emphasized that what is illustrated by these examples
is only a method, not the further ends which the method may serve.
These ends will vary from one critic to another, so that the passages
quoted cannot be taken to represent at all fully the purposes of their
authors. Professor Empson, it is true, is often interested in texture
for its own sake, as the phrase 'several pretty devices' suggests. But
in Dr Leavis's case the analysis of 'complexity,' 'concreteness,'
'realization,' operates in the service of a moral critique for which
'maturity' is a key term; while Professor Brooks's aim is to illustrate from various examples his view that the language of poetry is
always a language of paradox. Moreover, the critical method displayed in these extracts is not by any means something that belongs
solely to our own century. For example, Coleridge, whose work has
been widely and sometimes deeply influential on modern critics,
can be found using the very phrase 'practical criticism' in chapter XV
of *Biographia Literaria*; and elsewhere in the same work, and in his
notebooks, he carries out brief but genuine pieces of close reading.
Even Johnson, most generalizing of critics, offers in number 168 of
The Rambler a brilliant analysis of some lines in *Macbeth* in which he
contrasts the force of the ideas with what seems to him the imperfec-
tion of the diction. But this is an exception to prove the rule:
Johnson *could* carry out the most perceptive close reading if he
wished, but he was not normally interested in doing so. On the
whole, before the twenties and thirties of this century, the great
literary critics paid little conscious attention to the local texture of
their subject-matter: they must of course have been unconsciously
affected by it in their reading, but one will search almost in vain

[3] Cleanth Brooks, *The Well Wrought Urn* (London, 1949), pp. 147-8.

through the work of Dryden or Johnson or Arnold or even of
T. S. Eliot for examples of detailed verbal analysis. Nowadays
the situation is very different. The twentieth-century masters of
critical analysis—those quoted above, for example—have become
extraordinarily influential in their own lifetimes, and, like many
pioneers, they have attracted a swarm of inferior imitators, in whose
hands critical analysis has become a merely mechanical process, an
obsessive cataloguing of instances of ambiguity or concreteness.
What was once a fresh approach to literature has become the
commonplace of a thousand English lessons; and we have begun
to be aware that the concentration of attention on verbal detail has
often led to a neglect of the larger and simpler patternings of
narrative and argument. But for all this, the development of critical
analysis is emphatically not something to be regretted. It has had
many beneficial effects: it has cleared away much vague generality
from critical discussion, and it has made readers more sensitive than
ever before to the very taste and feel of literature, by enabling them to
see how a writer's distinctive vision may be expressed even in the
minutest details of his work, as well as in its larger outlines. These
beneficial effects, however, have not yet been felt in the criticism of
medieval literature, because the method of close reading has not so
far penetrated into that field. So far as medieval literature is concerned, we do not need reminding of the importance of narrative
and argument, but rather of the importance of stylistic detail, for
the criticism of medieval literature is still largely in a pre-twentieth-
century phase. This is so even in the work of critics who have shown
themselves most eager to apply to medieval authors approaches
that have proved fruitful when applied to more recent literature.
One might mention, for example, the work of Mr John Speirs.
Mr Speirs is a declared admirer of Dr Leavis, and his book *Chaucer
the Maker*[4] contains much that seems to have been arrived at by the
application of ideas of Dr Leavis's to Chaucer. It also contains much
lengthy quotation, involving a far closer reference to the texts
discussed than would probably have been found in a nineteenth-
century critical work; but there is still hardly anything that can be
called close reading. One of the aims of the present book will be to

---

[4] (London, 1951.) Mr Speirs acknowledges his 'inestimable debt to the work
of a great critic, Mr Leavis' (p. 9).

see how far the technique of close reading can be of service in a critical approach to medieval literature. There are various reasons why this technique has not been much used by critics of medieval literature—various qualities of medieval literature itself that have made it seem inapplicable—and we shall have to look at some of these. This will naturally lead us to consider medieval *ideas* about literature and the ways in which they differ from modern ideas, and to enquire how far they can be of service to the modern reader of medieval authors. But it will be more convenient to leave our discussion of medieval literary theories to later chapters, and to start with a survey of certain ways in which the literature itself differs from more recent literature, in its techniques of expression and in the relationship with its public that governs those techniques. Such a survey may in any case be useful as an introduction, since most people come to medieval writers with their ideas of what literature is like already formed (probably without their being aware of it) from a reading of works written between the age of Shakespeare and the present. These are the works to which close reading provides an effective method of entrance, and we must begin by considering what are the obstacles to the close reading of medieval literature. First we must mention the largest and most obvious of these.

Close reading of the kind we have been discussing clearly depends for its success on a delicate response to fine shades of meaning and tone. We may find that such a response comes naturally to us in reading the writers of our own age, because their language is ours; and we may even find that it is possible, though hardly easy, with literature going as far back as the age of Shakespeare. But to achieve such a response towards literature even older than that seems almost impossibly difficult, simply because of the barrier of language. The great period of medieval English literature—the fourteenth century —lies too far back in the past for us to be able to catch more than the dictionary definitions of most words; and there are still some of which we do not know even the dictionary definitions. By a long study of medieval literature (not only English, but also the Latin, French, and Italian sources of English) we may be able to supply something of that aura of association and suggestion which fills in the 'meaning' of a word for those who speak and hear it. And the situation may be more favourable than it appears, because fortunately to read great literature is often itself the best way of understanding the values of the dead civilization that produced it—great literature being the form of language in which words have the fullest and most exact meaning. It is perhaps *only* by reading great literary works that we shall come to grasp the meaning of words such as *curtesye, gentillesse,* or *fraunchise*—key terms, standing for some of the central ideas in the ethical and social thought of medieval Europe. But there remains a great host of words and phrases in medieval English which we may understand in the sense that we can provide a rough modern equivalent for them, but which we cannot be said to understand at all if by 'understanding' we mean that intimate and immediate response which more recent writing can evoke in the sensitive reader. All too often it may happen that what seems an intelligent response, one alert to tone and connotation, is in fact simply mistaken. A minor example may make this clearer. In *Sir Gawain and the Green Knight,* when the Green Knight comes riding arrogantly into Arthur's hall as the New Year's feast is about to begin, he looks high over the heads of the assembled lords and ladies, and the poet tells us that his first words are 'Wher is . . . the governour of this gyng?' We probably recognize the connection of *gyng* with our modern *gang,* we respond to the alliteration and perhaps to the modern slang sense of the word *governor* ('boss'), and so we are likely to think admiringly that the poet has achieved a wonderfully contemptuous turn of phrase, which exactly suggests the Knight's curl of the lip as he speaks it. Certainly it seems as if here the poet speaks directly to us, and we read him as we should read a contemporary. But if we now turn to two other poems found in the same manuscript as *Sir Gawain and the Green Knight,* written in the same dialect, and usually thought to be by the same poet, we shall begin to have doubts. For in *Pearl* the word *gyng* is used to refer to the company of the blessed virgins in heaven (*Pearl,* l. 455), while in *Patience* the word *governour* is used as an alternative to *god* (*Patience,* l. 199: the sailors ask Jonah as he sleeps through the storm, 'Has thou, gome, no governour ne god on to calle?'). Though attractive, this mistake is one that can be corrected; but we can only guess at the number of similarly mistaken responses that we do not notice and cannot correct.

This is a discouraging thought, and it is no doubt with this in mind that medievalists have generally steered clear of close reading. But, provided one is aware of the difficulty, and approaches the texture of medieval literature with a suitable tentativeness, it may be that close reading of a kind remains possible. Sometimes indeed it can be critical analysis of a perfectly familiar kind: the critic can sometimes call our attention to 'concreteness' of texture, or indicate how a medieval poet presents his meaning directly and dramatically through the interaction of sensuous images. Consider for instance the following lines from a late work of Chaucer's, the *Prologue* to *The Legend of Good Women*:

> Forgeten hadde the erthe his pore estat
> Of wynter, that hym naked made and mat,
> And with his swerd of cold so sore greved;
> Now hath th'atempre sonne all that releved
> That naked was, and clad him new agayn.
>
> (Text F, ll. 125–9)[5]

Here Chaucer is treating a completely traditional medieval theme, the return of spring after winter, and the imagery through which he presents this theme is itself traditional. The image of winter as a state of poverty suffered by the earth and then forgotten as soon as spring arrives, and the image of spring as providing the earth with new clothes, are both found in the French *Roman de la Rose*, which Chaucer had translated into English earlier in his career as a poet.[6] His version of the relevant lines had then run:

> And the erthe wexith proud withalle,
> For swote dewes that on it falle,
> And the pore estat forget
> In which that wynter had it set.
> And than bycometh the ground so proud
> That it wole have a newe shroud.
>
> (*Romaunt of the Rose*,
> ll. 59–64)

[5] This and all subsequent Chaucer quotations are taken from *The Complete Works of Geoffrey Chaucer*, ed. F. N. Robinson, rev. edn. (Cambridge [Mass.], 1957).

[6] The Middle English translation of the *Roman de la Rose* is not wholly, and may not be even partly, by Chaucer. It seems most likely that the passage quoted is genuinely Chaucerian, but my main argument is unaffected if it is not. We know that Chaucer wrote *a* translation of the *Roman de la Rose*.

It will be seen that in rehandling this passage for *The Legend of Good Women* Chaucer made it at once more complex and more compressed. In the *Romaunt of the Rose* version one image is succeeded by another, and then the first—that of the earth's pride—is repeated and expanded. But in *The Legend of Good Women* version we find not so much a succession of images as a fusion of images. The 'pore estat' of winter is developed further by the mention of nakedness, and then it merges rapidly into the 'swerd of cold,' and this in turn merges into the clothing image; and the point of view, or rather centre of activity, moves from the earth to winter and from winter to the sun. The poetry is of a kind which we might not unjustly call Shakespearean: its richness of texture is achieved by the rapid running together—the telescoping even—of a number of diverse images. But there is not merely diversity in the passage: as in the passage from *Macbeth* discussed above by Dr Leavis, the metaphorical complexity is unified by a single underlying image, an image which is submerged at first, and then comes to the surface in a pun. Mr Speirs, in commenting on the longer passage from *The Legend of Good Women* in which these lines occur, implies that its chief associations are pagan: he mentions 'the triumph of spring over winter immemorially celebrated in the annual dramatic rituals.'[7] But in fact the underlying reference here is to something which would have been much more familiar to Chaucer's audience, though it is perhaps less exciting for us: the Christian duty of relieving the poor and clothing the naked. The earth has been reduced by winter to a state of poverty and nakedness, but now the sun, like a charitable rich man, has 'releved' all that was naked and given the earth new clothing. And *releved* surely has a double meaning: the sun has relieved the naked trees by re-leaving them—covering them with a new dress of leaves. Here, it may be added, we begin to tread on dangerous ground, for, although *leave* in this sense exists in Middle English, the earliest example of *re-leave* given by the *Oxford English Dictionary* is as late as the seventeenth century. Moreover, the -ē- of *releved* meaning 'relieved' would have been close, while that of *releved* meaning 're-leaved' would have been open. It is thus difficult to be certain whether the pun we have just detected would have been possible for Chaucer

[7] *Chaucer the Maker*, p. 88.

or not: it may be simply an attractive illusion, like the contemptuous ring of 'governour of this gyng.' But whether or not the pun is really there, I believe I have indicated the general poetic method of the passage, and that it can properly be called Shakespearean in kind, though of course not necessarily in quality. And one can find similar poetry elsewhere in Middle English literature: let me quote as an example a line of Langland's about love, and a comment upon it by Mr D. A. Traversi. The line is: 'Tho was it portatyf and pershaunt as the poynt of a nelde' (Text C, II. 154). Mr Traversi comments: 'The effect of "pershaunt," preceded by "portatyf" and followed by "as the poynt of a nedle" is not so inferior to Hamlet's "bare bodkin"; it is certainly of the same kind, and depends upon a similar keen intensity of perception.'[8] Now this kind of poetry—the kind that depends for its effect on the unification of diverse sense-impressions—is precisely the kind that modern criticism has made most familiar to us. I have called it Shakespearean, but it is also a kind of poetry that we find in the work of Donne, Pope, Keats, or Hopkins—poets with whom twentieth-century critical analysis seems to have been most at home. We possess the right critical tools for appreciating this sort of poetic effect, and when it occurs in Middle English verse it is easy enough for Mr Traversi or me to point it out. But it cannot be said that poetic effects of this kind are really at all common in Middle English: they are rare even in Chaucer, and they are extremely rare in Langland, and indeed one might suggest that Mr Traversi's choice of that particular line from *Piers Plowman* for admiring comment and Shakespearean comparison is more a sign of what he is at home with as a critic than of what is most characteristic of Langland as a poet. I wish now to examine another and rather longer passage from Chaucer, which seems to me to contain a kind of poetry much more typical of Middle English. The greater length is significant, for reasons to be considered later. After that, I hope we shall be in a better position to see what the modern literary critic's problems are when he is faced with the typically medieval.

The passage I wish to look at is taken from one of Chaucer's earlier works, *The Book of the Duchess*. This poem was written as an elegy on the death of Blanche, Duchess of Lancaster, the first wife of John of Gaunt; and, unusually, it is an elegy in the form of

[8] From *The Age of Chaucer*, ed. Boris Ford (Harmondsworth, 1954), p. 143.

a dream. In considering this passage (lines 387–442 of the poem) it will be important to bear in mind its function in the work as a whole. It is a transitional passage, in which the Dreamer, the 'I' of the poem, passes out of the early stage of his dream—a fairly light-hearted hunting scene—into the main body of the dream, a much more serious section in which he meets a 'man in blak,' who is lamenting the loss of his lady and who presumably stands for John of Gaunt himself.

> I was go walked fro my tree, 387
> And as I wente, ther cam by mee
> A whelp, that fauned me as I stood,
> That hadde yfolowed, and koude no good. 390
> Hyt com and crepte to me as lowe
> Ryght as hyt hadde me yknowe,
> Helde doun hys hed and joyned hys eres,
> And leyde al smothe doun hys heres.
> I wolde have kaught hyt, and anoon 395
> Hyt fledde, and was fro me goon;
> And I hym folwed, and hyt forth wente
> Doun by a floury grene wente
> Ful thikke of gras, ful softe and swete,
> With floures fele, faire under fete, 400
> And litel used, hyt semed thus;
> For both Flora and Zephirus,
> They two that make floures growe,
> Had mad her dwellynge ther, I trowe;
> For hit was, on to beholde, 405
> As thogh the erthe envye wolde
> To be gayer than the heven,
> To have moo floures, swiche seven,
> As in the welken sterres bee.
> Hyt had forgete the povertee 410
> That wynter, thorgh hys colde morwes,
> Had mad hyt suffre, and his sorwes,
> All was forgeten, and that was sene.
> For al the woode was waxen grene;
> Swetnesse of dew had mad hyt waxe. 415
> Hyt ys no nede eke for to axe
> Wher there were many grene greves,
> Or thikke of trees, so ful of leves;
> And every tree stood by hymselve
> Fro other wel ten foot or twelve. 420

So grete trees, so huge of strengthe,
Of fourty or fifty fadme lengthe,
Clene withoute bowgh or stikke,
With croppes brode, and eke as thikke—
They were nat an ynche asonder—   425
That hit was shadewe overal under.
And many an hert and many an hynde
Was both before me and behynde.
Of founes, sowres, bukkes, does
Was ful the woode, and many roes,   430
And many sqwirelles, that sete
Ful high upon the trees and ete,
And in hir maner made festes.
Shortly, hyt was so ful of bestes,
That thogh Argus, the noble countour,   435
Sete to rekene in hys countour,
And rekened with his figures ten—
For by tho figures mowe al ken,
Yf they be crafty, rekene and noumbre,
And telle of every thing the noumbre—   440
Yet shoulde he fayle to rekene even
The wondres me mette in my sweven.

The first thing in this passage to catch the attention of a modern
reader will probably be the extremely vivid description of the
puppy. It gives the impression of being based on observation of a
real puppy, and we may be tempted to admire it simply as one of
those pieces of charming but extraneous 'realism' that are often
supposed to be typical of Chaucer. In particular we may be tempted
to think of it as what one might call a bit of 'late Chaucer' occurring
incongruously in the work of the early Chaucer. To admire it in this
way, though, is simply to dismiss it from the poem: we have to try
to see why Chaucer put it there. Realistic though it is, it is influenced
by certain literary sources—passages from works by the French poet
Guillaume Machaut, whom Chaucer often follows closely in *The
Book of the Duchess*. Thus Chaucer can hardly have put the description
in the poem simply because he had noticed a puppy's behaviour in
real life. It seems in fact to have a double function in the poem. The
unusually detailed descriptive technique arouses our attention so as
to suggest that now at last the poem is going to come to its main

point; a necessary device, because the preliminaries in *The Book of the Duchess* are particularly lengthy, though they eventually turn out to be perfectly relevant. And secondly this little dog continues the very theme of hunting that it seems to interrupt. The Dreamer has seen huntsmen and hounds, and now here is a miniature hunting hound, and the Dreamer as he follows it into the forest is embarking on a new hunt of his own. It is noticeable how at this point Chaucer speeds up the verse: the sudden flurry of action as the Dreamer tries to catch the puppy but has to chase after it is expressed through the breathless short sentences connected with *and*'s:

> I wolde have kaught hyt, *and* anoon
> Hyt fledde, *and* was fro me goon;
> *And* I hym folwed, *and* hyt forth wente. . . .   (395)

A decisive break has occurred, and now the pace slows again: the texture of sound is thickened in a way which suggests the richness and lushness of the forest without the use of any detailed description:

> Ful thikke of gras, *f*ul *so*ft*e* and swete,
> With *f*loures *f*ele, *f*aire under *f*ete.   (399)

The verse of this whole passage is generally lacking in imagery, except for a few similes of the simplest kind, and its sound-effects and rhythmic effects are also simple; there is very little enjambment in it, and very little verse that imitates action or sound. Now just as, within the basic regularity of an Augustan poem in heroic couplets, minute variations in rhythm stand out with unexpected force, so here, in the context of simplicity of sound, the thick alliteration of the lines just quoted stands out more vividly than it would elsewhere. In the next few lines we come upon something very characteristic of this passage and indeed of the poem as a whole: the narrator inserts an explanation that appears childish or garrulous or both:

> For both Flora and Zephirus,
> They two that make floures growe. . . .   (402)

The explanation seems superfluous; only a rather naive narrator could suppose it necessary. The same thing occurs a little later:

> For al the woode was waxen grene;
> Swetnesse of dew had mad hyt waxe.   (414)

There is a charmingly childish confidentiality in that last line. And
once again, towards the end of the passage, we have a similar and
longer explanation about 'Argus, the noble countour' (Chaucer is
referring to an Arabic mathematician, usually called Algus). The
narrator explains the decimal system with an enthusiasm which
seems naive (though it would have seemed less so in the fourteenth
century):

> For by tho figures mowe al ken,
> Yf they be crafty, rekene and noumbre,
> And telle of every thing the noumbre.   (438)

However, it may be necessary to remind ourselves that this naive,
childlike Dreamer is not Chaucer himself; he is, as G. L. Kittredge
has pointed out, 'a purely imaginary figure, to whom certain
purely imaginary things happen, in a purely imaginary dream . . . .
This childlike Dreamer, who never reasons, but only feels and gets
impressions . . . is not Geoffrey Chaucer, the humorist and man of the
world. He is a creature of the imagination, and his childlikeness is
part of his dramatic character.'[9] The Dreamer here, as in other
medieval dream-poems, is not the poet himself, but a mask or
persona of the poet; and he is deliberately presented as naive and
childlike so that he will be able to ask the man in black a series of
naive and childlike questions. This will permit the man in black to
unburden his heart by answering them, and will also permit
Chaucer to include in the poem, as part of his answers, a suitably
idealized vision of Blanche and of John of Gaunt's love for her. To
this naive Dreamer the world of his dream is one of endless 'wonders.'
This is the point he is making at the very end of the passage under
discussion, and which he also makes at various other places in the
poem. Through him, we are enabled to enter a world which has
the clarity and strangeness of a fairytale, and yet one which includes,
as fairytales often do, death and misery along with its wish-fulfilling
wonders. The bitter facts of death and human grief are absorbed
into a 'wonderful' fiction, so that John of Gaunt, and we, may be
reconciled to them. For the Dreamer the forest is enchanted, and so
it becomes enchanted for us. This enchantment is expressed most
fully in the almost anthropomorphic way in which the Dreamer

[9] *Chaucer and His Poetry* (Cambridge [Mass.], 1915), pp. 48 and 50.

sees the forest. Everything in it is quivering with an almost human life of its own. We have seen one example of this in the idea that the flowers do not just grow of their own accord or automatically—they are *made* to grow by Flora and Zephirus. Another example occurs further on in some lines which the reader will probably have recognized as once again making use of the *Roman de la Rose* passage about the poverty of winter and how it is forgotten in spring:

> Hyt had forgete the povertee
> That wynter, thorgh his colde morwes,
> Had mad hyt suffre, and his sorwes,
> All was forgeten, and that was sene.   (410)

In the *Legend of Good Women* version of this material, the metaphor of the earth's poverty was part of a sophisticated poetic texture; here it stands out from its simpler background as something to be taken as the Dreamer's literal belief. Because he keeps to the single image, instead of fusing several images together, the *Book of the Duchess* narrator makes us accept the personification of the earth more literally. And this giving of a life to the forest is completed when the Dreamer goes on to describe the actual trees:

> And every tree stood by hymselve
> Fro other wel ten foot or twelve.
> So grete trees, so huge of strengthe. . . .   (419)

The trees are presented as if they were giants on parade, each 'standing by himself.' Finally, when the beasts are described, we see that the forest is crammed with other lives as well as its own. The swarming creatures, part of the infinite plenitude of Nature, are semi-humanized:

> And many sqwirelles, that sete
> Ful high upon the trees and ete,
> And in hir maner made festes.   (431)

But only *semi*-humanized: they hold feasts *in hir maner*—in their own way, not our way. The Dreamer is giving himself up to a power outside himself.

This passage, then, has above all the effect of preparation or

initiation. The Dreamer is moving away from the superficially
meaningless fantasy with which his dream began into a more
serious region of the imagination. As he moves deeper and deeper
into the forest, in pursuit of the puppy, he does not simply pass
through a piece of natural scenery, described charmingly but
conventionally and in general terms; he passes into a realm quivering
with its own significance, a more sombre realm—'hit was shadewe
overal under' (426)—where an important experience is waiting for
him. Immediately after the passage ends, he suddenly comes upon
the man in black for the first time.

I have been trying to show in what way the method of close
reading can be applied to this passage from *The Book of the Duchess*;
but I have been faced with much greater difficulty than in examining
the shorter passage from *The Legend of Good Women*. The heart of
the difficulty seems to be simply that the passage from the *Legend*
is concentrated while that from *The Book of the Duchess* is diffuse.
Every line of the *Legend* passage yields an almost physically palpable
texture, while the poetic effects of *The Book of the Duchess* passage are
spread out over the whole. The 'poetry,' one might say, is not even
noticeable locally; by calling attention to single lines in the passage
I have maltreated it. That is not how it works; its most important
effects are cumulative. The personification of the forest, for example,
as we have seen, is built up only gradually, by one hint after another:
the separate hints are not intended to attract our attention. There is
an important reason why this should be so, a reason which also
explains why *this* is a more typical kind of medieval poetry than the
Shakespearean kind that we found in five lines from *The Legend of
Good Women* and that Mr Traversi found in one line of *Piers
Plowman*. The reason is that most medieval poetry was not written,
like most modern poetry, to be read silently by a private individual
from the printed page; it was written to be read aloud to a communal
audience of listeners. This fact is of course well known,[10] and so are
its causes. The most important causes are, first, that in the Middle
Ages most writers' audiences would contain a high proportion of
illiterate people, and, second, that before the invention of printing

[10] For more detailed discussion, see H. J. Chaytor, *From Script to Print*
(Cambridge, 1945), Ruth Crosby, 'Oral Delivery in the Middle Ages,'
Speculum XI (1936), pp. 88–110, and Marshall McLuhan, *The Gutenberg
Galaxy* (London, 1962), pp. 82ff.

manuscripts were too expensive for most people to be able to afford them, whether they could read or not. It must be added that throughout the medieval period literacy was gradually spreading. In England by the fourteenth century there existed a literate lay public large enough to call for the various vernacular devotional works of that period—those of Rolle, Hilton, and the author of *The Cloud of Unknowing*. Nevertheless, until the very end of the Middle Ages books were usually written to be read aloud to a group; and it takes some effort to recall that precisely this fact puts the twentieth-century literary critic at a severe disadvantage in dealing with medieval literature. The 'reading method' of the modern critic is of course that of the private reader in his armchair, not that of the listener forming one of a group. The twentieth-century critic is well equipped for dissecting the concentrated kind of literature that is normally written for an audience of private readers—readers who are in a position to pause over single lines and words, to compare one part of a work with another, and to reread passages as often as they like or need in order to grasp complexities of meaning. But a medieval listener was in a quite different position from this. He could not go back over something he failed to understand, and he had to be affected by literature immediately or not at all. It was with such a public in mind that the medieval poets had to write. This is not to say, of course, that all medieval literature is simple and lucid. The Provençal poets practised a style called *trobar clus*, which deliberately aimed at obscurity, while much of Dante's work, to take the supreme example of the greatest medieval poet, is extraordinarily difficult. And it is not to say, either, that medieval listeners to a poem were necessarily in the same helpless position that we should be in nowadays if we had to judge a literary work only from hearing it read aloud. Chaucer, for example, was in the first place a court poet, and his original audience would be made up of cultivated people, much more practised than we are in the art of listening, and presumably more competent at it. But, despite all these reservations, the fact is that most medieval English literature was written to have an immediate effect on an audience of listeners. This fact has a number of results observable in the nature of the literature produced. We have noticed some of these in looking at the passage from *The Book of the Duchess*; each presents its problem

to the modern critic, and in the rest of this chapter I propose
to consider them separately. In this way we may be able to see
more clearly what the critic's task is when he is confronted with a
medieval work.

One result we have certainly noticed already; it is simply that the
typical medieval literary work tends to be rather diffuse. We shall
see below, in chapter 3, how medieval theories about literature
encouraged diffuseness, and, in chapter 7, how Chaucer came to be
praised by his readers in the later Middle Ages as a miracle of
conciseness. Chaucer is indeed probably the most concise of medieval
English poets; and yet, compared with more modern poets, he
seems extremely diffuse, especially in early works such as *The Book
of the Duchess*. He had to be diffuse if his listening audience were to
be able to respond to his words. The attention of his audience moves
in a linear fashion, from one verse to the next, with no chance to
compare or contrast; and so at any particular point the texture
must be thin—the poetic effects must be cumulative, extended in
time. This means that the modern critic, to be fair to the poem,
must try to consider long passages as wholes, and not always expect
to find the effect of the whole present locally.

Another result of the fact that medieval literature was orally
delivered is that, as compared with poetry of the age of print, more
of the poet's meaning must be conveyed through the *sounds* of his
verse. These sounds are often those of speech itself. This is noticeable
particularly in alliterative poetry, where the freedom of rhythm
permits of a close approximation to the rhythms of speech. Poems
such as *Sir Gawain and the Green Knight* or *Piers Plowman* are full of
exclamations and interjections—words like 'What!', 'Wy!', 'Lo!',
'Baw!', and so on. The greatest English poets of the fourteenth
century, whether alliterative or not, are masters of dramatic speech;
however magnificent their rhetoric, they fall naturally into the
rhythm and idiom of speech at crucial points in their poems.
The descriptive passage from *The Book of the Duchess* which we
have just been looking at does not illustrate this; but at the heart of
The Book of the Duchess lies a human encounter, expressed in dialogue
between the Dreamer and the man in black, and the climax of the
poem comes in an utterly lifelike interchange of short phrases,
including many exclamations:

Man in Black:	God wot, allas! ryght that was she!
Dreamer:	Allas, sir, how? what may that be?
Man in Black:	She ys ded!
Dreamer:	Nay!
Man in Black:	Yis, be my trouthe!
Dreamer:	Is that youre los? Be God, hyt ys routhe!

(1307–10)

When Chaucer wants to express violent physical action, he normally does so directly through violence of sound. It has often been pointed out how he makes use of alliteration for this purpose; for instance, he describes the fatal tournament in *The Knight's Tale* as follows:

> Ther *sh*yveren *sh*aftes upon *sh*eeldes thikke;
> He feeleth thurgh the herte-spoon the prikke.
> Up *spr*yngen *sp*eres twenty foot on highte;
> Out goon the *s*werdes as the *s*ilver brighte;
> The *h*elmes they to*h*ewen and toshrede;
> Out *br*est the *bl*ood with *st*ierne *st*remes rede;
> With *m*yghty *m*aces the *b*ones they to*br*este.
> He *th*urgh the *th*ikkeste of the *thr*ong gan *thr*este;
> Ther *st*omblen *st*eedes *str*onge, and doun gooth al;
> He rolleth under foot as dooth a bal;
> He *f*oyneth on his *f*eet with his tronchoun,
> And *h*e *h*ym *h*urtleth with *h*is *h*ors adoun.

(*Canterbury Tales*, I 2605–16)

Here the imagery is of the simplest and most conventional—the swords are as bright as silver, an unhorsed knight rolls underfoot like a ball—and there is little dislocation of natural word-order, and no muscular straining of the sense across the gap between one line and the next, such as we might expect to find in a more recent poem. The genius of the passage lies in the selection of incident, the cinematic rapidity of movement between mass effects and individual sufferings (expressed grammatically in the variation between plural and singular forms), and above all in Chaucer's use of the methods of alliterative poetry. He employs the same alliterative technique elsewhere to express a more comic kind of violence, as in the hilarious chase with which *The Nun's Priest's Tale* comes to its conclusion:

> Of *b*ras they *b*roghten *b*emes, and of *b*ox,
> Of horn, of *b*oon, in whiche they *b*lewe and powped,
> And therwithal they skriked and they houped.
>
> (*Canterbury Tales*, VII 3398–400)

Another sign of the importance of sound in medieval literature is
the predominance among verbal effects of the simple repetition of
words and phrases. More will be said about this in chapter 5 below,
with reference to *Piers Plowman*, but it may be briefly illustrated
here by a quotation from the conclusion of Chaucer's *Troilus and
Criseyde*:

> Swich fyn hath, lo, this Troilus for love!
> Swich fyn hath al his grete worthynesse!
> Swich fyn hath his estat real above,
> Swich fyn his lust, swich fyn hath his noblesse!
> Swich fyn hath false worldes brotelnesse! . . .
>
> (V 1828–32)

It would be difficult to imagine a simpler rhetoric than this; though
one must note the art with which the homiletic power of the first
three 'Swich fyn hath's is unexpectedly intensified by the interrupting variation of the fourth line and the resumption of the original
pattern in the fifth. It is clear at least, I think, that this is an oral
rhetoric, and demands reading aloud if it is to be fully appreciated.
Unfortunately, critics of medieval literature are unlikely to be in a
position to have their subject matter read aloud to them.

We now come to a third result of the habit of oral delivery, and
one which is closely connected with the thinness of texture of medieval verse. If an audience of listeners is to be able to respond to a
poem on a single reading of it, not only must its expressive devices
be largely simple, they must also contain a high proportion of the
familiar. In such circumstances a poet cannot afford to be too novel,
too original, too individual in style: he must keep largely within a
stylistic convention which his audience will understand and accept
without consideration. Within the staple conventional idiom there
will of course still be wide scope for a gifted poet to express his
individual vision by gradual shadings, cumulative effects; but not by
a persistent use of sharply individual turns of phrase. If he is to keep
his audience with him, he must usually describe swords as being as

bright as silver, and an unhorsed knight as rolling like a ball. He must aim for much of the time at what Professor I. A. Richards has called 'stock responses';[11] and here again the modern critic is at a disadvantage, for, since Richards' ideas became influential in the nineteen-twenties, it has been one of the expressed or unexpressed assumptions of criticism that 'stock responses' are bad things. We can see a sign of the conventionality of style of medieval literature in the difficulty of distinguishing the work of one writer from another, even where great poets are concerned. For example, it seems quite impossible to tell from the subjective criteria that we should probably use with more recent writers whether *Sir Gawain and the Green Knight* and the three other poems found with it in the same manuscript are really by the same poet or not.[12] Many similarities in phrasing can be found between the four poems, but it is difficult to tell whether these are the mark of a single poet's individual style, or whether they belong to the literary dialect in which all the poems are written. This difficulty is particularly acute with alliterative poetry, and there is a special reason for this which may require explanation. Only in this century has it come to be realized that much of the poetry of largely illiterate peoples is not only orally delivered but also orally composed. What this means is that there is no single correct version of a poem, which is learnt by heart and repeated exactly at every recitation; nor, on the other hand, does the poet compose a completely new poem 'out of his head' on every occasion when a poem is required. The situation is that for a particular tale the poets of an illiterate society will possess in their minds a basic skeleton of plot and scenes, and they will elaborate round this a version composed in response to particular circumstances of delivery. (Thus for some occasions a short version would be more suitable, and for others a long version.) But for this oral composition of poetry to be possible, there must also exist a common pool of poetic material, out of which the particular elaboration will be made up. This pool has been divided by scholars into two categories: 'themes' and 'formulas.' The 'theme' has been defined

[11] See I. A. Richards, *The Principles of Literary Criticism* (London, 1924), pp. 202ff.

[12] In my *The Gawain-Poet* (Cambridge, 1970) I argue in favour of common authorship, largely on grounds of common subject-matter and a common attitude towards it.

by A. B. Lord as 'a subject unit, a group of ideas, regularly employed
by a singer, not merely in any given poem, but in the poetry as a
whole.' Examples from within a particular poetic tradition might
be the arming of a hero, the departure on horseback, the battle with
its traditional weapons and tactics, the storm at sea, the arrival of
strangers, and so on. And Milman Parry, the American scholar
who was a pioneer in this approach to primitive literature, defines the
'formula' as 'a group of words which is regularly employed under the
same metrical conditions to express a given essential idea.'[13] Such
phrases will make up a particular part of the metrical pattern of a
particular kind of verse (for example, a hexameter or an alliterative
half-line), and, to put the matter at its lowest, the poet can use them
without having to think of an individual phrase to express whatever
he is dealing with. This would seem to imply that an ideal assessment
of, say, an English alliterative poem would have to begin with a
critique of the traditional language-apparatus available to all alliterative poets, and could only after that proceed to discuss the use made
of the apparatus in any particular poem. This is perhaps an unattain-
able ideal; but it is certainly the case that an accurate critical reading
of any medieval poem must be based on an ability to recognize and
respond to the 'stock' elements in its language. However, in the
work of the best medieval poets the conventional ways of expression
are modified and extended as well as being repeated; and a highly
sophisticated poet, such as the later Chaucer, may well use conventional elements critically, and expect from his audience an alert
response to the fossilization of convention into cliché.[14] The pioneers
in the development of the concept of formulaic writing argued that
the very fact of its being composed in formulas would enable us to
identify a particular poem as being orally composed. More recently,

[13] Definitions from A. B. Lord, 'Homer and Huso II: Narrative Inconsist-
encies in Homer and Oral Poetry,' *Transactions and Proceedings of the American
Philological Association* LXIX (1938), p. 140, and Milman Parry, 'Studies in the
Epic Technique of Oral Verse-Making: I. Homer and Homeric Style,' *Harvard
Studies in Classical Philology* XLI (1930), p. 80. See also Lord's book, *The
Singer of Tales* (Cambridge, [Mass.] 1960); and, for a critique of the concept
of the formula, H. L. Rogers, 'The Crypto-Psychological Character of the
Oral Formula,' *English Studies* XLVII (1966), pp. 89–102.
[14] E.g. in *The Tale of Sir Thopas*; and see E. T. Donaldson's 'Idiom of
Popular Poetry in *The Miller's Tale*,' recently reprinted in his *Speaking of
Chaucer* (London, 1970).

scholars have come to recognize that the methods of orally composed poetry might continue to be used long after the advent of writing. They would be perpetuated in a culture based on manuscripts and oral delivery by their continuing usefulness for audiences of listeners, even if the poems to which they were listening had their existence in writing. Parry, with Homer in mind, wrote of a 'perfect narrative style, where no phrase, by its wording, stands out by itself to seize the attention of the hearers, and so stop the rapid movement of the thought.'[15] It will be seen how attractive such a style would continue to be to listeners, long after poets had become literate and even bookish. Parry's description excellently fits the style of the extract from *The Book of the Duchess* discussed above; and it is surely remote from any ideal suggested by modern critical analysis.

Now Old English alliterative poetry is highly formulaic, and it was undoubtedly at one stage orally composed. We have no direct evidence of an oral stage in the development of Middle English alliterative poetry, but, despite various differences, it represents essentially a later stage in the Old English tradition, and it retains a considerable formulaic content.[16] What kind of problem this raises for the modern critic can perhaps be made clear by a small example, taken from *Sir Gawain and the Green Knight*. When the lord of the castle (*alias* Sir Bertilak, *alias* the Green Knight) goes out hunting for the third time, his quarry is a fox. When the lord strikes at it with his sword, the fox swerves aside, away from the sharp edge. The poet's words are: 'And he schunt for the scharp, and schulde haf arered' (l. 1902). It has been suggested that in this the fox's behaviour is similar to Gawain's on the third day in the castle;[17] both resort to trickery, and both are undone by it, the fox falling into the hounds' mouths, and Gawain into the hands of his enemy.

[15] *Op. cit.*, p. 124.

[16] For discussion of formulaic elements in Old and Middle English, see F. P. Magoun, 'Oral-Formulaic Character of Anglo-Saxon Narrative Poetry,' *Speculum* XXVIII (1953), pp. 446–67; R. A. Waldron, 'Oral-Formulaic Technique and Middle English Alliterative Poetry,' *Speculum* XXXII (1957), pp. 792–804; R. D. Stevick, 'The Oral-Formulaic Analyses of Old English Verse,' *Speculum* XXXVII (1962), pp. 382–9; and R. F. Lawrence, 'The Formulaic Theory and Its Application to English Alliterative Poetry,' in *Essays on Style and Language*, ed. Roger Fowler (London, 1966), pp. 166–83.

[17] See H. L. Savage, *The Gawain-Poet* (Chapel Hill, 1956), pp. 37–8.

Now when Gawain finally meets the lord again, as the Green Knight at the Green Chapel, he behaves in just the same way as the fox had done when confronted by the same adversary. The Green Knight strikes at him and he swerves aside:

> Bot Gawayn on that giserne glyfte hym bysyde,
> As hit com glydande adoun on glode hym to schende,
> And schranke a lytel with the schulderes for the scharp yrne.
> That other schalk wyth a schunt the schene wythhaldes.
>
> (ll. 2265–68)

There are similarities in phrasing as well as in idea. The words *scharp* and *schunt* occur in both passages, and if one were giving the poem the sort of close reading that might be applied to a more recent work, I think one might argue that the similarity was deliberate and rather subtle. The argument would be that, on coming to the second passage, we are intended to be reminded of the first, and to have the idea recalled to us of Gawain as a fox, not an open-dealing knight. This seems convincing, until we remember the formulaic nature of the poem's style. In both passages the alliteration is on the sound *sch*, and it seems that for the poet the idea of evading a cutting edge is almost automatically expressed in a line alliterating on the words *scharp* and *schunt*. And the formulaic nature of this line is confirmed if we look at another alliterative poem from the same period, the *Morte Arthure*, and find there the same action described with the same alliteration and using the same two words: 'Bot the schalke for the scharpe he schowntes a littille' (l. 3842). It is striking, too, that the words 'schalke' and 'a littille' also occur in the second *Gawain* passage (though not in the first). There is no question here of the two poems being by the same author, or of one imitating the other: it is simply that both are written in the same specialized poetic idiom, and in that idiom the action of swerving aside from a blade is automatically expressed through a specific group of associated words. The lesson to be drawn from this example is not, of course, that we must abstain from any evaluative criticism of alliterative poetry and simply collect and tabulate formulaic systems. It is that, instead of merely blaming a particular poem for being conventional in its language, or praising it for being original, we must investigate what *use* it makes of its convention and try to decide how far it achieves the special kind of originality that may be possible within the bounds of convention.

Finally, I must mention one further effect that the habit of oral delivery has on medieval poetry. This is an effect not on texture but on structure. A long poem, composed to be read aloud, must inevitably, since there are limits to the amount that an audience of listeners can accept at one sitting, be composed to be read aloud *in instalments*. This means that a long work, such as, for instance, Chaucer's *Troilus and Criseyde*, will tend to be constructed less as a single whole than as a series of episodes. Each episode will be developed semi-independently, and we shall be unable to find in the complete work the Aristotelian kind of unity which has a single plot as its centre or 'soul.' There has been a tendency in recent scholarship to see in this sectional method of construction not merely functional necessity but the embodiment of a characteristically 'Gothic' aesthetic. Professor R. M. Jordan has written that 'The typical Chaucerian narrative is literally "built" of inert, self-contained parts, collocated in accordance with the additive, reduplicative principles which characterize the Gothic edifice.'[18] Certainly the medieval visual and plastic arts offer many analogies for a kind of structure which makes it the task of the spectator to synthesize a single meaning, if he can, out of a number of disparate and even mutually opposed parts. One may think of pictures (such as the well-known Wilton Diptych, from Chaucer's time) made out of two or three or more self-contained 'wings'; or of cathedrals, whose cruciform shape and large size make it impossible to take in the whole at once, so that they can be 'seen' only in the form of series of successive and different experiences of mass, space, and light. The very conception of history expressed in medieval typological interpretations of the Bible is not one of continuous, organic development, but of meaning emerging out of the juxtaposition *in the mind* of quite separate events: the sacrifice of Isaac prefiguring that of Christ, or Christ's descent into Hell completing the pattern established by the swallowing of Jonah by the whale.[19] In such cases, as

---

[18] *Chaucer and the Shape of Creation* (Cambridge [Mass.], 1967), p. xi.

[19] See Erich Auerbach, 'Figura,' in his *Scenes from the Drama of European Literature* (New York, 1959). One medieval literary form which was directly shaped by this conception of history was the cycle of 'mystery' or Corpus Christi plays: see V. A. Kolve, *The Play Called Corpus Christi* (London, 1966).

Jordan has written, 'The structural integrity of the part precludes a continuous, organic relationship among the parts and between the parts and the whole. The principle of creation is not growth but aggregation.'[20]

Even in shorter works, there is a tendency for the progression to be so linear that a story changes shape and focus halfway through, the beginning apparently being forgotten by the time the end is reached. This seems to happen in some of the *Canterbury Tales*. In *The Wife of Bath's Tale*, for example, we begin with a knight who has been sentenced to death for a brutal rape, but he is pardoned on condition that he finds out what thing it is that women most desire. He is told the answer to this riddle by an ugly old woman, but has to marry her in return. He protests, because she is of low birth as well as old and ugly, but she lectures him on the nature of true nobility, he is eventually reconciled to her, and she suddenly becomes young and beautiful. In the course of the tale, the focus of attention has shifted: the knight's original crime has been forgotten, and the question of nobility and of the ideal marriage-relationship has usurped its place. Similarly, in *The Franklin's Tale*, a story that first leads up to passionate questioning of God's purposes in the ordering of the world ends as a contest in generosity between a knight, a squire, and a scholar, with the philosophical questioning neither answered nor dismissed, but simply left behind. Yet in such cases the 'aggregative' structure need not imply a lack of concern for connected meaning. *The Franklin's Tale*, beginning with a quest for freedom in the sense of *libertee*, by a husband and wife who are dissatisfied with the dominance implied in the traditional conception of marriage, passes from that to a questioning of God's freedom in his governing of the world, and concludes with the achievement of freedom in a different sense— *fraunchise*, the generosity that frees men from the bonds of law. And it is perhaps not by accident that Chaucer attributes this story to a Franklin, or *free*holder. Evidently the Aristotelian kind of unity, with its basis in plot, is not necessarily the only possible kind. One of the questions we constantly find critics asking about long medieval works is whether they are unified, and, if so, what the principle of their unity is. This has been one of the major topics of critical

[20] *Op. cit.*, p. 80.

discussion with, for example, Langland's *Piers Plowman*, Malory's *Morte Darthur*, and Chaucer's *Canterbury Tales*. We shall be able to consider this question more fully in chapter 3, and particularly to see what kind of help, if any, medieval literary theories can give us in questions of structure.

I have been pointing out some of the problems—most of them connected with oral delivery—that have to be faced in an attempt to carry out practical criticism of medieval English literature. This has perhaps made my introductory chapter sound rather depressing: I have been largely concerned with what is not known or must not be said. In the chapters that follow a more positive approach will be adopted, but it has been necessary to begin in this negative way simply in order to avoid being hindered by preconceptions of what literature ought to be like, based on modern reading conditions. We shall find that the methods of practical criticism can still be used, but that if we are to deal satisfactorily with medieval literature they will have to be modified and extended in scope. It will emerge, I hope, that the modern critic of medieval literature has other choices open to him than either to pretend that it is of the same kind as the work of Shakespeare, Keats, or Hopkins, or to dismiss it entirely as lying beyond his powers. First I shall examine the style and meaning of one of the greatest Middle English poems, *Sir Gawain and the Green Knight*; then I shall look at medieval theories of poetry (as exemplified in *The Clerk's Tale*) and of preaching (in connection with another specific poem, *Piers Plowman*); and finally I shall consider two connected poems on the Troilus and Cressida story, one by Chaucer and the other by Henryson.

The texture of *Sir Gawain and the Green Knight* seems to conform much better than that of most medieval poems to the characteristic criteria of modern critical analysis. In part this is a matter of the literary tradition to which it belongs, for alliterative verse, with its freedom of rhythm and its accumulation of consonantal force, shows a special capacity for conveying a sense of physical objects and violent movements. *Sir Gawain and the Green Knight* is one of the great works of the fourteenth-century Alliterative Revival, and in its verse is bodied forth a world vividly present to all the senses, a world full of sharply defined things and actions. Thus we find Mr John Speirs referring to the description of the winter landscape through which Sir Gawain passes in his quest for the Green Chapel as 'dependent upon distinctness and accuracy of sensation, on the sharpness or piercingness of the sensory impressions and the subtlety with which these are distinguished and differentiated.'[1] Thus too Mr Francis Berry, in a contribution to a widely read critical survey of medieval literature, describes Gawain's experience on this same winter journey as being 'actualized in the muscular images and rhythms, in the firm grasp of concrete particulars.'[2] There can be no doubt that many of the *Gawain*-poet's most striking successes are of this kind. We might look, for example, at the scene in which Gawain, having accepted the Green Knight's challenge, prepares to strike a blow that will slice off his head:

The grene knyght upon grounde graythely hym dresses,
A littel lut with the hede, the lere he discoverez,
His longe lovelych lokkez he layd over his croun,
Let the naked nec to the note schewe.
Gawan gripped to his ax, and gederes hit on hyght,
The kay fot on the folde he before sette,

[1] *Medieval English Poetry* (London, 1957), pp. 231–2.
[2] *The Age of Chaucer*, p. 149.

Let hit doun lyghtly lyght on the naked,
That the scharp of the schalk schyndered the bones,
And schrank thurgh the schyire grece, and schade hit in twynne,
That the bit of the broun stel bot on the grounde.   (417–26)[3]

The Green Knight takes up his stance, bending down and throwing
his fine (though green) hair forward with a fluid movement
suggested in the *l*'s of 'his *l*onge *l*ove*l*ych *l*okkez he *l*ayd . . .'. Then
we follow the movement of the huge axe that he has lent to Gawain.
Gawain settles it in his hand, raises it with a great effort, and lets its
own weight bring it sweeping down, shearing through the bare
green neck and hitting the earth with a thud. The sound and
movement of the lines give the event an extraordinarily physical
presence: in particular one notices the crunching sound as the blade
shatters the bone ('the scharp of the schalk schyndered the bones'),
and the gradual increase in speed from the labouring movement of
'Gawan gripped to his ax, and gederes hit on hyght' to the monosyllabic and internally echoing plunge of 'the bit of the broun stel
bot on the grounde.' This impetus is slightly interrupted only when
the flesh is cut through and the vowels are lengthened by *r*'s ('sch*r*ank
thu*r*gh the sch*y*ire g*r*ece'), and by the caesura in the last line between
the two stressed syllables 'stel' and 'bot,' which at once suggests the
minute pause between the neck and the ground, and throws an
extra weight on to the fierce verb 'bot.' As Mr Speirs writes,
'This is poetry that must be read with the body; it conveys directly
a sense of physical actions and movements.'[4]

In attempting to analyse mimetic effects of this kind, we may run
the risk of imposing a merely fanciful interpretation on the pattern
of sounds and rhythms; nevertheless, the *Gawain*-poet's achieve-
ments of this kind are genuine and, I believe, widely recognized. It
seems, however, that an over-exclusive admiration for this side of
the poet's art tends to go with an interpretation of the poem as a
whole that places the Green Knight, rather than Gawain, firmly at
its centre. The connection is a very natural one, because the Green
Knight, more than any other character in the poem, is presented as
a source of violent energy, from the moment when he suddenly

[3] Quotations from the edition of J. R. R. Tolkien and E. V. Gordon, 2nd
edn., rev. Norman Davis (Oxford, 1967).

[4] *Op. cit.*, p. 227.

rides into Arthur's hall at Camelot, interrupting the service of dinner, to the moment when he rides out of the poem. He rushes away from Camelot 'with a runisch rout,' his horse's hooves striking fire from the stone floor (457–9); when, in his other role as Sir Bertilak de Hautdesert, he hears that the traveller who has come to his castle is Gawain, he bursts into a great laugh of joy (909); at the Green Chapel, returned to his former identity, he is not content to wade across a stream, but 'hypped over on hys ax, and orpedly strydez' (2232). On this view, it appears that the poet's imagination, and hence his skill, are most fully engaged in the figure of the Green Knight. In him the poem's characteristic violence and concreteness are most fully exemplified; and, from thus placing the Green Knight at the poem's imaginative centre, it is an easy step to placing him at the centre of its ethical scheme. This step is taken by Mr Berry, who tells us that the Green Knight 'testifies to an assumption that moral behaviour, though of vast importance, is subservient to and dependent on something even more primary— creative energy.'[5] Thus, as often happens, a particular (and, I believe, limited) kind of response to the verse of a poem is associated with a particular (and, I believe, misleading) interpretation of the poem's whole meaning. In this chapter I shall first develop a rather different interpretation of *Sir Gawain and the Green Knight*, and then try to support this interpretation with some critical analysis focused on qualities rather different from those noticed by Mr Berry and Mr Speirs.

In the only surviving manuscript, the poem has no title. It was called *Sir Gawain and the Green Knight* by its nineteenth-century editors, and yet from modern criticism such as Mr Berry's it would seem that a better title might be *The Green Knight and Sir Gawain*. But a very striking thing about the way in which the Green Knight is presented to us is that we almost never see the events of the poem through his eyes. On only two occasions are we told what he thinks or feels, and then only briefly and vaguely. The first is when Gawain comes to his castle and admits who he is, and then the Green Knight laughs aloud, 'so lef hit hym thoght' (909); the second is when, having received the return blow at the Green Chapel, Gawain leaps up ready to defend himself, and the Green Knight looks at him and 'in hert hit hym lykez' (2335). Apart from these two half-lines we

5 *The Age of Chaucer*, p. 158.

know nothing directly of the Green Knight's thoughts and feelings. This of course makes it easier for the poet to present him as a 'shape-shifter' and give him two different identities, but it makes it more difficult for us to understand what, if anything, he 'stands for'—what his place is in the poem's scheme of ideas. Unlike Gawain he is provided with no moralized emblem—no pentangle or other 'conysaunce.' When the Green Knight first arrives at Camelot the poet describes in minute detail what he looks like and what he says and does: he describes the fur-lining of his mantle, the embroidery of birds and insects on his clothing, the exact way in which his horse's hair is plaited, the tassels and knobs on his axe-handle, the way he stares insultingly at the company and asks which is Arthur, and so on; but of what lies behind the vivid outside of fashion and insolence and power we know nothing. All through, our attention is focused not on what is going on inside the Green Knight's mind but on his outward appearance and behaviour; and still more it is focused on other people's reactions to his appearance and behaviour. In particular, on his first arrival at Camelot, the poet presents in great detail the reactions of Arthur's court: how, after his first words, they stared at him in silence, wondering what his colour meant, and what he was going to do, and thinking that his appearance must be a matter of 'fantoum and fayryye' (240); how, after he had issued his extraordinary challenge, they were still more astonished and dumbfounded; how, when his head was cut off and rolled about the floor, they kicked it away with their feet; how, after he had galloped off, Arthur and Gawain 'laghe and grenne' (464), nervously trying to keep up the appearance of unconcern. After Gawain has been formally chosen by the court as Arthur's substitute in taking up the challenge, the chief centre of consciousness in the poem is unmistakably Gawain himself. We are given an intimate view of his thoughts and feelings, and, though he is as near perfect as a man may be—'On the fautlest freke that ever on fote yede' (2363)—we recognize in him someone like ourselves. When, in Sir Bertilak's castle, Sir Bertilak's wife comes creeping into his bedroom, he first peeps surreptitiously round the bed-curtains and then pretends to be asleep; on New Year's eve, as he lies in bed thinking of the ordeal he has to undergo in the morning, though he keeps his eyes closed, he cannot sleep;

when he learns that the Green Knight knows of his acceptance of the girdle, he feels not only shame but anger and bitterness. The Green Knight seems to be in the poem primarily in order that Gawain, and through him the whole Arthurian civilization of which he is the chosen representative, may react to him. For Gawain this reaction is quite explicitly a test, of which the Green Knight is the instrument. What we must now ask is, what are the qualities in Gawain that are being tested? It may turn out that the poet is more interested in these than in the instrument by which the test is carried out. Certainly this is suggested by the way in which the Green Knight, when finally questioned by Gawain, gives a purely personal explanation for his behaviour. He says that he was sent to Camelot by Morgan la Fay in order to terrify Guinevere—an explanation which appears to explain nothing in the poem as we have it (though there may be something in the suggestion that Gawain is eventually to be shamed by this reminder that he is kin to the evil enchantress Morgan as well as to King Arthur).[6] The direction of the poet's interest is also suggested by the plainly dismissive phrase with which the Green Knight is sent out of the poem once this unsatisfactory explanation has been given:

> Gawayn on blonk ful bene
> To the kyngez burgh buskez bolde,
> And the knyght in the enker-grene
> Whiderwarde-so-ever he wolde.   (2475–8)

Where that 'whiderwarde-so-ever' is we are evidently not to enquire. Whatever the modern critic may find most interesting, it appears that the poet's fundamental interest is less in 'the knyght in the enker-grene' than in Gawain and 'the kynges burgh,' the Arthurian civilization from which he came and to which we see him return.

It is well known that the plot of *Sir Gawain and the Green Knight* consists of two elements which are found separately elsewhere but which are not found in combination in any conceivable source for *Sir Gawain*. These two elements are the Beheading Game, in which Gawain's opponent is the Green Knight, and the Temptation,

---

[6] See L. D. Benson, *Art and Tradition in Sir Gawain and the Green Knight* (New Brunswick, 1965), p. 32.

in which his opponent is the Lady, the Green Knight's wife. The Beheading Game is essentially a test of physical courage, in which the danger is death. As Gawain sets off from Camelot to search for the Green Chapel, the ordeal he sees ahead of him is this physical test of completing the Beheading Game by receiving the Green Knight's return blow. This is also how the courtiers see the situation, as they lament

> That so worthé as Wawan schulde wende on that ernde,
> To dryye a delful dynt, and dele no more
> 　　　wyth bronde.　　　　　　　　　　　(559–61)

There is also, involved in the physical test, a test of Gawain's fidelity to his bond, since he is to seek the Green Knight, not be sought by him; but there is never any question that he will be at fault here. It is noticeable how easily he rejects the temptation offered when the servant sent to guide him to the Green Chapel suggests that he should run away, and nobody would be the wiser. Gawain is frightened, and so presumably he does not know whether the green girdle will really protect him, but nevertheless he is sustained without difficulty by his own conception of himself as a true knight:

> . . . helde thou hit never so holde, and I here passed,
> Founded for ferde for to fle, in fourme that thou tellez,
> I were a knyght kowarde, I myght not be excused.
> 　　　　　　　　　　　　　　　　　　　(2129–31)

For Gawain, the Beheading Game is the real test; and yet between the two parts of the Beheading Game—the blow Gawain gives and the blow he is to receive—is inserted the quite different theme of the Temptation. To Gawain, and to the poet's audience as they hear the work read for the first time, this is bound to seem a digression from the main subject. And yet the *Gawain*-poet austerely denies himself digression in any other respect: we are told on Gawain's journey out that

> So mony mervayl bi mount ther the mon fyndez,
> Hit were to tore for to telle of the tenthe dole,
> 　　　　　　　　　　　　　　　　　　　(718–19)

and similarly on his way back that he had

> . . . mony aventure in vale, and venquyst ofte,
> That I ne tyght at this tyme in tale to remene.
>
> (2482-3)

In fact, the Temptation is not a digression. It is itself the poem's main subject, though the audience, and Gawain, do not discover this until nearly the end of the poem, when the second part of the Beheading Game has already occurred. Then the Green Knight explains that the three blows he has dealt—two feints and one slight cut—do not themselves constitute the great test that Gawain has to undergo: they merely symbolize a greater test which has already occurred, a moral test, in which Gawain, superior though he is to all other knights, has failed. This is the function of that interweaving of the two plot-elements which, so far as we know, the *Gawain*-poet was the first to combine. The interweaving is not to be seen as a merely formal device. The poet's skill as a narrator, his manipulation of suspense, climax, and anticlimax, his linking of the two plot-elements by the green girdle, all this serves to emphasize the poem's moral significance. The poet constantly directs his audience's thoughts ahead, towards an expected climax in the form of a physical test, but it then turns out that the real climax lies in a moral test: the crucial conflict has been that with the Lady, not that with the Green Knight. If this is so, then the poem's 'muscular images and rhythms' may be less centrally important than the modern critical analyst will naturally take them to be. Moreover, since the Green Knight himself is absent during this real climax of the poem, and our attention is concentrated upon Gawain's own internal struggles, the Green Knight too may be further from the poem's ideological centre than is generally supposed.

But what is the nature of the test that Gawain undergoes in his conflict with the Lady? He is presented in the poem as a knight dedicated to the virtues of Christian chivalry, virtues which are secular as well as religious, but especially to chastity. To emphasize this dedication is the purpose of the elaborate description of his shield when he is being armed for his quest, and of the still more elaborate explanation of the symbolism of the pentangle painted on it. The poet thinks this explanation important enough to tarry

over, even though he will not stop to give us details of Gawain's
subsidiary adventures:

> And quy the pentangel apendez to that prynce noble
> I am in tent yow to telle, thof tary hyt me schulde
>
> (623–4)

The symbolism is moral and religious: the pentangle betokens the
knight's faultlessness and his faith. Moreover one of the five meanings
given to the five points of the pentangle is that they stand for the
five joys of the Blessed Virgin. This meaning is given a special
emphasis, because the poet further tells us that

> At this cause the knyght comlyche hade
> In the inore half of his schelde hir ymage depaynted,
> That quen he blusched therto his belde never payred.
>
> (648–50)

Gawain is specially devoted to the Blessed Virgin: he prays to her
for aid on Christmas Eve (736, 754), and at his moment of greatest
peril, when the Lady tempts him for the third time, he is referred to
as Mary's own knight:

> Gret perile bitwene hem stod,
> Nif Maré of hir knyght mynne.   (1768–9)

Moreover, Gawain himself is presented as celibate: he refuses to
defend himself against the Lady by saying that he already has a love
to whom he has pledged his faith (even when the Lady herself
suggests that defence to him), but insists that he neither has nor
intends to have a 'lemman' (1782–91). It is surely clear enough that
in the contest between Gawain and the Lady what is primarily at
stake is his chastity. If he succumbs to her he will in consequence
behave dishonourably towards her husband, who is his host and to
whom he is therefore particularly under an obligation; but the first
danger is to his chastity.[7]

---

[7] This view of the testing is not universally held. Compare B. J. Whiting,
'Gawain: His Reputation, His Courtesy and His Appearance in Chaucer's
Squire's Tale,' *Mediæval Studies* IX (1947), p. 203, n. 49: 'The test is not of
Gawain's chastity, but of his honor and in Gawain's case, as in medieval
romance generally, the two virtues are distinct.' More recently, a central
argument of Mr J. A. Burrow's important book, *A Reading of Sir Gawain and*

We have then, in Gawain, a celibate knight, under the protection of the Blessed Virgin, and determined to remain chaste. The question that immediately arises is, how is it that the Lady can bring such a knight into danger? There is a very obvious answer to this question in terms of the common humanity to which Gawain belongs: the Lady is attractive, and Gawain, who 'lappez [her] a lyttel in armes' (973) when they first meet, finds her desirable. This is true, and important; but the contest between Gawain and the Lady is a matter of values as well as impulses. This is hinted at in the description of his arming which we have just looked at. He may be protected by the Virgin whose image he bears on his shield, but there is a further, and different, symbolism in the embroidered covering that he wears over his helmet. This covering is decorated with

> bryddez on semez,
> As papjayez paynted peruyng bitwene,
> Tortors and trulofez entayled so thyk
> As mony burde theraboute had ben seven wynter
>   in toune.   (610–14)

The turtle-doves and truelove-knots,[8] embroidered with care by ladies, suggest Gawain's allegiance to a value quite different from chastity: the value of courtesy, or rather the quality called in medieval French *courtoisie* and in this poem *cortaysye*. This value indeed is among those included in the multiple symbolism of the pentangle (653). *Cortaysye* perhaps requires some explanation. In Arthurian literature generally, Gawain's reputation is not at all for chastity. In the *Canterbury Tales* Chaucer's Squire—an expert on chivalric matters—speaks of 'Gawayn, with his olde curteisye,' and what this

the *Green Knight* (London, 1965), is that the story is about the testing of Gawain's *trawthe*, his fidelity to his pledged word, not of his chastity.

It is difficult to understand Mr Speirs' assertion that 'chastity has here nothing very particularly to do with monastic asceticism. . . . The chastity theme is here complementary to the fertility theme' (*Medieval English Poetry*, p. 236). There can presumably be no doubt that for a medieval writer chastity might have nothing to do with fertility, and everything to do with asceticism; and while a twentieth-century critic may well feel that chastity is no very high value in itself, there seems no reason why he should expect a fourteenth-century poet to agree with him.

[8] Or possibly, as suggested by Norman Davis in his edition of the poem, flowers called 'true-loves'; but the symbolism remains the same.

curteisye consists of in the Arthurian romances has been summed up by Mr B. J. Whiting as follows: 'Gawain is the casual, good-natured and well-mannered wooer of almost any available girl. If she acquiesces, good; if not, there is sure to be another pavilion or castle not far ahead. Rarely indeed do the authors pass a moral judgment on the hero's conduct.' Mr Whiting goes on to remark that 'Because of Gawain's reputation as a lover he is the secret passion of many maidens who have never seen him in the flesh.'[9] The English *Gawain-*poet is doing something rather surprising (though there is precedent for it in the Gawain who sets off in quest of the Holy Grail in the earlier French romance *Perlesvaus*) in making his hero chaste and equipping him so fully with moral scruples; but this Gawain never-theless finds himself preceded by a reputation which really belongs to the 'casual, good-natured and well-mannered wooer.' At first it seems that his reputation is only for making courtly conversation, for, on his arrival at Sir Bertilak's castle,

> Uch segge ful softly sayde to his fere:
> 'Now schal we semlych se sleghtez of thewez
> And the teccheles termes of talkyng noble,
> Wich spede is in speche unspurd may we lerne,
> Syn we haf fonged that fyne fader of nurture.'
>
> (915–19)

But it soon becomes clear that *cortaysye* or *nurture* (good breeding) may imply more than conversation. When the Lady first visits him in his bedroom while her husband is out hunting, she says that she is beginning to wonder whether he really is Gawain. He is quick to ask why—so quick as to suggest that his traditional reputation means more to him than perhaps it ought—and she replies:

> So god as Gawayn gaynly is halden,
> And *cortaysye* is closed so clene in hymselven,
> Couth not lyghtly haf lenged so long wyth a lady,
> Bot he had craved a cosse, bi his *courtaysye*,
> Bi sum towch of summe tryfle at sum talez ende.
>
> (1297–1301)

Again, on her second visit she tells him,

[9] *Art. cit.*, p. 203.

> . . . ye, that ar so *cortays* and coynt of your hetes,
> Oghe to a yonke thynk yern to schewe
> And teche sum tokenez of trweluf craftes.   (1525-7)

Now *cortaysye* was a leading ideal among the aristocratic classes of
medieval Europe. It is an extremely rich and fluid concept, and for
that reason it is difficult to define. It meant the kind of behaviour
current in or appropriate to courts, and it could cover the whole
range of behaviour from politeness (what *we* should call courtesy),
thoughtfulness, generosity, through elegant conversation about love
with persons of the opposite sex, to the conduct of a real love-affair.
(Hence the Lady's assumption that courtly conversation is simply a
prologue of love-making.) The unifying element in this range of
activity seems to be an attitude towards women: deference, or even
devotion. Historically the development of *cortaysye* appears to be
connected with the rise in importance of the Blessed Virgin as an
object of devotion: the lady to whom deference was supremely due.
Thus Christianity and *cortaysye* could fuse into a single aristocratic
way of life, with no sense of incongruity. It is such a way of life that
we see symbolized in the intricately interlocking meanings of
Gawain's pentangle, and exemplified in the Camelot of the poem,
where Christmas is celebrated first with the singing of mass and then
with games (perhaps with kisses as forfeits) in which 'Ladies laghed
ful loude, thogh thay lost haden' (69). In this, Camelot is only an
idealized version of a medieval European court: the court of Edward
III or Richard II, or that of the provincial lord for whom *Sir Gawain
and the Green Knight* was perhaps written. The effect of the poem, I
would suggest, is to break the 'endeles knot' (630) of the pentangle,
which linked *clannes* and *cortaysye* in the same line (653); to under-
mine the pious gaiety or gay piety of Camelot, by driving a wedge
between courtliness and Christianity.[10] Gawain is chosen as the
supremely courtly or *cortays* representative of a courtly society

[10] This view has been attacked by W. O. Evans, ' "Cortaysye" in Middle
English,' *Mediaeval Studies* XXIX (1967), pp. 143-57, who claims that in
English *cortaysye* was normally used with reference to Christian virtue, and
writes: 'No "wedge" can be driven between Gawain's *cortaysye* and any other
virtue, for it has its source in Heaven' (p. 157). But this makes it impossible to
explain how the Lady is able to impose a quite different meaning on
cortaysye; if Gawain had shared Evans' opinion, he would surely have been
able to say, 'But everyone knows *that* isn't what courtesy means!'

to go on what seems an exploit demanding physical courage only. But the exploit turns out to be a moral test demanding the power to resist a woman; and *cortaysye* is based on devotion to women. The test that Gawain undergoes at the castle is one that sets his *cortaysye* against his chastity. If he were not devoted to *cortaysye* the Lady would have no power over him, since he would be able to reject her advances before they constituted a serious temptation. It is made clear that this is his dilemma at the feast at the end of the second day's hunting, when

> Such semblaunt to that segge semly ho made
> Wyth stille stollen countenaunce, that stalworth to plese,
> That al forwondered was the wyye, and wroth with hymselven,
> Bot he nolde not for his *nurture* nurne hir ayaynez,
> Bot dalt with hir al in daynté, how-se-ever the dede turned
> 　　towrast.　　　　　　　　　　　　　　　　　(1658–63)

Gawain is confronted with a situation for which the customary system of values at Camelot makes no provision. Though the Lady's physical attraction is perfectly real, he could presumably stand out against that, if it were not reinforced by his own *nurture*: hence his confusion and anger against himself. And this dilemma is clarified still further on the crucial occasion of the Lady's third visit to his bedchamber, when he succumbs to her so far as to accept the girdle and conceal it from her husband:

> For that prynces of pris depresed hym so thikke,
> Nurned hym so neghe the thred, that nede hym bihoved
> Other lach ther hir luf, other lodly refuse.
> He cared for his *cortaysye*, lest crathayn he were,
> And more for his meschef yif he schulde make synne,
> And be traytor to that tolke that that telde aght.
> 　　　　　　　　　　　　　　　　　　　　(1770–75)

Here the concepts involved are set out with schematic precision: if Gawain were willing to reject her advances *lodly* (discourteously), to be *crathayn* (churlish), he would be in no danger; but he is not willing to act thus, and so, for the sake of his *cortaysye*, he is in danger first of committing sin himself and second of behaving treacherously towards his host. One scholar has argued that lines

1774-5 do not in fact distinguish between (sexual) *synne* and disloyalty, but rather refer to a *synne* which *is* disloyalty.[11] The words
used by the poet are capable of bearing either meaning, but it seems
to me that the context—the Lady's low-cut dress, carefully chosen to
leave 'Hir brest bare bifore, and bihinde eke' (1741), Gawain's
ardent response ('Wight wallande joye warmed his hert' [1762]),
and the poet's warning that the Blessed Virgin had better look to her
knight—imposes the first. Of course, *synne* did not always mean
'sexual sin' in the Middle Ages, any more than it does today; but
that is what it has always been most likely to mean in a context concerning relations between a young man and a beautiful woman.
In *The Miller's Tale*, when Nicholas is persuading the carpenter that
he and his delectable young wife ought to keep apart, 'For that
bitwixe yow shal be no synne', there is no doubt about the nature of
the sin in question, even though the couple are married and the man
is old. Gawain, fortunately, does not literally accept the Lady as his
mistress, but, under the influence of a further motive—the wish to
live—does so symbolically, by accepting the girdle as a love-token
(*luf-lace* [1874, 2438]), thereby becoming her knight instead of the
Blessed Virgin's. Things would never have come to this pass if it
had not been for his *cortaysye*.[12]

   This interpretation of Gawain's testing, which is based on his own
interpretation of his experience, and which sees it as disclosing
a flaw in the Christian courtliness of the Camelot way of life, helps
to explain a part of the poem which many readers find baffling.
This is the angry speech with which Gawain greets the Green
Knight's final explanation of the test, a speech in which he lists the
great Old Testament figures who were deceived by women—Adam,
Solomon, Samson, and David—and says that this good company
ought to excuse him. Sir Israel Gollancz in his edition of the poem
comments in his note on this passage that 'Throughout this stanza
there runs a note of bitterness which is scarcely in keeping with the

----

[11] J. A. Burrow, *op. cit.*, p. 100.

[12] For a somewhat different view of *cortaysye* in *Sir Gawain and the Green
Knight*, see J. F. Kiteley, 'The *De Arte Honeste Amandi* of Andreas Capellanus
and the Concept of Courtesy in *Sir Gawain and the Green Knight*,' *Anglia*
LXXIX (1961), pp. 7-16.

knight of courtesy.'[13] Apart from the question of consistency of character, one might well feel that the poet was here being conventional in a limiting sense—that he was falling back into a traditional medieval misogynism (the natural converse of medieval *cortaysye*) which seems crude beside the subtle presentation of human behaviour in the rest of the poem. But in fact the antifeminism of this speech is its point, for in attacking women Gawain is rejecting *cortaysye*—not simply politeness, as Gollancz seems to suppose, but the whole courtly system of behaviour based on devotion to women. In leaving Arthur's court he has passed into a harsher world in which *cortaysye* is not enough; for *Sir Gawain and the Green Knight*, unlike *Pearl* (which is found in the same manuscript and may be by the same author), does not offer any means of bridging the gap between *cortaysye* and the absolute demands of Christian asceticism. In *Pearl*, though the religious lesson to be learnt is harsh, the central pearl-symbol has a heavenly as well as an earthly meaning, and the Blessed Virgin herself is 'Quen of cortaysye'; in *Sir Gawain and the Green Knight* there is no mention of this aspect of her nature, and Christianity is conceived of as an essentially ascetic, life-denying system. Thus the Green Knight's judgment on Gawain is more lenient than Gawain's judgment on himself. The Green Knight says that he accepted the girdle only because 'ye lufed your lyf; the lasse I yow blame' (2368), but Gawain, who now knows from experience how fragile a defence Christianity adulterated by *cortaysye* provides, vows to wear the girdle always so that

> . . . in syngne of my surfet I schal se hit ofte,
> When I ride in renoun, remorde to myselven
> The faut and the fayntyse of the flesche crabbed.
>
> (2433–5)

When he returns to Camelot, however, he finds that those who have not shared his experience do not understand it in the same way as he does: the courtiers take the girdle not as a badge of shame but as a badge of honour. By the end of the poem, Gawain is both wiser and sadder, and the gaiety of Camelot has come to seem rather shallow.

[13] Ed. I. Gollancz, M. Day, and M. S. Serjeantson, Early English Text Society 210 (London, 1940), p. 129.

To put it in these terms, however, is to adopt Gawain's own view of his adventure; and the poem does not force this view upon us, but indeed gives us some encouragement to consider alternative possibilities. If Gawain is, as I put it earlier, the poem's chief centre of consciousness, he is not its only centre of consciousness. We saw how at two brief but crucial moments the poem's normal perspective is inverted, to enable us to see Gawain through the Green Knight's eyes; again, there are moments when we see him through the eyes of other characters in the poem (for example, the courtiers at Camelot in lines 672ff. and at Hautdesert in lines 915ff. and 1987ff., or the Lady at lines 1283ff. and 1733ff.); and quite large parts of the poem's action—the hunting scenes, above all—occur unknown to Gawain, seen through the omniscient eyes of the narrator.[14] In consequence of these factors, and of the poet's whole handling of his story, we are permitted to see Gawain from the outside, and sometimes to see him in a critical or even a comic light. The bedroom scenes, in which the normal roles in the sexual hunt are reversed, so that woman becomes the pursuer and man the pursued, are permeated by a *Joseph Andrews*-like comedy. Gawain's heroism is a little tarnished by his acceptance of the girdle, and the courage with which he faces the Green Knight for the second round of the Beheading Game, though genuine, is obviously somewhat precarious. As the poem proceeds, it becomes clearer and clearer that Gawain is deeply concerned about his reputation, and perhaps even about his reputation rather than about the reality that underlies it. He is all too quick, as the Lady soon discovers, to establish that he really *is* the Gawain that everyone has heard of; and it may be that this concern for reputation makes it easier for him to slip into accepting the girdle in circumstances which make it appear certain that he will never be found out. The concern for reputation may even be found in the antifeminist speech we have just been considering, in which he puts himself on a level with the heroic sinners of the Old Testament. Once he has been found out—'tane in tech of a faute' (2488)—it is evidently not enough for him to be 'the fautlest freke that ever on fote yede' (2363); if he cannot be the perfect knight, he would rather be the worst of sinners, accusing himself of every

[14] For fuller accounts of 'point of view' in *Sir Gawain and the Green Knight*, see L. D. Benson, *op. cit.*, pp. 185ff., and my *The Gawain-Poet*, pp. 219ff.

failing under the sun, and wearing the shameful girdle with just a little ostentation. None of these possibilities is directly stated in the poem; it is rather the poet's method to envelop his story in a haze of uncertainties, and to leave his audience, very much as Chaucer does, to make up their own minds in the end. Is Gawain of full heroic stature, or is he, like Conrad's Lord Jim, 'an inch, perhaps two, under six feet'? The poem's studiously distant closing scene gives us no definite answers.

I have moved from one kind of critical analysis of *Sir Gawain and the Green Knight* to attacking a general interpretation of the poem with which it seems to be connected, and from there to substituting for it an interpretation which may be found more satisfactory. I have tried to show that for the poet the central interest in the poem is not the Green Knight but (however uncertain the poet's final verdict on him) Gawain and the *cortays* Arthurian civilization he represents. But even if this is accepted it may still be felt that, whatever the poet's conscious interests, the imaginative centre of his poem remains the Green Knight, and that the poem's poetry springs from him. In order to combat this view, it will finally be necessary to carry out some further critical analysis, by which it may be shown that, however impressive the poetry of muscular action that surrounds the Green Knight, there is another kind of poetry, at least as impressive, centring in Sir Gawain. There is, I believe, a poetry of *cortaysye* in *Sir Gawain and the Green Knight* as well as a poetry of muscular energy. For an illustration of this, let us look at Gawain's first speech in the poem, the speech in which, after Arthur has accepted the Green Knight's challenge and prepares to deal the blow, Gawain rises and begs to be substituted for the King:

'Wolde ye, worthilych lorde,' quoth Wawan to the kyng,
'Bid me bowe fro this benche, and stonde by yow there,
That I wythoute vylanye myght voyde this table,
And that my legge lady lyked not ille,
I wolde com to your counseyl bifore your cort ryche.
For me think hit not semly, as hit is soth knawen,
Ther such an askyng is hevened so hyghe in your sale,
Thagh ye yourself be talenttyf, to take hit to yourselven,
Whil mony so bolde yow aboute upon bench sytten,
That under heven I hope non hagherer of wylle,

Ne better bodyes on bent ther baret is rered.
I am the wakkest, I wot, and of wyt feblest,
And lest lur of my lyf, quo laytes the sothe—
Bot for as much as ye are myn em I am only to prayse,
No bounté bot your blod I in my bodé knowe;
And sythen this note is no nys that noght hit yow falles,
And I have frayned hit at yow fyrst, foldez hit to me;
And if I carp not comlyly, let alle this cort rych
          bout blame.'

                                                                    (343-61)

It will be seen that the purpose of this speech is to move towards a particular action—the substitution of Gawain for Arthur as the Green Knight's opponent—but to do so without giving any possible offence. A key word in it is *vylanye* (345), for *vylanye* is the opposite of *cortaysye;* just as *cortaysye* means in one sense the polite behaviour appropriate to a courtly person, so *vylanye* means the offensive behaviour appropriate to a *vilain*, a peasant. In both terms moral status is connected with social status, in accordance with the aristocratic structure of medieval society. It is *vylanye* above all that Gawain must avoid, and he does so, as far as the plain sense of the passage is concerned, by deferring successively to Arthur (*worthilych lord*), to Guinevere (*my legge lady*), and, at the very end, to the whole court. He argues that the Green Knight's challenge is foolish, and hence not suitable to be taken up by the King himself, and that Arthur's court is full of men brave enough to take it on themselves. Thus Gawain avoids claiming to be the only worthy opponent; indeed, he says that he is a suitable opponent only because the loss of his own life would matter least. And then, after all this, he puts his own claims, again in the most self-effacing way: he is Arthur's nephew (indeed, that is his only title to consideration), and he is the first to ask the boon of the King. The actual content of the speech, then, is supremely *cortays;* but Gawain's *cortaysye* is expressed most fully in the *way* in which he says what he says. The content of the speech can be easily translated into modern English, but the manner of expression (which is what turns the speech into a dramatic poem of *cortaysye*) is completely lost in translation. This may be illustrated by comparing the original with the modern translation by Mr Brian Stone—a version chosen not because it is particularly bad, and certainly not because I think it would be easy to do better, but simply to show how the very essence of the passage is to be found in its detailed phrasing, so that it demands from the reader or listener a subtlety of response which can be represented in writing only by the most minute critical analysis.

'If you would grant, great lord,' said Gawain to the King,
'That I might stir from this seat and stand beside you,
Be allowed without lese-majesty to leave the table,
And if my liege lady would likewise allow it,
I should come there to counsel you before this court of nobles.
For it appears unmeet to me, as manners go,
When your hall hears uttered such a haughty request,
For your great self to go forward and gratify it,
When on the benches about you so many bold men sit,
The best-willed in the world, as I well believe,
And the finest in the field when the fight is joined.
I am the most wanting in wisdom, and the weakest, I know,
And loss of my life would be least, in truth.
My only asset is that my uncle is my king;
There is no blessing in my body but what your blood accords.
And since this affair is so foolish that it should not fall to you,
And I first asked it of you, make it over to me;
And if I speak dishonourably, may all the court judge
            Without blame.'[15]

One of the first things one notices on looking at the original passage closely is the presence of a number of peculiarly circumlocutory phrases. Gawain does not simply ask the King's permission to rise and give him advice, he begs the King to *command* him to rise: 'Wolde ye, worthilych lorde, . . . Bid me bowe fro this benche.' Again, he does not merely ask the Queen's permission, but hopes that she will not be positively displeased if he rises: 'And that my legge lady lyked not ille.' The significant indirectness of both these addresses is lost when they are translated into the more straightforward 'If you would grant' and 'would likewise allow it.' A second noticeable aspect of the original passage is the length and complexity of its sentences. The manuscript is simply broken into lines and stanzas, but according to modern conventions the passage may reasonably be divided into three sentences only

[15] *Sir Gawain and the Green Knight*, trans. B. Stone (Harmondsworth, 1959).

(as in the edition quoted), and each of the three is full of subordinate clauses. The complexity of the syntax suggests the subtlety of the relationships that Gawain is establishing among a number of independent factors: the King's position, the Queen's position, the nature of the challenge, his own relationship to the King, the possible touchiness of the other leading nobles, and so on. These various and potentially opposing forces are woven by Gawain into a momentarily stable equilibrium, so that a particular action may follow. One observes how in the first sentence the main point—the wish of Gawain to offer advice to the King—is delayed until the very last line by a pair of conditional clauses (*If* the King would command it, *if* the Queen did not dislike it . . .), with a consecutive clause sandwiched between them (*So that* I might come forward without *vylanye*). Similarly in the last sentence the crucial claim (It falls to me) is delayed by subordinate clauses (*Since* the request is foolish, *since* I was the first to ask for it . . .), and immediately qualified by a further condition (*If* I am speaking unsuitably . .). The sense one has in moving through the passage is of the skirting of a series of obstacles, the overcoming or evading of one difficulty after another: the syntax seems to wind itself along, to move two steps sideways for every step forwards. This effect is heightened by the profusion of parenthetic phrases inserted before the main point of each clause is reached. For example, at the very beginning we are held up for the principal verb of the first conditional clause until the beginning of the second line, through the insertion of the polite address to the King and the poet's explanation of who is speaking to whom. There are parentheses and subordinate clauses even within the subordinate clauses. Throughout the speech we are delayed by phrases such as 'as hit is soth knawen,' 'Thagh ye yourself be talenttyf,' 'I hope,' 'I wot,' 'quo laytes the sothe.' The translator, even where he retains these, loses the main part of their effect by changing their position slightly: for example, in line 352, even though the phrase 'I hope' is lengthened to 'as I well believe,' its delaying effect is lost, because it is moved from the middle of the line to the end. Exactly the same thing happens to 'I wot' in line 354. The effect of the passage is gained or lost precisely in such minute details as these.

To suggest that Gawain's *cortaysye* is expressed in this way through tiny syntactical effects may make it sound rather bloodless. This would be a mistaken impression, however; for it is in fact very close to the physical—as close as the Green Knight's bluffness. This is particularly apparent in the use, twice in this passage, of the single word *body*. In line 353, where the translation has 'And the finest in the field when the fight is joined,' we find in the original 'Ne better bodyes on bent ther baret is rered.' The nobles are good fighting men in a realer sense than belongs merely to Gawain's politeness: they are so in a directly physical sense which has vanished in the translation. And, even more strikingly, in line 357 the translation has 'There is no blessing in my body but what your blood accords,' while the original reads 'No bounté bot your blod I in my bodé knowe.' Here the translation retains the word *body*, but once again the original line contains a physical conception which the translator has lost. For the *Gawain*-poet, Arthur's blood runs in Gawain's veins in a quite literal sense: the family relationship is conceived of as completely physical, and so what worth Gawain possesses is Arthur's not hyperbolically or metaphorically, but in simple truth. The modern translator is using a language which rejects such simplicity, and with his 'what your blood accords' he weakens it into something not quite physical and not quite metaphorical. This is a matter of language, as well as of what a particular poet does with it. Fourteenth-century English falls naturally into such physical conceptions of events, and more recent English does not. The change might be illustrated vividly by a comparison of one of Dryden's 'translations' from Chaucer with its original; but here a single example, from *The Wife of Bath's Tale*, must be enough. In Chaucer, the Queen tells the knight, 'Be war, and keep thy nekke-boon from iren' (*Canterbury Tales*, III 906), using an idiom in which the idea of execution is presented in terms of its physical constituents—the iron blade and the bone it will shatter. The equivalent line in Dryden runs: 'Beware, for on thy Wit depends thy Life'—and here the concrete has been completely replaced by the abstract.

We have seen from our analysis of Gawain's first speech how his character is declared as soon as he appears in the poem, partly by what he says, but still more by the way in which he says it. The extremely complex manner of expression, full of qualifications and delays, is typical of Gawain in the situations which most test his *cortaysye*. We can find it again, for example, in the speech he makes

in the second bedroom scene, after the Lady has twice referred to
him as *cortays* and suggested that he ought to display his *cortaysye* in
teaching her 'sum tokenez of trweluf craftes' (1528). Instead he
displays his *cortaysye* in a further show of sinuous politeness, a
politeness here devoted not to achieving action, as in the first
example, but to evading the action that the Lady would force upon
him:

> 'In goud faythe,' quoth Gawayn, 'God yow foryelde!
> Gret is the gode gle, and gomen to me huge,
> That so worthy as ye wolde wynne hidere,
> And pyne yow with so pouer a mon, as play wyth your knyght
> With anyskynnez countenaunce, hit keveres me ese;
> Bot to take the torvayle to myself to trwluf expoun,
> And towche the temez of tyxt and talez of armez
> To yow that, I wot wel, weldez more slyght
> Of that art, bi the half, or a hundreth of seche
> As I am, other ever schal, in erde ther I leve,
> Hit were a folé felefolde, my fre, by my trawthe.'   (1535–45)

Here he begins with polite exaggerations of phrasing, playing 'so
worthy as ye' against 'so pouer a mon,' and suggesting that any
attention she gives him must be a trouble to herself and the greatest
of pleasures to him. Then, in the second part of this single long
sentence, after the semi-colon, he uses exactly the same syntactical
devices as in his first speech, delaying the completion of the sense
until the last line by a series of noun and adjectival clauses. Further
delay is caused by the insertion, as before, of polite qualifying
phrases such as 'I wot wel,' 'bi the half,' and 'other ever schal.'
Finally, having reached the main clause with the guileful internal
assonance and alliteration of 'folé felefolde,' he at once adds two
further qualifying phrases, as if to muffle its force. As in his first
speech, the line of sense winds its way stealthily through a series of
obstacles: this is what the poet means when he tells us that in his
dealings with the Lady Gawain 'ferde with defence' (1282). We can
hardly be surprised that, by the parallelism of hunting and bedchamber scenes, he is eventually compared with the 'wylé' fox,
twisting and turning as Sir Bertilak hunts him on the third day. By
way of contrast, we might compare Gawain's manner of expression

with the Green Knight's way of talking in a characteristic speech of his. It is what he says when he makes himself known to Gawain at the Green Chapel:

> 'Gawayn,' quoth that grene gome, 'God the mot loke!
> Iwysse thou art welcom, wyye, to my place,
> And thou has tymed thi travayl as truee mon schulde.
> And thou knowez the covenauntez kest uus bytwene:
> At this tyme twelmonyth thou toke that the falled,
> And I schulde at this Nwe Yere yeply the quyte.
> And we ar in this valay verayly oure one;
> Here are no renkes us to rydde, rele as uus likez.
> Haf thy helme of thy hede, and haf here thy pay.
> Busk no more debate then I the bede thenne
> When thou wypped of my hede at a wap one.'
>
> (2239–49)

The most obvious comment on this is that it is completely different from Gawain's speeches. The Green Knight's bluffness is expressed through a series of short sentences, usually linked by 'and'—by co-ordination as opposed to the elaborate subordination of Gawain's idiom. Where Gawain's speeches are full of conditional and subjunctive verbs, the verbs here are most often in the simple present or past indicative, or else, significantly, in the imperative: '*Haf* thy helme of thy hede, and *haf* here thy pay.' Where Gawain is subtle, the Green Knight is brusque: in both cases, character is expressed through syntax rather than through imagery.[16]

The speeches I have chosen for analysis are fairly typical of their speakers, though naturally cases can be found where Gawain is brusque and paratactic, or the Green Knight subtle. Again, the insertion of qualifying phrases of the 'I wot' or 'bi the half' type is characteristic not simply of Gawain's speech, but of Middle English verse in general, and especially of alliterative verse. These phrases are formulas of the kind mentioned in Chapter 1: they belong to a style which still has its roots in a tradition of oral composition, and their original function is to fill a gap in rhythm and alliteration while enabling the poet to think ahead and his listeners to catch up with

[16] This analysis has been carried further by Cecily Clark, '*Sir Gawain and the Green Knight*: Characterisation by Syntax,' *Essays in Criticism* XVI (1966), pp. 361–74.

him. But in some of Gawain's speeches these conventional devices are put to an expressive purpose, in a way which is original as well as conventional. It is at least clear, I think, that, so far as the poetry of the poem is concerned, the Green Knight does not have things all his own way. I hope it is also clear that the modern critical method of close reading can be applied to this medieval poem with some profit, even though it must be directed upon characteristics of style different from those with which most modern critics have been concerned.

The reader will no doubt have noticed that while in the preceding chapter reference has been made to medieval ethical and social assumptions, none has been made to medieval ideas about literature. From the eighteenth century onwards, but particularly in this century, we have been becoming more and more conscious that the literature of the past was written according to the standards of the past, and that these were often different from our own standards. To try to recapture these standards may help to illuminate the literature itself, by showing us what the writers concerned were really aiming at. As an example of how twentieth-century scholarship has succeeded in this way, one might mention Miss Rosemond Tuve's *Elizabethan and Metaphysical Imagery*,[1] a study which throws real light for the modern reader on the purposes and ideals of Renaissance poetry, and thus helps to correct his expectations in reading that poetry. It is an obvious question, whether anything similar is possible in the case of medieval literature. There did in fact exist in the Middle Ages a body of works concerning the writing of literature, and these works were known to many medieval authors. It has in fact been claimed by modern scholars, as we shall see, that we can and should be guided in our judgments of medieval literature by the aims implied in this body of medieval literary theory. In the present chapter my purpose will be first to give a brief sketch of medieval theory about the composition of poetry, and then to enquire how far knowledge of this theory can help the modern reader towards an understanding of medieval English literature.

There existed in the Middle Ages three main groups of works about literature. All three are practical in intention; that is to say they are concerned with giving directions how to compose literary works rather than with theory about the nature, origins or effects of literature. All three are written in Latin, and written on

[1] (Chicago, 1947.)

the assumption that it is in Latin, not a vernacular language, that their readers will wish to write. One group, called the *ars dictaminis*, is concerned with the writing of elaborate prose, particularly in the form of letters; hence it is not of interest for the purposes of this book. The second group, called the *ars praedicandi*, is concerned with the making and preaching of sermons, and will be discussed at length in chapter 5. The third group, called the *ars poetica*, is concerned with the writing of poetry, and so it is with this that the present chapter will deal. We know that medieval poets were familiar with the *ars poetica*. Chaucer, for example, in *The House of Fame*, uses the phrase 'art poetical' (l. 1095), and that he has an established body of theory in mind is suggested by a famous ironical allusion in *The Nun's Priest's Tale* to the author of one of the most widely read *artes poeticae*. The lines refer to the capture of Chauntecleer by the fox, an event which takes place on a Friday:

> O Gaufred, deere maister soverayn,
> That whan thy worthy kyng Richard was slayn
> With shot, compleynedest his deeth so soore,
> Why ne hadde I now thy sentence and thy loore,
> The Friday for to chide, as diden ye?
>
> (*Canterbury Tales*, VII 3347–51)

'Gaufred' is Geoffroi de Vinsauf, author of a verse work called the *Poetria nova*, which includes as an example of *apostrophatio* or *exclamatio* a lamentation on the death of Richard I, which also occurred on a Friday. Chaucer's allusion is also a parody, since the lines quoted themselves make up an elaborate apostrophe of Geoffroi. It is true that, as a recent scholar has pointed out, Geoffroi's lament on the death of Richard was in circulation separately from the *Poetria nova* as a whole, and could have been known by Chaucer in that separate form; and it may also be the case that the *artes poeticae* as such were not widely read in England up to the fourteenth century.[2] On the other hand, there can be no doubt that the doctrines and terminology of the *ars poetica* had been available in some form or other to English writers from the twelfth century onwards;[3] and

[2] See J. J. Murphy, 'A New Look at Chaucer and the Rhetoricians,' *Review of English Studies*, n.s. XV (1964), pp. 1–20.

[3] The *Ancrene Riwle*, a devotional work of about 1200, uses the technical

Chaucer's own reference to Geoffroi necessarily implies an audience who would understand it, and would therefore know who Geoffroi was. A further sign of Chaucer's acquaintance with the *Poetria nova* as a whole is that in *Troilus and Criseyde* (I 1065–9) he translates some lines from another part of Geoffroi's treatise, comparing the composition of a poem to the building of a house—both need careful planning in advance. But Chaucer applies the house-building image instead to the planning of a love-affair; and this time he does not mention Geoffroi by name.

Several later medieval writers pay compliments to Geoffroi, in contexts devoid of Chaucerian irony. It may be revealing to look at the opinion of a more typical, because more mediocre, poet than Chaucer. Such a poet is Osbern Bokenham, author of a collection of *Legendys of Hooly Wummen*, which dates from 1443. Bokenham praises 'Galfridus Anglicus, in hys Newe Poetry [i.e. the *Poetria nova*]' for his use of the 'colours of rethoryk,' and goes on to say that as a rhetorician he is inferior to neither Cicero nor Demosthenes![4] Bokenham's very mediocrity as a poet may make his adulation less worth having, but the wide fame of Geoffroi's work is attested by the fact that there still survive over forty manuscripts of the *Poetria nova*. This, moreover, is only one of a whole group of works on the same subject. Among these may be mentioned Mathieu de Vendôme's *Ars versificatoria*, dating from the late twelfth century; the *Poetria nova* itself and another work by Geoffroi, in prose, called the *Documentum de modo et arte dictandi et versificandi*, both dating from the early thirteenth century; and Jean de Garlande's *Poetria*, dating from the mid-thirteenth century.

These works differ in many details, but they all propound the same basic teaching about the writing of poetry, and this teaching remained current until the beginning of the Renaissance. Then it was superseded by works based on the *Poetics* of Aristotle, and, with the elevation of Cicero as the supreme model for Latin style, by a

terms *antonomasice* and *hypallage*, and refers to amplification and adornment. See *The English Text of the Ancrene Riwle*, ed. Mabel Day, Early English Text Society 225 (London, 1952), pp. 90 and 142, and *Ancrene Wisse*, ed. Geoffrey Shepherd (London, 1959), pp. lxviff.

[4] Ed. M. S. Serjeantson, Early English Text Society 206 (London, 1938), ll. 83–96.

doctrine based on a fuller understanding of Cicero's own works on literary composition. In England, on the outer edge of Europe, where such influences arrived late, the early medieval doctrines continued to be put forward until the sixteenth century: there exists, for example, an anonymous late fifteenth-century poem called *The Court of Sapience* in which an allegorical figure called 'Dame Rethoryke' gives rules for composition of an entirely traditional medieval kind. The medieval *ars poetica* originated, then, in the early Middle Ages, and in fact it was a product of what is often called the 'Twelfth-Century Renaissance.' This early efflorescence of classical and humane learning took as one of its forms a revival of education, and the *artes poeticae* belong firmly to this educational movement. One of the most important facts about them is that they were mostly written by schoolmasters for use in the schoolroom. Medieval education was based on the study of Latin authors. It began with 'grammar,' which taught how to understand the meaning of texts and how to write and speak Latin correctly. It then passed on to 'rhetoric,' and the *artes poeticae* are aids to the teaching of rhetoric to schoolboys. This may help to explain the affectionately derisive tone of Chaucer's invocation of 'Gaufred' —it is as if a modern author were to invoke Kennedy, or North and Hillard. Mathieu de Vendôme has a section on *correctio*, a process which consists in the examination by the master of verses composed by his pupils, so that he may help them get rid of their faults and put beauties in their places. The master's duties are to notice mistakes and to suggest how they may be put right, while the pupils must admit their errors without any kind of concealment and accept the master's rebukes. From such a source, preoccupied with the practical problems of the classroom, we have no right to expect any very deep thought about literature. The *artes poeticae* contain a large proportion of exercises for imitation; they are directed not towards understanding the nature of literary values, but towards the teaching of a specific skill. Our feeling nowadays will probably be that, if poetry is an art, it is not one that can be taught—not an art in the sense of a technique or skill. This is a Romantic view of the nature of poetry, a view which pictures the poet as pouring his soul forth, like Shelley's skylark, 'in profuse strains of *unpremeditated* art.' Such a view, with its emphasis on 'spontaneity,' 'sincerity,' or 'naturalness,' and its tendency to reject much of the literature of the past as 'contrived,' is quite foreign to the Middle Ages. One reason why it is worth knowing something of the *artes poeticae* is that they make us realize vividly that there was an age (it lasted down to the eighteenth century) in which 'rhetoric' and 'artifice' were not thought of as qualities obviously to be avoided, but as the very basis of literature. Such a realization may make us understand our own views more clearly, and avoid hasty dismissals. But, for all this, we must remember that, because of their original humble function, we cannot expect from the *artes poeticae* any very penetrating thought about the rules they offer to teach.

The chief interest of the *artes poeticae* is in literary style, and in style conceived of purely as a matter of local verbal arrangement. A subject about which they say very little explicitly is one which was mentioned in chapter 1 as a frequent matter for controversy among readers of medieval literature, and which will be discussed again below—that of the unity or lack of it to be found in the structure of literary works. Their remarks about structure (*dispositio* in the technical language of the *ars poetica*) consist merely of directions for beginning a work—for example, with a statement of some general truth, such as a proverb (*sententia*), or with an illustrative story (*exemplum*)—and for attaching the middle to the beginning and the end. As an instance of such a way of beginning a work one might mention the opening lines of Chaucer's *Legend of Good Women*:

> A thousand tymes have I herd men telle
> That ther ys joy in hevene and peyne in helle,
> And I acorde wel that it ys so. . . .   (Text F, 1–3)

These form a *sententia* as such the *ars poetica* recommends; though it is typical of Chaucer at once to undercut the confidence of this assertion attributed to 'men' in general with his own personal dubiety:

> But, natheles, yet wot I wel also
> That ther nis noon dwellyng in this contree,
> That eyther hath in hevene or helle ybe,
> Ne may of hit noon other weyes witen,
> But as he hath herd seyd, or founde it writen.   (4–8)

Even from this small example one can see a great poet at work, not simply following the *ars poetica* but *using* it. Equally one can see how valuable it was to Chaucer that this form of conventional opening existed, for without it his ironic qualification would have far less effect.

After dealing with beginnings and endings, a typical *ars poetica* will go on to list methods of abbreviating or amplifying a work. This distinction between abbreviation and amplification was a familiar one to medieval poets. Chaucer, for example, in *Troilus and Criseyde* claims no more than to be translating what he finds in his source, and invites his audience to undertake the task of *correctio* by amplifying or abridging his words as they think fit:

> For myne wordes, heere and every part,
> I speke hem alle under correccioun
> Of yow that felyng han in loves art,
> And putte it al in youre discrecioun
> To encresse or maken dymynucioun
> Of my langage, and that I yow biseche. (III 1331-6)

Similarly, John Lydgate, in his *Complaynt of a Loveres Lyfe*, probably written twenty or thirty years after the *Troilus*, claims only to be repeating what he heard said by someone else:

> For evenlych wythout addissyon
> Or disencrese, outhir mor or lesse,
> For to reherse anon I wol me dresse.   (201-3)

And towards the end of the fifteenth century, Robert Henryson, in the Prologue to his *Morall Fabillis*, explains that he is only translating what Aesop wrote, and that, because he himself knows nothing of 'eloquence nor rethorike,' he begs his readers to 'correct' his work if it is found to be too much abbreviated or too much amplified:

> Thairfoir meiklie I pray your reverence,
> Gif that ye find it throw my negligence
> Be deminute, or yit superfluous,
> Correct it at your willis gratious.   (39-42)

In all three cases, the assumption is that the poet has some given material to work on; and this is a fundamental postulate of the medieval *ars poetica*. Indeed medieval authors (like Shakespeare) did normally retell an existing story rather than invent a new one. Even the *Gawain*-poet, as we have seen, does no more than to combine two traditional plots.

The retelling usually involved *amplificatio* rather than *abbreviatio* —a fact connected with the diffuseness of medieval literature noted in chapter 1. Thus the *artes poeticae* have much more to say about amplification than about abbreviation; and indeed there *is* much more to be said about the former than about the latter. Amplification is to be carried out by the use of periphrasis, comparison, apostrophe, digression, descriptions of characters, things, or places, and similar devices. To give an idea of the kind of help offered by the *artes poeticae* in this field, it may be useful to quote some samples from Geoffroi de Vinsauf. Of *descriptio* he remarks: 'Descriptions spread out one's material. For when one has to make the brief statement that "Such a woman is beautiful," if a description of her beauty is given, then the brevity will be expanded.' And he adds an all-purpose verse example, describing in order a lady's round head, gold hair, milk-white forehead, black eyebrows, bright eyes, regular nose, gold and silver (i.e. peaches and cream) complexion, kind lips, and ivory teeth. Of periphrasis (*circumlocutio*) he writes:

> Periphrasis similarly expands one's material. For periphrasis occurs when we do not make some necessary statement straightforwardly, but, as it were, wander round in a by-path and ease it in by mentioning several details in a fuller verbal arrangement. Thus Virgil gives a periphrasis for Aeneas—'I sing of arms and of the man who first sailed from the land of Troy to Italy and came to its Lavinian shore' [the opening lines of the *Aeneid*]. Which is to say nothing other than 'I will write about Aeneas.'

Again, he writes as follows about the sub-species of apostrophe called *conduplicatio*: '*Conduplicatio* is the rhetorical colour used when we repeat the same word, sometimes through grief, sometimes through love, sometimes through indignation.' Geoffroi illustrates this 'colour'—a term often used, through the analogy between embellishing a narrative with rhetorical devices and colouring in a drawn outline—with quotations from Ovid and Juvenal, with a misquotation from Virgil, and with some verses of his own.[5] We may illustrate it from the prologue to Book II of *Troilus and Criseyde*:

> Owt of thise blake wawes for to saylle,
> O wynd, o wynd, the weder gynneth clere. (II 1-2)

Finally, the *artes poeticae* go on to catalogue and illustrate the various ornaments of style—figures of words (consisting of various kinds of verbal repetition, rhyming, and word-play) and figures of thought (such as metaphor, allegory, synecdoche, and so on). Some of these will be illustrated below, so there is no need to pause over them here.[6]

Only a complete reading of one of the *artes poeticae*—a task not likely to be undertaken by most modern readers—would bring out fully what comprehensiveness they aim at. Despite the 'colour' metaphor, it would hardly be possible to go through a poem written according to their precepts and to separate the 'rhetoric' from the main substance, because ideally 'rhetoric' would include and classify everything—all conceivable forms of speech except for the barest and most straightforward narrative. Thus the whole of any poem might be an intricate web of rhetorical devices, in the sense that the whole of it would be capable of being described in the terms of the *ars poetica*. Now because this theory of poetic composition was so familiar to educated poets and audiences in the Middle Ages, one result of its comprehensive nature is a keen awareness of the rules that are being followed *as* they are being followed. This produces a phenomenon which has been noticed by Professor Erwin Panofsky

---

[5] E. Faral, *Les arts poétiques du XIIᵉ et du XIIIᵉ siècle* (Paris, 1924), pp. 271-2, 273 and 276. There is an English translation of the *Poetria nova* by Margaret F. Nims (Toronto, 1967).

[6] For further information about the *artes poeticae*, see J. W. H. Atkins, *English Literary Criticism: the Medieval Phase* (London, 1943); C. S. Baldwin, *Medieval Rhetoric and Poetic* (New York, 1928); E. R. Curtius, *European Literature and the Latin Middle Ages*, trans. W. R. Trask (New York, 1953); E. de Bruyne, *Études d'esthétique médiévale*, vol. II (Bruges, 1946); R. O. Payne, *The Key of Remembrance* (New Haven, 1963).

as characteristic of two other medieval arts, namely architecture and scholastic philosophy. The phenomenon is what he calls *manifestatio*, the 'gratuitous clarification of function through form.' Panofsky points out that the scholastic philosophers, 'in contrast to Plato and Aristotle, felt compelled to make the orderliness and logic of their thought palpably explicit,' and they did this through a minute division into interrelated members, as in the *Summae* of St Thomas Aquinas. The same is true of Gothic architecture: 'the membrification of the edifice permitted [a medieval man] to re-experience the very processes of architectural composition just as the membrification of the *Summa* permitted him to re-experience the very processes of cogitation.'[7] One finds a very similar explicitness of form in the *artes poeticae* themselves, with their elaborately hierarchical classification of rhetorical devices, and one also finds it in the poems which were written under their influence. For example, in Chaucer's short poem *The Complaint of Mars*, Mars begins his actual *compleynt* or lamentation by saying,

> The ordre of compleynt requireth skylfully
> That yf a wight shal pleyne pitously,
> Ther mot be cause wherfore that men pleyne.
>
> (155–7)

If we take this naturalistically it sounds touchily on the defensive; in fact it simply shows a consciousness that in a lamentation, as in anything else, there are rules to be followed. At the beginning of *Troilus and Criseyde*, after the narrator has invoked Tisiphone and the lovers among his audience, he remarks, 'For now wil I gone streght to my matere' (I 53), thereby showing his consciousness of the need for an explicit transition from the introductory section of a poem to its main substance. In *The House of Fame* there is also an invocation near the beginning, but it follows a general discussion of dreams, and Chaucer marks the transition between the two sections with the lines

[7] E. Panofsky, *Gothic Architecture and Scholasticism* (London, 1957), pp. 59–60, 34, and 59. Jordan (*op. cit.*) has subsequently made a somewhat more ambitious application of Panofsky's ideas to the structure of Chaucer's poetry.

> But at my gynnynge, trusteth wel,
> I wol make invocacion,
> With special devocion,
> Unto the god of slep anoon.   (66-9)

In the *Canterbury Tales*, the Physician, having given a single *exemplum* to illustrate his argument about the need to protect innocence, remarks:

> Suffiseth oon ensample now as heere
> For I moot turne agayn to my matere.
>
> (*Canterbury Tales*, VI 103-4)

The Franklin explains in his prologue that, being a plain simple chap, he knows nothing of rhetoric:

> I lerned nevere rethorik, certeyn;
> Thyng that I speke, it moot be bare and pleyn.
> I sleep nevere on the Mount of Pernaso,
> Ne lerned Marcus Tullius Scithero.
> Colours ne knowe I none, withouten drede,
> But swiche colours as growen in the mede,
> Or elles swiche as men dye or peynte.
> Colours of rethoryk been to me queynte.
>
> (*Canterbury Tales*, V 719-26)

And yet when he comes to tell his tale he not only uses *circumlocutio* with the greatest accomplishment, but shows that he is perfectly conscious of what he is doing:

> But sodeynly bigonne revel newe
> Til that the brighte sonne loste his hewe;
> For th'orisonte hath reft the sonne his lyght—
> This is as muche to seye as it was nyght!   (1015-18)

The last line seems to recall deliberately such remarks by the rhetoricians as Geoffroi's frigidly reductive comment on the opening lines of the *Aeneid*, quoted above. Chaucer at least tends to expose rather than conceal the simpler structural and decorative relationships of his work (though this is not to say that he could learn from the *ars poetica* how to organize a complete poem). This habit of his is partly connected no doubt with the prevalence of oral delivery, for a listening public would require to have such relationships made unmistakably clear to them; but it would not have been possible without the existence of a rigid and familiar theory of composition.

We have seen that the *ars poetica* was a branch of 'rhetoric' in the medieval school curriculum, and that, although it consisted strictly speaking of rhetoric as applied to poetry, it was often referred to simply as 'rethoryk.' This subsumption of poetry into rhetoric is important for our understanding of medieval literary theory, and what kind of importance it has may be seen from a glance at the ancestry of the *ars*. The medieval *ars poetica* is not derived in any direct way from Aristotle's *Poetics*, but from various later classical works on rhetoric. Among its chief sources are the *Ars poetica* of Horace and a work called the *Rhetorica ad Herennium*, which in the Middle Ages was attributed to Cicero, but which is now generally supposed to be by an anonymous contemporary of Cicero. Now for Aristotle 'poems' form a special class of independent objects with their own internal structure, in which the governing principle is the plot or fable. Thus for him rhetoric is only a minor branch of poetics. The approach of the rhetoricians is very different: what they teach is the art of speaking persuasively in specific situations. The art of rhetoric does not itself provide these situations: they are provided by real life—a particular case has to be defended in the law-court, or a particular line of action advocated in the senate. This is why the medieval *ars poetica*, following classical rhetoric, has so little to say about *dispositio*, for this will vary according to the external circumstances. Moreover, even in classical times, rhetoric had largely ceased to have any vital social purpose—under the Caesars, for example, political oratory had ceased to be of any practical significance. Thus rhetoric had become directed not towards decision but towards verbal display. This was still more the case in the Middle Ages, when, as we have seen, rhetoric had become simply a school exercise. A contrast may be suggested here (it will be pursued in chapter 5) between the *ars poetica* and the *ars praedicandi*; the art of preaching still possessed a supremely important purpose outside itself, namely the saving of souls, and if only for this reason we might expect to find among writers of *artes praedicandi* clearer and harder thought about their art than among writers of *artes poeticae*. For the medieval rhetoricians the pressure of narrative or argument had ceased to be important, and thus they advocated a constant turning aside from the main path of a work into descriptive digressions. For them, indeed, the art of poetry is above all an art

of description: a poem is a peg on which descriptions are to be
hung, and the shape of the peg is of little importance. We can see
this assumption operating most clearly in the naive mind of
Bokenham. Having embarked on the legend of St Margaret, he
remarks:

> Wherfore, if the crafth of descrypcyounn
> I cowde as weel both forge and fyle
> As cowd Boyce in his Phisycal Consolacyounn,
> Or as Homer, Ovyde, or elles Virgyle,
> Or Galfryd of Ynglond, I wolde compyle
> A clere descripcyounn ful expressely
> Of alle hyr feturys evene by and by.[8]

Description is evidently the characteristic power of the supreme
poets: Boethius, Homer, Ovid, Virgil, and Geoffroi de Vinsauf.
Another way in which, for us, the usefulness of the *artes poeticae* is
limited is that, because they are textbooks, they exclude value-
judgments. This is so even by comparison with their sources. For
example, in classical rhetoric *amplificatio* and *abbreviatio* refer to
importance: material is 'amplified' by being given more dignity.
But in the *ars poetica*, as we have seen, these terms refer simply to
length. Again, both classical and medieval rhetoric divide literary
styles into three kinds, high, middle and low. In classical rhetoric
these too are a matter of intrinsic importance, and of the orator's
powers. Thus the *Ad Herennium* explains:

> There are, then, three kinds of style, . . . to which discourse, if
> faultless, confines itself: the first we call the Grand; the second,
> the Middle; the third, the Simple. The Grand type consists of a
> smooth and ornate arrangement of impressive words. The Middle
> type consists of words of a lower, yet not of the lowest and most
> colloquial, class of words. The Simple type is brought down even
> to the most current idiom of standard speech.
> A discourse will be composed in the Grand style if to each idea
> are applied the most ornate words that can be found for it,
> whether literal or figurative; if impressive thoughts are chosen,
> such as are used in Amplification and Appeal to Pity; and if we
> employ figures of thought and figures of diction which have

[8] Ed. Serjeantson, ll. 407–13.

grandeur. . . [9]

In the medieval *ars poetica*, on the other hand, the three styles have been reduced to referring to social status. Jean de Garlande writes: 'Thus there are three styles, according to the three human estates; the low style belongs to the life of shepherds, the middle to that of farmers, and the high to that of high persons who are superior to shepherds and farmers.'[10] A similar social distinction between styles is assumed by the Host in the *Canterbury Tales* (though he seems to have the *ars dictaminis* in mind), when he tells the Clerk,

> Youre termes, youre colours, and youre figures,
> Keepe hem in stoor til so be that ye endite
> Heigh style, as whan that men to kynges write.
> *(Canterbury Tales*, IV 16–18)

The *ars poetica* offers, then, a conception of literature which is severely limited. Despite this, however, various suggestions have been made by twentieth-century scholars as to how our own judgment of medieval literature should be affected by this conception. We may take, as representative of these, the sweeping claim made by Mr D. A. Pearsall when he argues that in reading medieval literature the modern reader should abandon all other standards of judgment and substitute for them 'the single criterion of efficacy within a conventional framework.'[11] It is true that such an approach might help us to exclude the preconceptions of our own time where these are irrelevant; it might help us, for example, to exclude the demand for directly personal expression in literature. As E. R. Curtius has written, 'Merely from the rhetorical character of medieval poetry, it follows that, in interpreting a poem, we must ask, not on what "experience" it was based, but what theme the poet set himself to treat.'[12] But the criterion of 'efficacy' is in itself, of course, essentially subjective, and it must be remembered that it was not a concept much treated by the medieval rhetoricians. For example, in the various treatments by rhetoricians of *descriptio*,

---

[9] Trans. Harry Caplan (London, 1954), pp. 253 and 255.
[10] *Poetria*, ed. G. Mari, *Romanische Forschungen* XIII (1902), p. 920.
[11] D. A. Pearsall, 'Rhetorical "Descriptio" in *Sir Gawain and the Green Knight*,' *Modern Language Review* L (1955), p. 134.
[12] *Op. cit.*, p. 158.

Mathieu de Vendôme alone comes near to raising the question of its efficacy, and all he says is that 'the description of a character is often timely and often superfluous' (Faral, p. 118). He offers no further help as to the criteria for judging timeliness and superfluity, and it is plain that the rhetoricians generally have little interest in such matters, for they possess neither the notion of a poem as an object with its own internal structure nor the notion of any external purpose for poetry. Mr Pearsall, however, has tried to show how a knowledge of the *ars poetica* can be of use to a modern reader of a specific medieval poem; and the poem he has chosen is, conveniently enough, that which we were discussing in the last chapter, *Sir Gawain and the Green Knight*. He is particularly interested in the poet's use of *descriptio*. He writes:

> ... the poet does not describe the winter in the mountains because he is fond of wild, romantic scenery and wants us to share his pleasure in it, but because the narrative demands at this point an illustration of the discomforts of Gawain's 'anious vyage.' The description is functional in the strict *rhetorical* sense. . . . The winter-scene at the opening of Fit IV is likewise a *rhetorical* amplification of Gawain's state of mind. . . . A similar *rhetorical* motive can be seen in most of the nature-descriptions in *Gawain*.[13]

It is perfectly true that the various *descriptiones* in *Sir Gawain and the Green Knight* are not extraneous but functional; they have work to do within the total economy of the poem, and are not there simply because the poet liked them, any more than the little dog is in *The Book of the Duchess* simply because Chaucer liked little dogs. But to call this functionalism 'rhetorical' is quite misleading, because the rhetoricians have so little to say about it—only that descriptions are sometimes timely and sometimes superfluous. And even if they said more about it, we should hardly need to go to them to be informed of such a commonplace as that descriptive passages in a narrative ought to have some purpose connected with the narrative. A modern reader who was ignorant of that would be beyond any help that the *artes poeticae* might give him. I might indeed, in discussing *Sir Gawain and the Green Knight* in the last chapter, have argued like Pearsall that one needed the help of the *artes poeticae* to understand it,

[13] *Op. cit.*, pp. 132–3 (my italics).

but for a different purpose. I remarked that the Temptation element seemed to be inserted by the poet into the Beheading Game element as a digression away from the main story, and that the audience would not realize that it was not really a digression until Gawain arrived at the Green Chapel and had his interview there with the Green Knight. Then Gawain, and the listeners, learned that the Temptation formed the real test he had to undergo, and that he had already failed it. Now I might have argued that in arranging his story thus the *Gawain*-poet was following the precepts of the rhetoricians. Geoffroi de Vinsauf writes:

> If we wish to employ digression, let us see to it that this digression is suitable and relevant to the subject, and thus we shall avoid the fault which is called 'unsuitable digression.' ... This fault is often incurred by many writers when they digress in describing this or that thing which is described readily and customarily, when however the description has little or no application to the matter in hand.[14]

These remarks are true enough, and even display a certain practical shrewdness, which a beginner in composition would do well to take advantage of. But, so far as the principles of literary construction are concerned, they say nothing that a competent poet would not already know in his bones. The *Gawain*-poet, certainly, would know well enough that digressions must not be irrelevant without having to be told so by Geoffroi.

There have been other modern attempts to find in the *artes poeticae* a guide to our understanding of medieval literature. In particular, scholars have been concerned to find in them some clues towards the structure of medieval works, even though, as we have seen, this is a subject about which on the surface the *artes poeticae* seem to have little to say. For example, in medieval prose romances we find a somewhat baffling narrative structure, in which a large number of stories are treated simultaneously, being interwoven like the threads of a tapestry. The English reader will probably be most familiar with this narrative method in some parts of the work of Malory. Now Professor Eugène Vinaver has pointed out that this method meant that 'each episode appeared to be a digression from

[14] Faral, *op. cit.*, pp. 314–15.

the previous one and at the same time a sequel to some earlier unfinished story,' and he has claimed that it can be explained by reference to the rhetorical conception of *digressio* which we have just seen Geoffroi de Vinsauf discussing.[15] Geoffroi distinguishes between two different kinds of *digressio*, and writes about them as follows:

> One method of digression is when we digress *within* the subject-matter to another part of the subject-matter; the other method is when we digress *from* the subject-matter to something else outside it. We digress from the subject-matter to another part of the subject-matter when we omit that part that comes next and take up first another part which follows. . . . And we digress from the subject-matter to something else outside it when we introduce comparisons or similitudes, so that we fit them into the subject-matter.[16]

But the example of 'comparisons or similitudes' suggests that by *digressio* here Geoffroi means something on a very small scale—far smaller than the structural interweavings of prose romance. And this is supported by the examples he gives of the first kind of digression. He remarks, for instance:

> When one has to say that 'Acteon was tired out with hunting and went to get his breath back beside a delightful fountain,' after one has said that he is tired, and before one says that he went to the fountain, there should be a digression about the fountain, so that its beauty may be described, and it must be explained afterwards that he went there to get his breath back. . . . Similarly, when one has to say that 'The lovers separated from each other in the springtime,' first the springtime must be described, and after that one must say, 'Then they separated.'[17]

Clearly Geoffroi is not thinking of *narrative* digression at all, but of *stylistic* digression, the insertion of descriptions, comparisons, and

---

[15] See E. Vinaver, Introduction to *Le Roman de Balain*, ed. M. D. Legge (Manchester, 1942), p. xiii, and Introduction to *The Works of Sir Thomas Malory* (Oxford, 1947), vol. I, pp. li-lii. The quotation is from the latter, p. lii.

[16] Faral, *op. cit.*, pp. 274–5.

[17] *Ibid.*, p. 274.

the other amplifying devices with which the *ars poetica* is so largely concerned. Vinaver himself admits that 'It is doubtful whether Geoffroi de Vinsauf or any other medieval rhetorician had in mind anything approaching the methods of thirteenth-century romance writers;'[18] and in fact there is no evidence at all that the influence of such teaching is to be found in the narrative methods of the prose romances.

A different link between the *ars poetica* and the actual structure of medieval poems has been suggested by the late Miss Dorothy Everett. Miss Everett argues that the *dispositio* of some of Chaucer's poems could best be understood as exemplifying Geoffroi de Vinsauf's instructions for a particular kind of amplification called *expolitio* or *interpretatio*. In the *Poetria nova* Geoffroi writes: 'When the meaning is single, let it not come forth content with one garb, but let its garments vary and let it put on changing clothes; resume what has been said before in different words; repeat a single thing in many sentences; conceal the same idea in manifold shapes; be various and yet the same' (Faral, p. 204). (In writing thus he is, incidentally, exemplifying his own instructions, by repeating the same command in as many forms as possible.) Miss Everett suggests that this principle underlies the structure of, for instance, *The Book of the Duchess*, where a story read by the narrator to cure insomnia is followed by a dream, and the story and the dream form 'two examples of the same theme—the loss of a loved one and the grief of the one who is left.'[19] The story is Ovid's tale of Ceyx and Alcyone, and the dream concerns a 'man in blak' who has lost his beloved wife; thus the story concerns a wife's loss of her husband, and the dream a husband's loss of his wife. Now the connection Miss Everett makes with Geoffroi's teaching seems to me to demand two comments. The first is that such a parallelism between a dream and an experience enjoyed immediately before falling asleep is

[18] *Malory*, vol. I, p. li.
[19] Dorothy Everett, *Essays on Middle English Literature* (Oxford, 1955), p. 162. Another attempt to find in the *ars poetica*, and particularly in *expolitio*, a key to the structure of a medieval poem has been made by Professor A. M. F. Gunn in his *The Mirror of Love* (Lubbock, 1952). The poem in question is the *Roman de la Rose*, which most readers would regard as something less than an ideal example of coherent literary form.

precisely what we should be led to expect both from medieval theories about dreams[20] and from our own experience of dreaming. Indeed the whole structure of *The Book of the Duchess* reflects the subtle thematic correspondences that medieval people expected to find, and that are really found, between dreams and real life and within dreams themselves. Thus there is no need to turn to the *ars poetica* for an explanation of the *dispositio* of *The Book of the Duchess*. And the second comment is that, as Miss Everett herself points out, when Geoffroi gives his instructions for *expolitio* 'he is almost certainly thinking only of verbal variation,' so that the most one can claim is that 'a creative mind, occupied with problems of organization, might have found in his words a hint for variation on a larger scale.'[21] We shall shortly be considering an example of *expolitio* in another poem, and we shall see that it is quite different from any principle of structure to be found in *The Book of the Duchess*. Whether a 'hint' passed from Geoffroi to Chaucer is something we are never likely to know.

These examples seem to lead us to the conclusion that only if one had a preconceived notion that medieval poets *must* have learnt something significant about literary structure from the *artes poeticae* would one insist on connections such as those made by Vinaver and Miss Everett. So far as general precepts about the organization of poems are concerned, the rhetoricians have little to offer but commonplaces—helpful for schoolboys but offering to modern readers only the temptation to wring out of them meanings more sophisticated than they originally possessed. But we have insisted that the chief concern of the *artes poeticae* is not with poetic organization at all, but with the details of literary style, and we have seen one or two examples of how their stylistic precepts are followed by a poet such as Chaucer. It is here, on their own ground, that we could reasonably hope to get most help from them. For this purpose, I think it will be useful to take as an example a rather longer passage of medieval poetry, and see what help the *artes poeticae* can give us in analysing its style. The passage I have chosen comes from an anonymous early medieval poem called *The Owl and the Nightingale* —one of the finest English poems of its period. It dates from about

[20] See below, pp. 139–47
[21] Everett, p. 162, n. 2.

1200, and is itself, like the *artes poeticae*, a product of the Twelfth-Century Renaissance, so that we might hope to find close connections between the two. The poem takes the form of a disputation between the two birds of its title, and the particular passage chosen comes about a third of the way through it; it is a speech by the narrator himself, inserted between a long and triumphant oration by the Owl and the Nightingale's reply to it.

He mot gon to al mid ginne,
Wan the horte both on winne;   670
An the man mot on other segge:
He mot bihemmen and bilegge,
Yif muth withute mai biwro
That me the horte noght niso.
An sone mai a word misreke   675
Thar muth shal agen horte speke,
An sone mai a word misstorte
Thar muth shal speken agen horte.
Ac notheles, yut upe thon,
Her is to red wo hine kon,   680
For never nis wit so kene
So thane red him is a wene;
Thanne erest kumeth his yephede
Thone hit is alre mest on drede.
For Alfered seide of olde quide—   685
An yut hit nis of horte islide:
'Wone the bale is alre hecst
Thonne is the bote alre necst;'
For wit west among his sore,
An for his sore hit is the more.   690
Forthi nis nevere mon redles
Ar his horte bo witles,
Ac yif that he forlost his wit
Thonne is his redpurs al toslit:
Yif he ne kon his wit atholde   695
Ne fint he red in one folde.
For Alferid seide, that wel kuthe—
Evre he spac mid sothe muthe:
'Wone the bale is alre hecst
Thanne is the bote alre nest.'   700
   The Nightingale al hire hoghe

Mid rede hadde wel bitoghe;
Among the harde, among the toghte,
Ful wel mid rede hire bithoghte,
An hadde andswere gode ifunde   705
Among al hire harde stunde.[22]

A man whose heart is troubled must always go to work with cunning; such a man must not speak what he thinks: he must trim his words and explain them away, if the mouth can cover things up on the outside, so that people cannot perceive the heart within. For a word can quickly go astray when the mouth speaks against the heart, and a word can quickly go wrong when the mouth speaks against the heart. But nevertheless, as against that, here is a way out for whoever understands it, for never is one's intelligence so keen as when one is in doubt what to do; its cunning appears for the first time when it is most frightened. For Alfred remarked in an ancient saying, which even now is not forgotten: 'When trouble is at its height, then the remedy is nearest'; for intelligence grows when it is in trouble, and it grows because of the trouble it is in. And so a man is never helpless unless his heart lacks intelligence, but if he loses his intelligence his bag of tricks is slit open: if he cannot retain his intelligence he will not be able to find a plan in any fold of it. For Alfred, who was very wise, said—and he always spoke the truth—'When trouble is at its height, then the remedy is nearest.'

The Nightingale in her anxiety had gone to work well and wisely; in these difficult and strained circumstances she had pondered well and wisely, and had found a good answer at this difficult time.

Clearly this passage is enormously diffuse. Its prose content is very small, and could probably be summarized quite adequately in a sentence or two, but it has undergone the process of amplification and been drawn out to nearly forty lines. It might indeed stand as an example of *amplificatio* in a vernacular rhetoric. The last six lines of the passage refer to the Nightingale's particular situation—the difficult position she has been put in by the Owl's clever arguments —but the earlier lines form a more general discussion arising out of her situation. The amplification in these first thirty-two lines consists of two main phases or movements. The first, down to line 678,

[22] Ed. E. G. Stanley (London, 1960).

turns on an antithesis between *muth* (mouth) and *horte* (heart), and involves much repetition of these words. The second phase turns on an antithesis between *wit* (intelligence) and *red* (advice, or a plan), and again involves repetitions of these key words. Now verbal repetition of the kind found here is among the most common 'figures of words' treated by the *artes poeticae*. The use of verbal repetition is defended by the *Rhetorica ad Herennium* as follows: '... frequent recourse to the same word is not dictated by verbal poverty; rather there inheres in the repetition an elegance which the ear can distinguish more easily than words can explain.'[23] It does indeed require the ear to respond to these repetitions, and not simply the eye: this aspect of the *ars poetica* is closely connected with the prevalence of oral delivery. The two movements I mentioned are closely connected with each other. According to medieval physiology the heart (in the first movement) is the seat of *wit* (in the second movement), and *wit* in turn is of course the origin of *red*. Now the passage as a whole makes use of one particular means of amplification, the device called *expolitio*. We have already seen what Geoffroi de Vinsauf has to say about this. It is defined more lucidly in the *Ad Herennium*:

> [*Expolitio*] consists in dwelling on the same topic and yet seeming to say something ever new. It is accomplished in two ways: by merely repeating the same idea, or by descanting on it. We shall not repeat the same thing precisely—for that, to be sure, would weary the hearer and not refine [*expolire*] the idea—but with changes.[24]

These are exactly the methods we find used in the passage from *The Owl and the Nightingale*. The poet produces elegant variations on his two basic themes, but only once does he exactly repeat the same idea. This is when he quotes the proverb attributed to Alfred in line 687 and again in line 699. The use of such a proverb is itself an example of the 'figure of words' called *sententia*, 'a saying drawn from life, which shows concisely either what happens or [what] ought to happen in life.'[25] This is one of the figures most commonly used

[23] Trans. Caplan, p. 281.
[24] *Ibid.*, p. 365.
[25] *Ibid.*, p. 289. See also Faral, p. 113.

in medieval poetry, and not only as a way of beginning a poem: Chaucer's works, for example, are full of *sententiae*, usually with the air of being pieces of folk-wisdom. We can recognize in the passage many other figures named by the *artes poeticae*. Take for example lines 675 to 678. Here we have two couplets, of which the second almost but not quite exactly repeats the first:

> An sone mai a word misreke
> Thar muth shal agen horte speke,
> An sone mai a word misstorte
> Thar muth shal speken agen horte.

Alternate lines begin with the same words; that is an example of *repetitio*. In lines 676 and 678 the same words are used, but in a different order; this device is called *transgressio*. Line 677 repeats line 675 except that it replaces *misreke* with a word of almost the same meaning, *misstorte*; that is an example of the 'figure of words' called *interpretatio* (for *interpretatio* is the name of this small figure as well as being a synonym for the larger-scale *expolitio*). There is perhaps another example of *interpretatio* in lines 693 to 696, where the second couplet exactly repeats the meaning of the first. In line 694 the word *redpurs* is probably one invented by the poet of *The Owl and the Nightingale*—at least it has not been found anywhere else in Middle English—and it means literally 'plan-purse' or 'bag of tricks.' To invent a word in this way is to use the device called *nominatio*; there is an amusing example of it earlier in the same poem, when the Owl says that the Nightingale, because she chatters so much, ought to be called not *nightingale* but *galegale*, which we might translate as 'gabblegale' or 'gabbingale.' In the two lines 689–90, with the repetition of the word *sore* in two different positions, we have an example of the figure called *traductio*. And so on; one could pick out many other named verbal devices from the passage, but no doubt enough has been done to show how comprehensively it might be analysed in the terms of the *ars poetica*.

We must now ask, however, what would be the use of such an analysis? What is the point of being able to identify all these verbal devices? We may guess that an educated medieval listener to the poem, perhaps brought up at school on Mathieu de Vendôme, would have been able to identify them, and would have been thinking to himself as he heard the poem read, 'What a neat *traductio*!' or 'That was a cunning *interpretatio*!' This is possible; but it is perhaps more likely that a listener, however expert, would not have been able to grasp more than that general 'elegance' (*festivitas*) noted by the author of the *Ad Herennium* as a product of verbal repetition. In either case we may well feel that, as Butler puts it in the well-known couplet from *Hudibras*,

> All a rhetorician's rules
> Teach nothing but to name his tools.

When the tools have been named, what follows? What an acquaintance with the medieval *ars poetica* can do for us is to arouse a general attentiveness to the patternings of sound and syntax. It can sharpen the 'auditory imagination' and make us more aware of the elaborate echoing that goes on inside much medieval verse. But for the use, beyond the merely decorative, to which these intricacies of sound are put, we shall have to resort as usual to our own critical judgment. The passage we are looking at does have a function within *The Owl and the Nightingale* as a whole, a function which is partly practical and partly more strictly literary. The practical side of it is that these lines come about a third of the way through a poem of nearly 1800 lines. It is likely that, after hearing over six hundred lines of argument in verse, an audience of listeners would welcome some sort of interlude. The passage under discussion would provide this by demanding from them a different kind of attention from that required by the argument which precedes and follows, and thus supplying them with a less taxing form of literary pleasure—music between the acts, as it were. The literary function is that this passage marks a turning-point in the development of the poem's meaning. At the beginning of *The Owl and the Nightingale* it is the Nightingale, with its associations with summer and young love, that seems the most attractive of the two birds, but gradually we come to see that the poet is on the side of the moralizing Owl. It is in this passage, with its emphasis on the difficulties the Nightingale has in answering the Owl's arguments, that the change in sympathy first becomes clear. Thus the verbal elaboration, the amplification through *expolitio*, is necessary to emphasize a crucial change in the poem's direction. But of course the *artes poeticae* cannot tell us this;

in order to discover the function of the passage we must analyse the poem for ourselves.

What emerges from this discussion of the *ars poetica* is, I think, that while a study of elementary medieval textbooks on poetry is certainly of some value to a modern reader of medieval literature, that value is somewhat specialized. It would be a great mistake, I am sure, to erect the *artes poeticae* as a barrier between modern readers and medieval authors—to suggest that a study of the *ars poetica* is a necessary preliminary to a true understanding of medieval poetry. Indeed, we have seen in this chapter how modern scholars, who are perfectly capable of analysing the structure of poems for themselves, have had to distort the *artes poeticae* in order to find in them some warrant for their own interpretations of medieval works. Yet the *artes poeticae* are of real value for the things they assume and imply rather than for the things they say, because they can bring us close to the unexamined assumptions on which medieval poetry was written. They assume that the poet's role will not be that of a creator or inventor. He will begin with a pre-existing *materia*, and his task will be to re-present and reinterpret that *materia* for the benefit of his audience. Thus the situation of the poet is the humble one of a mediator or middleman; and perhaps medieval vernacular poets felt this even more than the writers of Latin verses envisaged by the *artes poeticae*. So much of the work of a French or English poet was a matter of 'translation' from revered Latin originals: how could such poets see themselves as more than 'dwarves standing on the shoulders of giants,' as Bernard of Chartres is reported to have said about his contemporaries in the twelfth century? We shall see in the next chapter how in Chaucer's work this role becomes itself part of the dramatic fiction of the poem. And another assumption built into the *artes poeticae*, which also puts the poet in a humble position, is that poetry is less a matter of inspiration than of craftsmanship: it is a job to be done, like the work of a ploughman or carpenter. Chaucer may toy with grander ideas from time to time, as in *The House of Fame*, when he appeals to Apollo, the 'god of science and of lyght' to aid him with his 'devyne vertu' (1091, 1101), but fundamentally he and his fellow-poets of the Middle Ages saw poetry as an art defined as 'a collection of precepts by which we are informed how to do something more easily than by nature.'[26] This identification of art with craft leaves its marks everywhere in the deliberate and unconcealed artifice of medieval poetry, though it does not, of course, relieve us of the responsibility of deciding for ourselves which medieval poems have permanent value, and which are no more than respectably workmanlike constructions. It remains the case that the usefulness of the *artes poeticae* for what they explicitly say is limited. On the one hand they have no means of considering poems as objects with their own internal structure; on the other hand they can suggest no purpose by which their art may be governed. These deficiencies are not present in another branch of medieval theory about literature, the *ars praedicandi* or art of preaching, and in chapter 5 I shall turn to examine this. But first I wish to take one of Chaucer's poems as an example of how a great poet can make use of the underlying conceptions of the *ars poetica* rather than of its precepts.

[26] Anonymous twelfth-century definition, quoted in de Bruyne, vol. II, p. 372.

4 Chaucer's Clerk's Tale as a Medieval Poem

We have seen in the previous chapter that the medieval *ars poetica* begins from the assumption that the writer would not be the inventor of his own material, but would be reworking some already existing story or argument, by amplification, or by abbreviation, or by some combination of the two. His prime task, in theory at least, would be to pass on matter that he had received from some existing source, some authority or *auctour*. If the poet is telling a story, then that story is fixed and, in essentials, unalterable; the writer's creative work (as we would see it) comes in the way he tells it. Perhaps the most obvious example of this can be found in the great medieval cycles of Arthurian romance (of which *Sir Gawain and the Green Knight* forms a small but highly distinguished offshoot). Writer after writer, for century after century, takes up the same body of stories, adds or omits a little here and there, but essentially retells, reshapes, reinterprets the same body of material. And the retelling could be a matter of reinterpretation. If medieval *rhetorica* taught all possible literary devices, medieval *grammatica* taught the interpretation of existing literary texts, the finding of an appropriate *sen* in an existing *matiere*. Professor Vinaver has noted, in the case of Arthurian romance, 'the striking contrast between the continuity in the transmission of the *matiere* and the corresponding degree of instability in the position of the *sen*'; and elsewhere he has written that when an educated medieval writer

set himself the task of making a traditional or a classical story into a romance nothing seemed more important to him than the process of interpreting his material in the way he had been taught to do [when he studied Latin texts as part of *grammatica*]. In practice this meant either commenting on the narrative or letting the characters themselves explain their feelings and their behaviour.[1]

[1] *Works of Sir Thomas Malory*, vol. I, p. lxvi, and 'From Epic to

Thus the kind of skill which nowadays goes into literary criticism went in the Middle Ages partly into commentary on Scripture, but partly into retellings of existing stories, which incorporated the findings of the writer's critical and interpretative reading of his *auctours*. A Dr Leavis of the Middle Ages, for example, would have embodied his creatively sensitive interpretations of existing literary works not in critical essays on *Middlemarch* or *Women in Love* but in rewritten versions of those novels; and a medieval Professor Wilson Knight would not have published several volumes of Shakespeare criticism but would simply have rewritten Shakespeare's plays so as to bring out more clearly the meanings he sees in them. The new versions might have borne the same relation to their originals as, say, the anonymous *Perlesvaus* to Chrétien de Troyes' *Perceval*, or as Chaucer's *Troilus and Criseyde* to Boccaccio's *Il Filostrato*.

The medieval poet then is a mediator, and perhaps a critical mediator, between his story and his audience. The audience is extremely important, because, as we have seen, most medieval literature was written to be read aloud to a group of listeners. Paradoxically, as it may seem, this mediatory position tended to give the medieval writer much more prominence in his own work than modern writers usually have. In reading a medieval narrative poem, we are often very much aware of the narrator's presence, as someone who calls himself 'I' and addresses us as 'lordings,' or 'this fair company,' or simply as 'you':

> And ye wyl a whyle be stylle
> I schal telle yow how thay wroght.
> (*Sir Gawain and the Green Knight*, 1996–7)

The narrator is always bustling around, moving us on from one part of the narrative to the next, making sure we are listening, offering his own suppositions about the characters' motives, and so on. The narrator may himself be a dramatic construct, a *persona* or 'creature of the imagination,' as Kittredge called the naive narrator of *The Book of the Duchess*, though even then he may be developed out of

Romance,' *Bulletin of the John Rylands Library*, XLVI (1963–4), 476–503, p. 493. Vinaver has developed these ideas more systematically in a book just published at the time of writing, *The Rise of Romance* (Oxford, 1971).

the face the poet habitually presented to the world. Doubtless Chaucer was in the habit of pretending to be simpler than he really was; it would have been a valuable skill for a diplomat. By his own presence in the poem, whether genuine or dramatic, the poet will tend to draw his audience into it too, to join with him in finding the true motivation or the true *sen* that will render the existing story fully intelligible. Indeed, for the very reason that the story exists separately from its teller, being *given* in the same way as real life is given, it will seem natural that more than one way of interpreting it should be possible. Ideally, the audience will have the sense of participating in the re-creation of the story. At first sight it may seem that a writer who felt bound to work only with stories that already possessed a fixed and unalterable outline would be in an intolerably constricted situation; but in fact the role of middleman, master of ceremonies, or critical commentator, could leave the poet a remarkable freedom to 'colour' the outline (rhetorical devices, as we have seen, were frequently called *colores*) in any way he chose, and to establish a truly personal rapport with his listeners.

Some of Chaucer's poems—*The Miller's Tale* or *The Summoner's Tale*, for instance—may have had as their *materia* a folktale or other popular form of story, transmitted by word of mouth; and in such cases the 'colouring' of the finished version would be all his own. Much more often, though, Chaucer began with a literary source, which was already highly coloured; and indeed in many cases he seems to have compared different literary versions of the same narrative, to have used now one and now another, and to have added his own critical commentary to those already present in his sources. In such cases the finished work has something of the nature of a palimpsest, or, better, of a medieval Scriptural text, in which the text itself is surrounded by layers of later commentary by various theologians. This is the situation with *Troilus and Criseyde*, which we shall be considering in the next chapter, and also with *The Clerk's Tale*. It is true, in the case of *The Clerk's Tale*, that there are many folktale or fairytale versions of the story of the patient Griselda, which cannot have been unknown to Chaucer and his audience. But Chaucer's actual *materia* for *The Clerk's Tale* was not something of this kind, existing only in bare outline; it consisted of two sophisticated literary documents. One was a Latin work by Petrarch, called *De obedientia ac fide uxoria mythologia* ('A Fable of Wifely Obedience and Devotion'); the other was a French translation of Petrarch's Latin, *Le livre Griseldis*.[2] In these sources a great deal of colouring and explanatory work had already been done. The motives of the characters had been examined, they had been supplied with speeches, the setting of the story had been described, and its *sen* or inner meaning had already been expounded. The purpose of the story, for Petrarch, was to supply in Griselda a model for human constancy towards God. In his conclusion he writes:

> This story it has seemed good to me to weave anew, in another tongue, not so much that it might stir the matrons of our times to imitate the patience of this wife — who seems to me scarcely imitable — as that it might stir all those who read it to imitate the woman's steadfastness, at least; so that they may have the resolution to perform for God what this woman performed for her husband.[3] (pp. 310-11)

In that sentence, Petrarch refers to himself quite openly as 'I', and presents himself not as the creator of the story but as its re-writer: it comes naturally to him, evidently, to adopt the role of mediator between story and audience. On the other hand, he addresses not a listening, but a reading public: partly because he is writing in a learned language, and partly perhaps because in Italy, even before the invention of printing, there already existed a larger reading public than in England, so that Petrarch had already begun to approach our modern situation of the independent writer writing for readers whom he might never meet.

[2] The Latin and French texts can be found in W. F. Bryan and G. Dempster, *The Sources and Analogues of Chaucer's Canterbury Tales* (Chicago, 1941). The translation of the Latin used here is that of R. D. French, *A Chaucer Handbook*, 2nd. edn. (New York, 1947), pp. 291-311. For a parallel text of part of the *Tale* and the corresponding part of *Le livre Griseldis*, see *The Clerk's Prologue and Tale*, ed. James Winny (Cambridge, 1966), pp. 91-9.

[3] Petrarch speaks of re-writing his version 'in another tongue' because he was himself translating it from the Italian of Boccaccio (*Decameron*, Day X, Story 10—the final tale of the collection). The Latin phrase corresponding to 'in another tongue' is *stylo nunc alio*; but it would appear that in the manuscript used by Chaucer this read *stylo nunc alto*, 'in a high style', and that it was this false reading that led Chaucer to refer to Petrarch's *heigh stile* (*Canterbury Tales*, IV 41).

Chaucer's sources for *The Clerk's Tale*, then, were not mere
outlines, but were already fully 'coloured'. The consequence of this
was a change in his role as the latest of many retellers of an old story.
Instead of being a mere mediator, who expands and contracts,
dramatizes and explains, as he thinks fit, he becomes a critical commentator on his source. He feels obliged to pass on to us not just the
bare events of the story, but the colouring which the distinguished
authority Petrarch gave them; but he also feels free to comment in
a critical and even subversive way on Petrarch's treatment of the
story. In *The Clerk's Tale* Chaucer, or the Clerk, exercises this free-
dome from the very beginning. Henceforward, in order to avoid
confusion, I shall refer to the narrator of *The Clerk's Tale* as the
Clerk rather than as Chaucer. This is not in the least to suggest
that we are meant to be interested in the *Tale* chiefly, or even at all,
as an expression of the personality of the Clerk; but, whatever may
be said about the possibility that Chaucer wrote his version before
he had thought of *The Canterbury Tales* at all, we are certainly very
much aware in reading it of the presence of a teller in the *Tale*, and in
the actual context of *The Canterbury Tales* that teller is not Chaucer
(who tells two other stories) but the Clerk. The Clerk, then, acts
from the very beginning as a critical commentator on his source.
He mentions only the Latin version, and it will be a convenient
simplification if we follow him in this. He unashamedly begins by
telling the pilgrims that he did not invent the story himself—a
medieval audience would have thought worse rather than better of
him if he had invented it—but got it from the 'worthy clerk, . . .
Fraunceys Petrak, the lauriat poete' (27, 31).[4] He comments appreci-
atively on the 'heigh stile' (41) of Petrarch's version; and at the end
of the story he repeats this reference to Petrarch and his high style
(1147–8). These allusions to 'heigh stile' are somewhat mischievous,
no doubt, since the Host has particularly asked the Clerk *not* to use
the 'termes, . . . colours, and . . . figures' (16) that belong to the high
style, but to tell his tale 'so pleyn . . . That we may understonde
what ye seye' (19–20). For our present purpose, however, their main
point is to show that there is no attempt whatever to claim for the
narrator any higher role than that of a commentator on an estab-

---

[4] This and all subsequent *Clerk's Tale* line-numbers refer to *Canterbury Tales* IV.

lished and classical text. But he is a *critical* commentator. He begins, almost as soon as he has praised Petrarch's high style, by criticizing the amplification which is its consequence. Petrarch has begun with a 'prohemye' (43), in which he describes the geographical setting of the story. The Clerk repeats some of this, and then somewhat sharply comments that it is not really relevant, but is only used as a way of introducing his *materia*:

> And trewely, as to my juggement,
> Me thynketh it a thyng impertinent,
> Save that he wole conveyen his mateere. (53–5)

He therefore cuts it short. Once again, in the dramatic context of the pilgrimage, the Clerk no doubt has his eye on the Host, who is presumably getting impatient with all this elevated *amplificatio*. The Clerk is teasing him; he judges very well the point at which the Host is about to explode, and at that precise moment he cuts the 'prohemye' and gets to the plain tale the Host has asked for. But at the same time this business with the 'prohemye' has established the presence of the Clerk as a commentator who will not hesitate to introduce his own personal responses to his source—

> And trewely, as to *my* juggement,
> *Me* thynketh it a thyng impertinent.

The Clerk begins as a literary critic; he very quickly proceeds to become a moral critic of his source.

The *Tale* proper begins with three stanzas about 'Saluces' (Saluzzo) and its marquis, Walter, who was full of the virtues that belong to noble youth, 'Save in somme thynges that he was to blame' (76). And then a whole stanza is devoted to explaining in what he was to blame:

> I blame hym thus, that he considered noght
> In tyme comynge what myghte hym bityde,
> But on his lust present was al his thoght,
> As for to hauke and hunte on every syde.
> Wel ny alle othere cures leet he slyde,
> And eek he nolde—and that was worst of alle—
> Wedde no wyf, for noght that may bifalle. (78–84)

Now that criticism of Walter is in Petrarch too, but it is not presented as having the personal feelings of the narrator behind it.
Petrarch writes that Walter was 'marked out . . . for leadership in all
things, save that . . . he took very little care for the future . . . and—
what his subjects bore most ill—he shrank even from a hint of marriage' (p. 292). In Petrarch there is no narrator saying '*I* blame hym,'
and the special reprehension of his unwillingness to marry—'and that
was worst of alle'—is not attributed to the narrator but to Walter's
people. In Chaucer's version, even at this early stage, the effect is not
of Petrarch's judicious neutrality, but of a personal intervention into
the story by the Clerk, as a partisan, and one who disapproves of the
part that Walter plays in it. He cannot alter Walter's actions—they
are in the source—but he can at least express his disapproval of them.
He goes on doing so, wherever he finds it necessary, throughout the
Tale. Walter marries Grisilde, having extracted from her a promise
of total and ungrudging obedience, and he finds that she keeps her
promise. Nevertheless, after she has borne him a daughter, he decides
to test her further. Now Petrarch once more treats this decision in a
carefully detached way, deliberately withdrawing from any personal judgement: 'Walter was seized with a desire more strange
than laudable—so the more experienced may decide—to try more
deeply the fidelity of his dear wife, which had been sufficiently made
known by experience, and to test it again and again' (p. 299). But
the Clerk is vehemently personal and partisan in his comment, and of
course thoroughly disapproving of Walter:

> Nedelees, God woot, he thoghte hire for t'affraye.
>
> He hadde assayed hire ynogh bifore,
> And foond hire evere good; what neded it
> Hire for to tempte, and alwey moore and moore,
> Though som men preise it for a subtil wit?
> But as for me, I seye that yvele it sit
> To assaye a wyf whan that it is no nede,
> And putten hire in angwyssh and in drede.   (455–62)

We are forced to be conscious of the personal intrusion of the narrator into the story: 'as for *me*, *I* seye . . .'. This pattern is exactly
repeated when Walter, having found Grisilde steadfast on having

her daughter taken away from her and apparently murdered, decides to repeat the experiment with her second child, a son. With his usual neutrality, Petrarch writes simply, 'the father fell back into his former caprice. And again he said to his wife . . .' (p. 301). The Clerk inserts a vehement comment of his own:

> O nedelees was she tempted in assay!
> But wedded men ne knowe no mesure,
> Whan that they fynde a pacient creature.   (621–3)

The effect of that sad generalization—'married men don't know when to stop when they find a wife who will put up with anything' —is to relate the events of the story to our own experience of life, and to encourage us to judge them in the light of that experience, rather than to keep them in a separate compartment labelled 'Literature Only.' The narrator's personal engagement in the story encourages us too to become personally involved with it. This effect is intensified when Walter's second test of Grisilde has been completed, and she is still steadfast. Petrarch's comment implies disapproval, but still keeps it cool and impersonal: 'These trials of conjugal affection and fidelity would have been sufficient for the most rigorous of husbands; but there are those who, when once they have begun anything, do not cease; nay, rather, they press on and cling to their purpose' (p. 303). The Clerk intervenes with far greater fervency, and in a way that directly invokes the natural human responses of the women in his audience:

> But now of wommen wolde I axen fayn
> If thise assayes myghte nat suffise?
> What koude a sturdy housbonde moore devyse
> To preeve hir wyfhod and hir stedefastnesse,
> And he continuynge evere in sturdinesse?   (696–700)

It is almost as if he were urging his female listeners to rebel against the monstrous acts that the story he is telling would force them to accept. In becoming a partisan for Grisilde and against Walter the Clerk seems to have stumbled into being a partisan in the sex-war itself—a war being carried on among the Canterbury pilgrims in most of the tales concerning marriage. In the final stanza of Part V, after Grisilde has been sent back to her father, the Clerk settles more firmly into this role, the angry supporter of the female sex against his own sex, and indeed against his own profession (which is also Petrarch's), that of 'clerk' or scholar:

> Men speke of Job, and moost for his humblesse,
> As clerkes, whan hem list, konne wel endite,
> Namely of men, but as in soothfastnesse,
> Though clerkes preise wommen but a lite,
> Ther kan no man in humblesse hym acquite
> As womman kan, ne kan ben half so trewe
> As wommen been, but it be falle of newe.   (932–8)

This stanza has no equivalent at all in Petrarch.

Finally I wish to mention two occasions on which the Clerk intervenes with some comment on the reactions of Walter's subjects to his treatment of his wife. Petrarch mentions two such occasions in particular. The first is after Walter has taken away both the children, and the story goes round among his people that he has had them both killed, because he was ashamed of their mother's humble origins. Now Petrarch calls this 'an ugly rumour' (p. 304); but to the Clerk it seems, on the contrary, that the people are fully justified in their suspicions, and he therefore expands the rumour itself, and indicates that there was nothing surprising in its prevalence:

> The sclaundre of Walter ofte and wyde spradde,
> That of a crueel herte he wikkedly,
> For he a povre womman wedded hadde,
> Hath mordred bothe his children prively.
> Swich murmur was among hem comunly.
> No wonder is, for to the peples ere
> Ther cam no word, but that they mordred were. (722–8)

That 'No wonder is . . .' strikes characteristically the note of spontaneous personal comment. So when, according to Petrarch, Walter's subjects take an unfavourable opinion of him, the Clerk defends them for doing so. Later on, however, when Walter produces his supposed second bride and her brother, Petrarch tells us that some of the subjects took a more favourable view of his con-

duct, admittedly on somewhat cynical grounds: 'There were those
who said that Walter had been fortunate and prudent in the change
he made, since this bride was more delicate and of nobler breeding,
and had so fine a kinsman into the bargain' (p. 308). Once more, this
is something the Clerk cannot alter because it is in his source; but
equally he cannot restrain himself from a passionate condemnation
of their approval of Walter. Like many of his other comments, the
condemnation is exclamatory in form (nearly all the exclamations in
The Clerk's Tale are the Clerk's own additions):

> O stormy peple! unsad and evere untrewe!
> Ay undiscreet and chaungynge as a fane!
> Delitynge evere in rumbul that is newe,
> For lyk the moone ay wexe ye and wane!
> Ay ful of clappyng, deere ynogh a jane!
> Youre doom is fals, youre constance yvele preeveth;
> A ful greet fool is he that on yow leeveth.   (995–1001)

These are the Clerk's words; and then he suddenly remembers that
he is supposed to be telling a story, not preaching a sermon, and
hastily explains that this was what the reliable members of the public
said—'Thus seyden sadde folk in that citee . . .' (1002). When the
people are against Walter, the Clerk intervenes to defend them;
when they are for Walter, he intervenes to condemn them.

Again and again, then, the Clerk pushes his way into the story as a
deeply engaged and sometimes angry critical commentator on his
auctour, Petrarch. But besides these open interventions, which make
us aware of him as a distinct personality, of lively responses and
definite (usually critical) opinions, he is also at work throughout,
reproducing, modifying or even changing the 'colouring' Petrarch
has given to the story of the patient Griselde. One well known
example of this is the Clerk's considerable elaboration of Petrarch's
final scene, in which the children are restored to Grisilde and she is
restored to her husband's open favour. The Clerk does not alter the
main events of the scene, but he colours them so as to intensify their
pathos. He makes Grisilde swoon twice, where in Petrarch she does
not swoon at all. He elaborates the second swoon still further by
adding the detail that, when she swooned, she was holding her

children so tightly that they could not be prised out of her arms. He
gives her a pathetic exclamatory speech of thanks to Walter, which
passes into an *apostrophatio* of the children themselves:

> 'Grauntmercy, lord, God thanke it yow,' quod she,
> 'That ye han saved me my children deere!
> Now rekke I nevere to been deed right heere;
> Sith I stonde in youre love and in youre grace,
> No fors of deeth, ne whan my spirit pace!
>
> 'O tendre, o deere, o yonge children myne!
> Youre woful mooder wende stedfastly
> That crueel houndes or som foul vermyne
> Hadde eten yow; but God, of his mercy,
> And youre benyngne fader tendrely
> Hath doon yow kept . . .'.   (1088–98)

The Clerk has previously added, also in exclamatory form, his own
personal reaction to the scene:

> O which a pitous thyng it was to se
> Hir swownyng, and hire humble voys to heere!   (1087–6)

And he alters the reactions of the onlookers within the poem, to
make them accord with his own. Where in Petrarch the only reactions mentioned are that 'the ladies gathered about her with alacrity
and affection' and that 'The most joyous plaudits and auspicious
words from all the throng resounded all about' (p. 310), the Clerk
has the spectators full of tearful pity, expressed yet again with an
exclamation:

> O many a teere on many a pitous face
> Doun ran of hem that stooden hire bisyde;
> Unnethe abouten hire myghte they abyde.   (1104–6)

In this final scene of the poem, then, we can see the Clerk taking the
opportunity to apply a great deal of *amplificatio* to an event which
Petrarch had left as a brief outline. One of the chief means he uses is
apostrophatio or *exclamatio*, which Geoffroi de Vinsauf discusses and
exemplifies at great length as a means of amplification, and one of
whose functions, he writes, is to 'languish in tearful complaint

against all that is harsh.'[5] His purpose is to heighten the pathos of the scene, to present it as a great and, it must be admitted, enjoyable emotional experience; but in doing this he is not in any way criticising the story Petrarch has handed on to him. Here, for once, precisely because Petrarch has left only a bare outline, he can easily mould the story to suit his own purposes.

But there are other points in the *Tale* at which the Clerk's 'colourings,' as much as his interventions, function as an adversely critical commentary on his source. I shall not attempt to mention all of these, but shall consider briefly two of them, one obvious, the other perhaps less obvious. The obvious one is a speech the Clerk invents for Grisilde in the scene where Walter informs her that he has decided to cast her off and send her back to her father. Petrarch gives Grisilde a long speech of patient and completely unreproachful acceptance; the Clerk reproduces this, but he inserts into the middle of it some lines (yet once more exclamatory in form) which intensify the pathos of her situation, and at the same time imply, though without stating, a definite reproach to Walter:

> O goode God! how gentil and how kynde
> Ye semed by youre speche and youre visage
> The day that maked was oure mariage!
>
> But sooth is seyd—algate I fynde it trewe,
> For in effect it preeved is on me—
> Love is noght oold as whan that it is newe.　　(852–7)

The generalization—'Love isn't the same when it's old as it is when it's new'—has a similar effect to the Clerk's generalization about married men mentioned above: it encourages us to see the story as one of real life, and to judge Walter's behaviour accordingly. It must be the case, as often happens, that he has simply stopped loving Grisilde as he used to. Grisilde's sad acceptance that this is the way of the world only lowers Walter still further in our estimation, for the story has claimed that he is someone out of the common run of men.

The second, less obvious 'colouring' of Petrarch's story is a matter of thematic significance, which begins as far back as the Clerk's prologue. The Clerk presumably has in mind what tale he is going to tell, and he has in mind particularly that one of its themes will be authority. The tale will again and again display Walter in an attitude of dominance, not only towards Grisilde, but towards his people in general. He demands of them that they shall 'neither grucche ne stryve' (170) against his choice of a wife, just as he later demands unquestioning submission from her—'And nevere ye to grucche it, nyght ne day' (354)—however he treats her. He is constantly shown commanding and being obeyed: obeyed by his household when he tells them to prepare for his marriage ('And they to his comande-ment obeye' [194]), by Janicula when he says that he wishes to marry Grisilde, by the sergeant when he tells him to take the children away. What the tale seems to imply is that there can be no limits to the demands of authority. This indeed is what the sergeant tells Grisilde, as being an accepted truth:

> Ye been so wys that ful wel knowe ye
> That lordes heestes mowe nat been yfeyned;
> They mowe wel been biwailled or compleyned,
> But men moote nede unto hire lust obeye,
> And so wol I; ther is namoore to seye.   (528–32)

Now in his prologue the Clerk has already touched on this theme of obedience to authority. So far as the story-telling contest on the road to Canterbury is concerned, authority is embodied in Harry Bailly, the Host, who has been made 'oure governour,/And of oure tales juge and reportour' (I 813–14) by the common agreement of the pilgrims. The Clerk now presents himself as being obedient to that authority, but with a highly significant reservation:

> 'Hooste,' quod he, 'I am under youre yerde;
> Ye han of us as now the governance,
> And therfore wol I do yow obeisance,
> As fer as resoun axeth, hardily.   (22–5)

For the Clerk himself, human authority is not absolute, it is limited by the demands of reason, and what those demands are each man must judge for himself. This is the attitude he adopts in his choice of tale. He will obey the Host's command to tell the next story, but he will not necessarily make it 'som murie thyng of aventures' (15), because, although it was agreed that the Host should be the 'governour' of the contest, it was never stated that he should be entitled to lay down what kind of story each pilgrim should tell. By raising in this light-hearted way in his prologue the question of the limits of lawful authority, the Clerk gives us a slight but sufficient hint that we are not necessarily to accept the *Tale's* apparent premise that Walter can rightfully command whatever he chooses. Incidentally, it would be quite wrong to suppose that in the Middle Ages it was generally thought that princes or husbands had *absolute* authority over their subjects or wives, even to the extent of cruelty. In Chaucer's work, so far as princes are concerned, this subject is discussed at some length in *The Legend of Good Women* (*Prologue*, Text G, 356–97), where Alceste asserts, without contradition, that a 'kyng or lord . . . oughte nat be tyraunt and crewel,' and that it is his duty to his people to show them 'pleyn benygnete.' The orthodox view of the authority of husbands is clearly stated, with only a touch or two of Chaucerian slyness, by the Parson in his *Tale*:

> Now comth how that a man sholde bere hym with his wif, and namely in two thynges, that is to seyn, in suffraunce and reverence, as shewed Crist whan he made first womman. For he ne made hire nat of the heved of Adam, for she sholde nat clayme to greet lordshipe. For ther as the womman hath the maistrie, she maketh to muche desray. Ther neden none ensamples of this; the experience of day by day oghte suffise. Also, certes, God ne made nat womman of the foot of Adam, for she sholde nat been holden to lowe; for she kan nat paciently suffre. But God made womman of the ryb of Adam, for womman sholde be felawe unto man. Man sholde bere hym to his wyf in feith, in trouthe, and in love, as seith Seint Paul, that a man sholde loven his wyf as Crist loved hooly chirche, that loved it so wel that he deyde for it. So sholde a man for his wyf, if it were nede.   (X 925)

One final way in which the theme of authority comes up on *The Clerk's Tale* is of course in the Clerk's attitude towards the authority of his source. Here too, as we have been seeing, the Clerk does not take Petrarch's authority as absolute and unlimited. He judges what Petrarch says by the light of his own understanding, and that is why he adds the interventions and 'colourings' which we have so far been discussing.

The general picture that emerges from what has been said so far is, perhaps, of a Clerk who is somewhat at odds with the tale he tells. He is not entirely at odds with it, certainly: he seems to welcome the opportunities it gives him for pathos in the treatment of Grisilde's sufferings, her endurance in face of them, and the eventual happy ending. But he cannot bring himself to sympathize with the motive force of the whole story, the part played by Walter in causing Grisilde's sufferings; and his disapproving attitude towards Walter emerges in the form of a largely personal commentary on Petrarch's story. It might appear, in fact, that the Clerk would have done better to have chosen some other story for his *Tale*—perhaps a story in which an innocent heroine's suffering and longsuffering were brought about either by pure chance, or by the actions of admittedly wicked people, rather than by a man who is supposed to be her loving husband. He would have been better suited, that is to say, by some such tale as the Man of Law tells, about the sufferings and eventual reward of Constance, or the one told by the Second Nun about the martyrdom of Saint Cecilia. But if this is so, it may be asked, why did the Clerk tell the story of Grisilde, rather than one of the Constance or Cecilia type (there were many such tales available in Chaucer's time)? One kind of answer to this question has been given in a penetrating and important study of *The Clerk's Tale* by Professor Elizabeth Salter. Her explanation for the apparent disharmony between the teller and his tale is that Chaucer allowed this to happen because he could not help it. In *The Clerk's Tale* he was telling a story towards which he himself had mixed feelings, and which aroused in him conflicting impulses. For Petrarch, the purpose of the story was to function as a parable concerning man's attitude towards God, which 'might stir all those who read it to imitate the woman's steadfastness, at least; so that they may have the resolution to perform for God what this woman performed for her husband' (p. 311). Chaucer recognized and accepted this purpose:

> For, sith a womman was so pacient
> Unto a mortal man, wel moore us oghte
> Receyven al in gree that God us sent;
> For greet skile is, he preeve that he wroghte. (1149–52)

But on the other hand, his sympathies were so strongly aroused by Grisilde's undeserved suffering that he could not help also treating the story in terms of human realism; and in those terms Walter's part becomes quite unacceptable. And so, as Professor Salter writes, 'The *Tale* is constantly pulled in two directions, and . . . the human sympathies so powerfully evoked by the sight of unmerited suffering form, ultimately, a barrier to total acceptance of the work in its original function.' According to Professor Salter, this conflict of purposes in the *Tale* was not something planned by Chaucer or under his control. She writes, for example, that the 'strong desire to present Walter and his servant in terms of harshest realism . . . seems to grow as the poem gets under way, and although . . . Chaucer makes sporadic attempts to control it, he cannot rid himself of it.' At times, Chaucer sees the story he has undertaken in the symbolic perspective of religious parable; at other times, he sees it in the opposing perspective of human realism; and, Professor Salter concludes, 'Chaucer does not seem to recognize the problem he sets himself and his readers by attempting to juxtapose, rather than to relate, both perspectives upon the narrative.'[6] Professor Salter has written by far the most sensitive critical study of *The Clerk's Tale* known to me; it records most acutely what is actually in the poem; but in my view the conclusion drawn from this evidence is unconvincing. Chaucer, after all, was not at this stage of his career a completely amateur writer, who had no idea how to choose material that would suit his general outlook on life. He was not merely a gifted gentleman, like Sir Thomas Malory a century later, who evidently had to translate from the French two lengthy books of the tale of Sir Tristram before discovering that it was not in accordance with his own view of life. On the contrary, he was an accomplished poet, who had learned from the literary theory of his time (and no doubt from his own experience) the importance of careful planning of a literary work in advance:

> For everi wight that hath an hous to founde
> Ne renneth naught the werk for to bygynne
> With rakel hond, but he wol bide a stounde,

[6] *Chaucer: The Knight's Tale and The Clerk's Tale* (London, 1962), pp. 50, 55, 62.

And sende his hertes line out from withinne
Aldirfirst his purpos for to wynne.[7]

In the case of *The Clerk's Tale*, it cannot be that Chaucer was writing
in a great hurry, so that he did not have time to notice that his source
was often one he disapproved of, for, as we know, he took the
trouble to compare at least two versions of the Griselda story, one in
French and one in Latin. There is no evidence, lastly, that here he
was writing under orders from some great patron, as may con-
ceivably have been the case with *The Legend of Good Women*, so
that he had no freedom of choice. He *could* have chosen a quite
different story for the Clerk; why did he fail to do so?

To answer this question, it is necessary to return to the fact that the
story of Grisilde is presented by Chaucer not as his own tale, but as
the Clerk's tale. Whatever separate existence it may have had
previously, it has come down to us as part of *The Canterbury Tales*;
and the whole framework of *The Canterbury Tales* is designed to
relieve Geoffrey Chaucer of the responsibility for the tales told, and
to hand that responsibility over to the various pilgrims. The pilgrims,
of course, are fictional characters (though it is possible that some of
them were based on real people); and one purpose of the pilgrimage-
fiction is to make the narrator of each tale, and his whole method of
narration, part of the meaning of the poem. Let me repeat that to
say this is not to imply that Chaucer intends us to be primarily
interested in the individual psychology of the pilgrims, or in the
tales as revealing expressions of their characters. Indeed, in many
cases it might be better to think of the pilgrims as being merely convenient personifications of possible attitudes towards the tales they tell.
What Chaucer has done is to take the situation envisaged by the
artes poeticae, of a storyteller as being a commentator on an already
existing *materia*, rather than a completely original creator, and to
turn it, in multiple form, into a dramatic fiction. Whatever Chaucer's
own, personal attitude towards the story of the patient Grisilde as
recounted by Petrarch, so far as *The Clerk's Tale* is concerned the
Clerk's disapproval of some aspects of his source is part of the fiction.
It is therefore part of the meaning of the fiction; and if there appears

[7] *Troilus and Criseyde*, I 1065–9, adapted from Geoffroi de Vinsauf,
Poetria nova, lines 43ff. Cf. p. 53 above.

to be a somewhat tense relationship between the teller and his tale, then that tension is part of the meaning of the poem. In this case, I would wish to say that the tension is an essential part of the meaning of *The Clerk's Tale*.

The fact must be faced that there *is* a tension within *The Clerk's Tale*. It is a tension between two contradictory demands, or, as Professor Salter puts it, between two perspectives, one absolute and symbolic, the other relative and realistic. There is the perspective whose claim is embodied in the monstrous marriage-agreement between Walter and Grisilde, stated in Grisilde's promise,

> heere I swere that nevere willyngly,
> In werk ne thoght, I nyl yow disobeye,
> For to be deed, though me were looth to deye. (362-4)

And there is the perspective established by the instinctive reactions on which we base our everyday judgments of human behaviour. It is easy enough to see how this second perspective gets into the poem: it is there through the Clerk's often indignant reactions to his source, reinforced by the whole 'real life' context of the pilgrimage to Canterbury. But how is it that we are persuaded to accept the monstrous contract between Walter and Grisilde, even as a premise for a work of fiction? Chaucer uses a number of means, some of which have been analysed by Professor Salter. We are persuaded by the ritualistic and symbolic nature of the action of the story: the deliberate repetitions, such as the sergeant's two parallel visits to Grisilde, to take away first one and then the other of her children, and the persuasive symbolism of such events as Grisilde's three changes of clothes. Events such as these, giving the tale such a noticeable shapeliness, like that of a fairy-story, help to persuade us that it is following a predetermined and unalterable pattern. While we are under the spell of the tale, it is unimaginable that things should be otherwise; and the spell is strengthened by the slow-moving, ostentatiously patterned and yet finely austere language used, which also has its telling repetitions. '"This is ynogh, Grisilde myn," quod he' occurs twice: once at the beginning of Grisilde's test, when Walter accepts her promise of obedience (365), and again at the end of the test, when she finally satisfies him of her ability to keep her promise

(1051). 'That day that maked was oure mariage' is similarly used twice: once by Walter when he is about to submit Grisilde to her first trial (497), once by Grisilde at the moment when she comes nearest to breaking under the strain:

> O goode God! how gentil and how kynde
> Ye semed by youre speche and youre visage
> The day that maked was oure mariage! (852–4)

Thus the poem's language conspires to point back to the marriage-promise as a fixed landmark; and a similar cadence reminds us of it yet again after Walter has disclosed everything to Grisilde and to his people:

> For moore solempne in every mannes syght
> This feste was, and gretter of costage,
> Than was the revel of hire mariage. (1125–7)

In entering the poem, we enter a world of language within which only certain kinds of feeling are possible. Or, to put it differently, reading the story of the patient Griselda as told by Petrarch is like putting on a special pair of spectacles, which will allow only a strictly limited range of colours to be seen. Every so often the Clerk takes them off, and is horrified at what he sees without them; but until he reaches the end of the story, he always puts them on again.

It must be added, though, that in *The Clerk's Tale* we do not find simply a tension between two kinds of language, each conveying its own perspective upon the action—the ritualistic and impersonal language of acceptance, and the vehement and personal language of protest. We also find signs of tension *within* the staple language of the *Tale*—the language of acceptance that is. This is particularly true of the language used by and about Grisilde. It is most striking how often Grisilde's virtues, and especially her patience, are expressed not positively but negatively—in the form, that is, of a denial of the corresponding vices. Even while it is emphasizing Grisilde's perfection, the language of the *Tale* is implying that it is something abnormal, for what would be normal must be strenuously excluded in order to achieve it. Some examples will make this clear. When Grisilde's character is first described, it is largely in terms of what she is not, rather than of what she is:

> No likerous lust was thurgh hire herte yronne.
> Wel ofter of the welle than of the tonne
> She drank, and for she wolde vertu plese,
> She knew wel labour, but noon ydel ese. (214–17)
>
> She wolde noght been ydel til she slepte . . . (224)
>
> And made hire bed ful hard and nothyng softe. . . . (228)

Lines such as these seem to imply that sensual delight, in the form of gluttony and sloth, is the normal human aim, and that Grisilde is highly unusual in rejecting it. Again, the marriage-agreement that Walter presents to her is expressed in negative terms. He may freely treat her as he wishes,

> And nevere ye to grucche it, nyght ne day;
> And eek whan I sey 'ye' ne sey nat 'nay,'
> Neither by word ne frownyng contenance. (354–6)

Walter obviously thinks that the normal thing would be for a wife to say 'No' at some point; and the experience of married men throughout history confirms that he is right. Grisilde's behaviour when her daughter is taken from her is again expressed as a negation of what is clearly assumed to be normal behaviour:

> Ne of hir doghter noght a word spak she.
> Noon accident, for noon adversitee,
> Was seyn in hire, ne nevere hire doghter name
> Ne nempned she, in ernest nor in game. (606–9)

Her behaviour when she is divorced and sent back to her father is expressed in exactly the same way:

> . . . neither by hire wordes ne hire face,
> Biforn the folk, ne eek in hire absence,
> Ne shewed she that hire was doon offence;
> Ne of hire heighe estaat no remembraunce
> Ne hadde she, as by hire contenaunce. (920–24)

And again, a little later:

> No tendre mouth, noon herte delicaat,
> No pompe, no semblant of roialtee. . . .   (927–8)

Many other examples might be mentioned: the whole treatment of
Grisilde echoes with all those words of negation beginning with *n*-:
no, noon, ne, neither, nor, nevere, noght. (In Middle English, as con-
trasted with modern English, they can be multiplied freely without
cancelling each other out.) The effect of this persistent rhetoric of
negation is to stress the uniqueness of Grisilde's virtue, of course; but
it is also to convey a sense of the unending strain that is necessary to
assert it.

In other ways, however, the wording of the *Tale* does help to
persuade us towards acceptance. It is not only in an epilogue explaining its purpose that *The Clerk's Tale* is justified as being a religious
parable. In the course of it, too, there are numerous hints that the
pattern the action is following is spiritual as well as aesthetic. There
are elusive but highly suggestive hints that Grisilde's sufferings and
her humility are comparable to those of the Blessed Virgin, who
also gave up her child in conformity with the will of her Lord:

> And thus she seyde in hire benigne voys,
> 'Fareweel, my child! I shal thee nevere see.
> But sith I thee have marked with the croys
> Of thilke Fader—blessed moote he be!—
> That for us deyde upon a croys of tree,
> Thy soule, litel child, I hym bitake,
> For this nyght shaltow dyen for my sake.'   (554–60)

And she is compared, to her advantage, with Job, who was also
tested by intolerable suffering: 'Men speke of Job, and moost for his
humblesse' (932), but women are capable of still greater humility
and *trouthe*. Finally, and paradoxically, the Clerk's very bewilder-
ment and indignation when faced with the problem of finding some
intelligible motivation for Walter's behaviour also help to make the
course of events seem inevitable. Walter, it appears, is acting under
an inner compulsion as powerful as the external compulsion he has
imposed on Grisilde. It is an impulse, evidently, as mysterious to

him as it is to us that causes him to go on testing her so cruelly long
after her obedience has manifested itself; he is as helpless as one
'bounden to a stake,' as Chaucer puts it (in another of his additions
to Petrarch), and all that can be said by way of explanation is that
there *are* people like that:

> But ther been folk of swich condicion
> That whan they have a certein purpos take,
> They kan nat stynte of hire entencion,
> But, right as they were bounden to a stake,
> They wol nat of that firste purpos slake.   (701–5)

And it must be added, I think, that we are able to accept Walter's
monstrous conduct as a premise for the story because, though
mysterious and intolerable, it is not totally implausible. I do not
mean that we can imagine any real husband doing exactly and in
detail what Walter does to his wife and children; but it is surely
perfectly possible to see his behaviour as following a pattern which
is also followed in some real-life marriages, in which cruelty on one
side is met with submission on the other, and that in turn provokes still
greater cruelty on the first. I suspect that some of the indignation and
incredulity the *Tale* has aroused among modern critics—'too cruel,
too incredible a story,' Professor Coghill exclaims, and 'It is, of
course, a grotesque and quite unbelievable tale,' Mr Speirs assures
us[8]—arises not from its implausibility but from their unwillingness
to recognize how plausible it is. It must be accepted, of course, that
the story 'stands for' real life, rather than representing it directly;
but, given that, what is surprising about it is not so much that
Walter treats Grisilde as he does, as that, having started, he ever stops.
For me, at least, a large part of the disturbing power of *The Clerk's
Tale* derives from the fact that it bears a recognizable symbolic
relationship to the darker side of real life—the side that may be
studied in nightmares and in certain of the Sunday papers. Like the
Clerk, I feel moved to protest against the course of the story because
I believe in it; if I found it unconvincing, I should remain unmoved.

I have been arguing that *The Clerk's Tale* conveys an effect of
tension rather than of harmony, and, more important, that that

[8] Nevill Coghill, *The Poet Chaucer* (Oxford, 1949), p. 139; John Speirs,
Chaucer the Maker, p. 152.

tension is an effect sufficiently pervasive and sufficiently consistent for us to see it as a result of Chaucer's deliberate intentions. It certainly cannot have been the case that, in his eagerness to present an extreme situation, he failed to notice the effect of tension, for it is noticed by the Clerk, the fictional teller of the *Tale*; and, precisely because the Clerk is a fiction, and part of an elaborately devised fictional structure, it seems unlikely that his unease is nothing more than a direct reflection of Chaucer's awareness that something had gone wrong. It remains to consider why Chaucer should have composed a work whose aim is to create an effect of tension, of disharmony. Medieval writers and their audiences were very fond of stories in which an unbreakable promise imposes on the person who has made it conduct that may seem irrational or even monstrous.[9] Another example in Chaucer is *The Franklin's Tale*, in which the wife Dorigen, in order to comfort the young squire Aurelius, who has fallen in love with her, even though she loves only her husband, tells him in jest that she will love him in return if he removes all the rocks from the coast of Brittany. By magic he does so; and in consequence both Dorigen and her husband consider her promise so absolutely binding that they decide it is her duty to beome Aurelius's mistress. One advantage of such stories is that they permit the display, to an extreme degree, of the virtue of truth to one's word; another is that they provide opportunities for sensational scenes of pathos when the promise is kept, or when the victim is released from it. But it might also be suggested that such stories were popular even with highly sophisticated poets such as Chaucer because in them could be found an image of the human condition in general, as this was often seen in the Middle Ages. Though God had created Nature, and had made human nature in his own image, Nature was corrupted, and the divine image in man was corrupted too, as a consequence of Adam's sin. Thus the human condition itself was one of tension between the divine law and the law of the flesh, or between Grace and Nature. In this way, the state of man in general could be seen as similar to that of the hero-victim of promise-stories, or, more subtly, as in the case of *The Clerk's Tale*, to that of the unhappy witness and narrator of such a story: a state of divided values, of tension, of disharmony.

[9] For a discussion of such stories, see J. A. Burrow, *op. cit.*, pp. 160ff.

I have no wish to claim, then, that *The Clerk's Tale* is by any means a unique kind of work, though I believe it to be an unusually successful example of its kind.

There are in fact many other examples to be found. An obvious parallel to the story of the patient Griselda is to be seen in the Biblical story of Abraham and Isaac. Like Griselda, Abraham is commanded to give up his child to death, in order to show his total commitment to an absolute system of values; and like her, having displayed his willingness to commit an act which by normal human standards is cruel and unnatural, he is eventually released from the test. According to the typological interpretation of Old Testament events which formed a central part of medieval understanding of Scripture, this story was a prefiguration of God's sacrifice of his Son on the cross; and it seems to have been this figural significance which gave plays of Abraham and Isaac such a prominent place in medieval religious drama. As the Expositor of the Chester cycle of plays explains,

> This deed you se done in this place,
> In example of Ihesu done yt was,
> That for to wyn mankinde grace
> Was sacrifised on the rode.
>
> By Abraham I may understand
> The Father of heaven that can fand
> With his Sonnes blood to break that band
> The Devil had brought us too.
>
> By Isaac understand I may
> Ihesu that was obedyent aye,
> His Fathers will to worke alway,
> His death to underfonge.[10]

This interpretation may be said to correspond roughly to the per-

[10] *The Chester Plays*, vol. I, ed. H. Deimling, Early English Text Society, Extra Series 62 (London, 1892), IV 465–76. On typology see the works by Auerbach and Kolve listed in Chapter 1, note 19; and on its place in plays of Abraham and Isaac see Rosemary Woolf, 'The Effect of Typology on the English Medieval Plays of Abraham and Isaac,' *Speculum* XXXII (1957), pp. 805–25.

spective of religious symbolism which is incorporated in *The Clerk's Tale*, and which leads towards acceptance of what seems an intolerable narrative. It is embodied in the dramatic content of some medieval plays, such as the emblematic and exemplary *Abraham and Isaac* of the 'Ludus Coventriae' cycle, where Isaac, when told he must be sacrificed, exclaims

> Almyghty God, of his grett mercy,
> Ful hertyly J thanke the sertayne.
> At Goddys byddyng here for to dye
> I obeye me here for to be sclayne.[11]

But in other plays the story of Abraham and Isaac is also seen in terms of a different perspective, that of sympathetic human realism. In such cases, Isaac's reaction is much closer to that of a real little boy, begging to be beaten for what he supposes to be his fault, not killed:

> Yff I have trespassyd agens yow owt,
> With a yard ye may make me full myld;
> And with yowr scharp sword kyll me nogth,
> For, iwys, fader, I am but a chyld.

Once he has learned that his death is God's will, this Isaac submits, though not without a muted reproach of God which may well remind us of Grisilde's attitude towards Walter:

> Now, fader, agens my Lordes wyll
> I will never groche, lowd nor styll.
> He mygth a sent me a better desteny
> Yf yt had a be hys plecer.

And in the same play Abraham, faced with God's command, endures an inner conflict not unlike that experienced by the Clerk confronted with the demands of the story he has to tell:

> A! Lord God, my conseons ys stronly steryd!
> And yit, my dere Lord, I am sore aferd
> To groche ony thyng agens yowre wyll.

[11] *Ludus Coventriae*, ed. K. S. Block, Early English Text Society, Extra Series 120 (London, 1922), IV 145–8.

At the end of this version, a 'Doctor' draws out the moral rather than the typological sense, in a way which relates the story to the everyday lives of the audience, and implies a contrast between 'Nature' or 'Kinde' and some higher system of values:

> Trowe ye, sores, and God sent an angell
> And commawndyd yow yowr chyld to slayn,
> Be yowr trowthe, ys ther ony of yow
> That eyther wold groche or stryve thereageyn?
> How thyngke ye now, sorys, therby?
> I trowe ther be thre or fowr or moo.
> And thys women, that wepe so sorowfully
> Whan that hyr chyldryn dey them froo,
> As Nater wool and Kynd,
> Yt ys but folly, I may well awooe,
> To groche agens God or to greve yow.[12]

The partial similarity of this to the Clerk's moralization of the story of Grisilde will be obvious; and the play as a whole seems to articulate quite consciously a conflict between two opposed ways of looking at the story it has to tell—a conflict which it evidently expects to be enacted in the lives of its audience.

A second kind of parallel to the tension conveyed by *The Clerk's Tale* may be found in a number of the parables of the New Testament. Professor Salter, and others who have written about the *Tale*, have given the impression that its disharmony arises from an attempt to achieve two incompatible kinds of harmony—that of human realism and that of the religious parable. But in fact it is surely a mistake to see the New Testament parables as harmonious allegories, which expound the behaviour and purposes of God in such a way as to make them perfectly intelligible and acceptable to earthly eyes. On the contrary, if we translate a parable from the human terms in which it is couched into the divine terms towards which it seems to point, we shall often find that it makes the workings of God seem irrational and even monstrous, and certainly unacceptable to our everyday notions of justice and common sense. Consider the parable

---

[12] *The Sacrifice of Isaac* (Brome MS.), ed. J. Q. Adams, *Chief Pre-Shakespearean Dramas* (Cambridge [Mass.], 1924), lines 169–72, 190–93, 78–80, and 443–53.

of the talents, for example. Judged by human standards, the servant who, knowing that his master was 'an hard man', hid the talent that had been given to him in the earth and returned it to his master intact, does not seem to have acted badly. But what happens to him?

His lord answered and said unto him, Thou wicked and slothful servant, thou knewest that I reap where I sowed not, and gather where I have not strawed:

Thou oughtest therefore to have put my money to the ex-changers, and then at my coming I should have received my own with usury.

Take therefore the talent from him, and give it unto him which hath ten talents.

For unto every one that hath shall be given, and he shall have abundance: but from him that hath not shall be taken away even that which he hath.

And cast ye the unprofitable servant into outer darkness: there shall be weeping and gnashing of teeth.   (Matthew, xxv 26–30)

Like Walter, the lord of this parable must surely be interpreted, in any 'translation,' as standing for God; yet, like Walter, in this case he seems to have behaved with irrational cruelty. Is God really a hard-faced capitalist? Similarly with the parable of the vineyard. Here the lord insists on paying exactly one penny to each of the labourers in his vineyard, even though some have been working all day, but others have started work only late in the evening. Has the harsh capitalist been transformed into a totalitarian leveller? In fact, of course, parables such as these do not aim to soothe us with the sense that the divine order can be understood in terms of the human order, or even that it is continuous with the human order, but to shock us into a recognition that the divine order is mysterious and alien. Each of the two parables quoted leads us towards an inextric-able paradox, a mystery: in the parable of the talents, 'For unto every one that hath shall be given, and he shall have abundance: but from him that hath not shall be taken away even that which he hath'; and in the parable of the vineyard, 'So the last shall be first, and the first last: for many be called, but few chosen' (Matthew, xx 16). As Professor C. H. Dodd has written, 'the parable has the character of an argument, in that it entices the hearer to a judgment upon the situation depicted, and then challenges him, directly or by implication, to apply that judgment to the matter in hand.'[13] Here Professor Dodd is contrasting parable with allegory; and it must be admitted that in the Middle Ages the New Testament parables were often read as if they were allegories, mere illustrations or clarifications of accepted truths. But they were not always read in this way; and in Chaucer's time we find evidence of this in the treatment of the parable of the vineyard in *Pearl*. Here the parable is recounted by the Pearl Maiden with the purpose of indicating to the Dreamer that the notions of justice he has brought with him from his earthly world will not apply to the justice of God, which can make a two-year-old child a queen in heaven. In the retelling, full weight is given to that element of human realism in the parable which makes us feel that the point of view of the workmen who have laboured all day, and are aggrieved at being paid no more than the latecomers, cannot be lightly dismissed. Their speech, with its ponderous repetitiousness, gives a convincing sense of the human feeling of medieval labourers:

> And thenne the fyrst bygonne to pleny
> And sayden that thay hade travayled sore:
> 'These bot on oure hem con streny;
> Uus thynk uus oghe to take more.
>
> 'More haf we served, uus thynk so,
> That suffred han the dayez hete,
> Thenn thyse that wroght not hourez two,
> And thou dotz hem uus to counterfete.'[14]

The effect of the whole is that of an argument or challenge; we are being asked, as at the end of the last Abraham and Isaac play mentioned above, 'How thyngke ye now, sorys, therby?' *The Clerk's Tale*, similarly, is an argumentative and challenging work; and it is surely so by intention, rather than because Chaucer has lost control, or because of his 'inability to decide upon and abide by one single set of moral standards.'[15] It is about a world divided against itself,

---

[13] *The Parables of the Kingdom*, rev. edn. (London, 1961), p. 21.

[14] *Pearl*, ed. E. V. Gordon (Oxford, 1953), lines 549–56.

[15] Salter, *op. cit.*, p. 61.

and articulates a view of human life of which a distinctive feature is
precisely that it feels the pull of more than one single set of moral
standards.

In this discussion I have been happy to follow Professor Salter's
treatment of the double standard of values in *The Clerk's Tale* in
terms of two 'perspectives' upon the story. The word 'perspective'
implies an analogy with the visual arts; and the last parallel I wish to
suggest to the tension conveyed by the *Tale* is taken from this field.
In the late fourteenth century, when Chaucer was writing *The
Canterbury Tales*, the basically linear art of North-western Europe
was gradually being penetrated by influences from Italian art, which
had already developed a greater mastery of the representation of
three-dimensional space and of the relationships among objects within such space. One beautiful example of this transitional art is Pol de
Limbourg's *Fall of Man*, an illumination in the manuscript known as
Les Très Riches Heures of Jean, Duc de Berri. This picture, dating
from the early fifteenth century, has recently been discussed by Dr
George Henderson.[16] It depicts within a single frame four stages in
the Fall: the temptation of Eve by the serpent, the temptation of
Adam by Eve, God's reproof of Adam and Eve, and their expulsion
from Eden. Eden itself thus becomes not a real but a symbolic
space, within which successive events occur in apparent simultaneity,
as if seen by the eye of God in his 'eterne present.'[17] It is corres-
pondingly represented as a flat, two-dimensional circle, 'a design,'
as Dr Henderson puts it, 'which is basically no more than a histori-
ated initial,' comparable to those found in manuscripts of two or
three centuries earlier. Yet within this linear design (and indeed to
some extent bursting out of it into a different imaginary space) the
gates of Eden, an exquisitely wrought architectural structure over its
central fountain, and above all the repeated figures of Adam and
Eve themselves seem solid, substantial, three-dimensional. Within
the symbolic space a real drama is being transacted, and one that
demands from us sympathy rather than contemplation. There is, of
course, a clash of styles, which the art historian cannot help seeing
just as Professor Salter sees *The Clerk's Tale*: as an inability to decide

[16] *Gothic* (Harmondsworth, 1967), pp. 127–34. The illumination in question
is reproduced as figure 79.
[17] Chaucer's translation of Boethius, V pr. 6, 136.

upon and abide by one single set of standards (whether spatial or moral). Dr Henderson writes that 'The firm skilfully modelled figures and the substantial architecture are . . . out of scale and out of character with their setting,' and he adds, 'Pol de Limbourg is trying to have the best of both worlds. But we may feel that the two can never really blend.' We may indeed feel that; but we shall only think it a fault or a historical accident if we assume that the necessary purpose of art is blending, or harmony. In fact, the double nature of the Fall, as a dramatic and pathetic human event, and as a foreseen element in the divinely ordained pattern of history, finds appropriate expression in an art of double perspective. So it is, I believe, with *The Clerk's Tale*: the stylistic tensions convey a double view of the meaning of the story of the patient Griselda, and that double view is itself the meaning of the poem.

Appendix: *The Clerk's Tale* and *Le Livre du Ménagier de Paris*

An interesting parallel to *The Clerk's Tale* is to be found in the version of the story of Griselda included in a French work of the early 1390s, *Le livre du ménagier de Paris*.[1] This anonymous text dates from the same period as Chaucer's work, and, like *The Clerk's Tale*, is presented by its author as being translated from 'master Francis Petrarch, who was crowned poet at Rome' (p. 113). Moreover, the relationship between the story and its context is very similar to that found in *The Clerk's Tale*. The tale is told, by its French reteller as by Petrarch, as an *exemplum* to show that if a woman could endure patiently such a trial by her husband, 'by how much the greater reason behoveth it for men and women to suffer patiently the tribulations which God . . . sends to them'. Yet it is told in a context which implies that it relates directly to the ethics of human marriage, for it occurs in the section of the book in which the Ménagier is instruct-

---

1 Ed. Juste de Noailles, *Le Ménagier de Paris* (Paris, 1848). There is an English translation, *The Goodman of Paris* (London, 1928), by Eileen Power, who has also written an essay on the work in her book *Medieval People* (London, 1924). Quotations in this appendix are from her translation, with appropriate page-references.

ing his young wife in her duty of obedience to her husband: a
context, that is to say, analogous to the discussion of sovereignty in
marriage among the Canterbury pilgrims. The result is a distinct
embarrassment on the part of the Ménagier. He has to explain to his
wife that 'I, that have set the tale here merely to lesson you, have
not set it here to apply to you, nor because I would have such
obedience from you, for I am not worthy thereof, and also I am no
marquis nor have taken in you a shepherdess'—for him evidently
the social disparity between husband and wife is some justification
for their behaviour—'and I am not so foolish, so overweening, nor
of so small sense that I know not well that 'tis not for me to assault
nor to assay you thus . . .' (p. 137). And he goes on to express his
sense that the tale is one of excessive cruelty, but to explain that
nonetheless he has to tell it as it is set down in his source: 'And
excuse me if the story telleth of cruelty too great (to my mind) and
above reason. And wot you that it never befel so, but thus the tale
runs, and I may neither correct it nor make another, for a wiser than
I compiled and told it.' (pp. 137–8).

It is valuable to have this independent testimony to the discomfort
which the story of Griselda might arouse in a late fourteenth-century
reader, and to such a reader's strong feeling that he was nevertheless
not free to alter it. But in the case of the Ménagier, this discomfort
is expressed only in an epilogue; it does not penetrate into the telling
of the story itself, in which he keeps far closer to Petrarch's Latin
than Chaucer does. A comparison of the two versions brings out
clearly to what an extent the doubleness of perspective in Chaucer's
version is a sustained and pervasive effect, associated with the intru-
sive personality of the fictional narrator, rather than a mere accident
resulting from Chaucer's spontaneous reactions to the human element in the story.

5 The Art of Preaching and Piers Plowman

Piers Plowman is one of the most fascinating, and also one of the most difficult, of fourteenth-century poems. Its difficulty does not lie primarily in individual passages; for what could be more attractively accessible to the modern reader than the grotesquely heightened realism of this description of Avarice?

> And thanne cam Coveytise; can I hym noughte descryve,
> So hungriliche and holwe Sire Hervy hym loked.
> He was bitelbrowed, and baberlipped also,
> With two blered eyghen as a blynde hagge;
> And as a letheren purs lolled his chekes;
> Wel sydder than his chyn thei chiveled for elde;
> And as a bondman of his bacoun his berde was bidraveled.
> With an hode on his hed, a lousi hatte above,
> And in a tauny tabarde of twelve wynter age,
> Al totorne and baudy, and ful of lys crepynge;
> But if that a lous couthe have lopen the bettre,
> She sholde noughte have walked on that welche, so was it
>   thredebare.   (B V 188–99)[1]

And what could be more immediately moving than the Dreamer's humble reply to a rebuke from Conscience?

> 'That ys soth,' ich seide, 'and so ich byknowe
> That ich have tynt tyme, and tyme mysspended;
> And yut ich hope, as he that ofte haveth chaffared,
> That ay hath lost and lost, and atte laste hym happed
> He bouhte such a bargayn he was the bet evere,

---

[1] *Piers Plowman* quotations are from *The Vision of William Concerning Piers the Plowman in Three Parallel Texts*, ed. W. W. Skeat (Oxford, 1886). There are three main texts of the poem, called A, B, and C, and probably representing different versions written by the same author (William Langland) in the course of his life. I normally quote from the latest text, C.

And sette hus lost at a lef at the laste ende,
Suche a wynnynge hym warth thorw wordes of hus grace; . . .
So hope ich to have of hym that is almyghty
A gobet of hus grace, and bygynne a tyme
That alle tymes of my tyme to profit shal turne.'

(C VI 92–101)

The difficulty is not here, for nothing could appeal more directly than the joke about the louse or the piercing humility of the word 'gobet.' The difficulty in *Piers Plowman* is where it so often is with medieval poems: in the problem of organization, *dispositio*. *Piers Plowman* is a very long poem—in each of the complete versions, called the B- and C-texts, it has over seven thousand lines—and it is a poem in which the modern reader will almost certainly get lost. Like *The Book of the Duchess*, it is a dream-poem, a poem presented to us as the experience of an 'I' who is never fully in control of what happens to him. But Langland's Dreamer finds more to baffle him than the sudden appearance of a little dog or a 'man in blak' in the forest: 'helped' by authorities with whom he is usually at cross-purposes, he is engaged in an immense quest whose object is never quite clear—for the question 'Who is Piers Plowman?' is never asked and seems incapable of being answered. And yet the poem ends with the promise of a further and perhaps never-ending continuation of the quest:

'By Crist,' quath Conscience tho, 'ich wol bycome a pilgryme,
And wenden as wide as the worlde regneth,
To seke Peers the Plouhman, that Pruyde myghte destruye.'

(C XXIII 380–83)

It is as if the bafflement of the Dreamer were a reflection of that of the poet; and certainly *Piers Plowman* gives a stronger impression than almost any other medieval poem of being a 'spontaneous overflow of powerful feelings.'

Piers Plowman begins with the Dreamer falling asleep in the Malvern Hills; like *Sir Gawain and the Green Knight*, this poem belongs to the West Midland 'Alliterative Revival,' but while *Sir Gawain* comes from the North-west, *Piers Plowman*, as this initial setting suggests, belongs to the South-west. The Dreamer dreams that he is in a 'fair feld ful of folke' (C I 19), situated between a tower and a dark valley; an image, fairly clearly, of the world, 'Myddelerde' as Langland calls it elsewhere, placed between heaven and hell. Suddenly the people in the field are replaced by rats and mice, and he sees an enactment of the familiar fable of 'belling the cat.' Next a beautiful and awe-inspiring lady appears—'Ich was aferd of hure face, thauh hue faire were' (C II 10)—and the Dreamer asks her the first of what is to be an interminable series of questions: 'what may thys be to mene?' (C II 11). She is called Holy Church, and she explains that the tower is the dwelling of Truth; and in fact the first part of the poem, which is usually called the *Visio*, resolves itself into a quest for Truth. Truth is another name for God Himself, and it eventually emerges that He dwells in the human heart:

> And yf Grace graunte the to go yn thys wise,
> Thow shalt se Treuthe sytte in thy selve herte,
> And solace thy soule, and save the fro pyne.
>
> (C VIII 254–6)

But this knowledge is arrived at by the most devious route conceivable, through visions of the trial of Lady Meed (payment or reward, either just or unjust), a sermon by Reason, the confessions of the Seven Deadly Sins, and the first appearance of Piers himself, a ploughman who agrees to guide the community to Truth if they will first help him to cultivate his half-acre. Piers receives what seems to be a pardon from Truth Himself, the text of which is simply:

> *Qui bona egerunt ibunt in vitam eternam:*
> *Qui vero mala, in ignem eternum.*   (C X 287)
>
> [Those who do well shall go into eternal life,
> while those who do evil shall go into eternal fire.]

But doubt is cast on whether this is really a pardon at all. Now the direction of the poem changes, and the quest for Truth becomes a quest for the quality of 'Do-well' suggested by the pardon. The Dreamer seeks for three aspects of this quality, namely Do-well, Do-better, and Do-best, and in the second part of the poem, called the *Vita*, he makes enquiries about these three of a whole host of allegorical figures such as Intelligence, Study, Scripture, Learning, and so on, and also of such non-allegorical figures as some friars and a learned but greedy Doctor of Divinity. After many such encounters, he eventually achieves a vision of the Crucifixion and Harrowing of Hell, in which Christ appears as a knight dressed in the armour of Piers the ploughman. This vision might make a triumphant conclusion to the poem; but instead the direction again changes, and the Dreamer is returned from the historic events of the period of the Incarnation to the world of his own day, where a barn called Unity, built by Piers, is being attacked by the deadly sins, and at the same time the Dreamer is being attacked by Old Age and Death. Defeat seems imminent; but the poem ends, as we have seen, with the promise of a new quest.

When the course of events in *Piers Plowman* is summarized briefly in this way, the poem sounds like the most confused phantasmagoria conceivable—a nightmare rather than a dream. And not even a single nightmare, for the Dreamer has waking intervals, and in these too he sometimes meets allegorical figures, and sometimes indeed it is not clear whether he is supposed to be dreaming or awake. It is true that certain themes seem to recur throughout the poem—images of pilgrimage and ploughing, for example, or formulas such as the seven deadly sins—but despite these 'foretastes and echoes' [2] it appears impossible to call the method of the poem anything more complimentary than 'kaleidoscopic': [3] the same elements may recur in different combinations, but the combinations seem to bear only an arbitrary relation one to another. It hardly needs arguing that the *ars poetica* is unlikely to give us any help towards grasping the principle of structure of such a work, for we have seen that *dispositio* is a topic about which the rhetoricians say little. If, however, we turn to consider the *content* of *Piers Plowman*, we find (except in the case of Piers himself) not something peculiar and baffling, but something much more familiar. It has been shown by Professor G. R. Owst that in its content *Piers Plowman* is extremely close to the sermons of medieval preachers. The ideas of the poem, even when they sound, as they sometimes do, most revolutionary, most

[2] Nevill Coghill, 'The Pardon of Piers Plowman,' *Proceedings of the British Academy* XXX (1944), p. 312.

[3] E. M. W. Tillyard, *The English Epic and Its Background* (London, 1954), p. 164.

closely related to the surges of revolutionary feeling that underlay
the Peasants' Revolt and the Lollard movement, are in fact 'in
perfect accord with . . . the most commonplace orthodox preaching
of the times, indeed a perfect echo in every respect of the Church's
message to the world.'[4] This can be taken as established; but in
other respects too *Piers Plowman* displays its closeness to the medieval
sermon. The poem contains certain passages which are explicitly
described as sermons. In passus C VI Reason, 'revested ryght as a
pope,' delivers a sermon 'byfor al the reame' (ll. 112, 114). Again,
in C XIII we find the following passage:

> 'He seith soth,' quath Scripture tho, and skypte an hy, and
>   prechede, . . .
> Of here teme and of here tales ich took ful good hede;
> Hue seide in here sarmon selcouthe wordes:—
> '*Multi* to a mangerie and to the mete were sompned,
> And whan the peuple was plener come the porter unpynnede the
>   gate,
> And plyghte in *pauci* pryveliche, and leet the remenant go rome.'
>   (C XIII 40, 44-8)

Although Scripture's sermon itself is not reported, but only its
'teme'—Matthew xxii 14—expanded sufficiently to recall the whole
parable in which it occurs, the passage suggests some interest on
Langland's part in the art of preaching. The 'teme' or *thema* is what
we should now call the text of the sermon, and the 'tales' or *exempla*
are a regular feature of medieval sermons, and one strongly recommended by the writers of *artes praedicandi*. Langland's interest in
preaching shows itself more pervasively throughout his poem. We
might expect the many personified abstractions who appear in it to
do so in order to take part in an allegorical action which would
demand some effort of interpretation from the reader; but in fact
they appear most often simply as preachers. They do not have to be
interpreted allegorically themselves, but are more likely to *use* the
medieval preacher's technique of allegorical exegesis on Scriptural
texts. Thus in passus C XI Intelligence explains Matthew vii 18 ('A
good tree cannot bring forth evil fruit, neither can a corrupt tree

[4] G. R. Owst, *Literature and Pulpit in Medieval England* (Cambridge, 1933),
pp. 548-9.

bring forth good fruit') as referring to illegitimate children. The poem is largely made up of such expository, sermon-like speeches. It contains specifically narrative passages, of course, but even when the poet seems most deeply engaged in narrating some action 'really' seen in his visions, he is always ready to turn aside into homiletic discourse. He does this, for example, in the Harrowing of Hell episode, when, to Satan's accusation that it is Lucifer's lies that have brought about the misery of the fallen angels, he adds a general disquisition on lying, only to pull himself up apologetically with

> A lytel ich overlep for lesynges sake,
> That ich ne segge as ich seih, suynge my teme!
>
> (C XXI 360–61)

The poet's apology for not simply 'saying as he saw' shows his awareness of his own tendency to let narrative slide across into homily. And indeed, when we think back over *Piers Plowman* after reading it, we find it difficult to distinguish narrative from homily; even so vivid an action as the Harrowing of Hell leaves behind it the impression of being an *exemplum* illustrating some larger argument.

Facts such as these suggest, I think, that it may be useful to examine medieval teachings on the art of the sermon to see whether they can give us any help in understanding *Piers Plowman*; and help will most be needed in grasping the *dispositio* of the poem. On the face of it, *Piers Plowman* does not seem to possess either a single coherent argument or a single coherent plot; indeed, one might borrow a remark of Dr Johnson's about Samuel Richardson, and say that if you were to read Langland for the story your impatience would be so much fretted that you would hang yourself. Perhaps then a study of the *ars praedicandi* might help us to see how to read Langland.

There can be little doubt that Langland would have been familiar with the art of preaching either directly or indirectly.[5] The *ars praedicandi*, unlike the *ars poetica*, played no part in medieval education, but it was well known in England. Owst has pointed out that 'Tracts by Englishmen on the formal art of preaching . . . are so numerous from the second half of the thirteenth century onwards, that the practice might almost be looked upon as a speciality of our

[5] Compare Elizabeth Salter, *Piers Plowman—An Introduction* (Oxford, 1962), pp. 26 ff.

pulpits.'[6] The two *artes praedicandi* I shall be referring to are both by Englishmen of the early fourteenth century: the *De modo componendi sermones* of Thomas Waleys, and the *Forma praedicandi* of Robert de Basevorn. But Langland would not have had to study these tracts themselves in order to grasp the principles of the art of preaching. He would simply have had to listen to a number of sermons in which those principles were reflected; and nothing can be more certain than that a medieval man, with Langland's deep interest in religious problems, would have heard thousands of sermons preached in his lifetime. Sermons in the Middle Ages were listened to, at least by the 'judicious' among their congregations, with a keenly appreciative and critical attention. Indeed, a convenient way into our subject may be to quote a comment made by an educated listener of the late twelfth century on a sermon he had heard preached. The listener was one Peter of Cornwall, who had heard a sermon given at a synod by Thomas à Becket's enemy, Gilbert Foliot. He afterwards wrote about it as follows: 'The whole sermon was varied by certain *distinctiones*, adorned with flowers of words and sentences, and supported by a copious array of authorities. It ran backwards and forwards on its path from its starting-point back to the same starting-point.'[7] What this makes clear, first, is that for a medieval listener the art of the sermon was genuinely an art. It goes without saying that the preacher's ultimate goal was practical, not artistic— the moral and spiritual improvement of his congregation. But within the limits set by this purpose, an aesthetic organization was possible, and might be appreciated by the listeners, or at least by some of them. There is some evidence, too, that with the growth of a class of educated laymen, congregations had become more exacting by the fourteenth century than they were in Peter of Cornwall's day.[8] A second point emerging from Peter of Cornwall's comment is that he seems to have been struck by Gilbert Foliot's use of a particular method of composing a sermon—a method which

[6] G. R. Owst, *Preaching in Medieval England* (Cambridge, 1926), p. 314.

[7] Quoted by R. W. Hunt, 'English Learning in the Late Twelfth Century,' *Transactions of the Royal Historical Society* 4th s. XIX (1936), pp. 33–4, now reprinted in *Essays in Medieval History*, ed. R. W. Southern (London, 1968), p. 120.

[8] See Beryl Smalley, *English Friars and Antiquity in the Early Fourteenth Century* (Oxford, 1960), pp. 28–29.

involved great complexity of structure, and a special kind of circling or spiralling movement. This technique of composition was a new one when he heard it—hence his evident surprise and delight—and it is one of two methods distinguished by the *artes praedicandi*. The writers on preaching divide sermons into two types: the 'ancient' type and the 'modern' or 'university' type. The 'ancient' type of sermon is descended from the homilies of the early Church, and in it, as Thomas Waleys puts it, 'the whole gospel passage that is read in the Mass is taken as the *thema*, and the whole of it is expounded.' [9] In other words, the *dispositio* of this type of sermon is provided by the Scriptural passage discussed; the preacher will simply go through the passage verse by verse. Thus the 'ancient' sermon has no distinctive structure of its own, needs no art of preaching to explain it, and hence is discussed no further by the writers of *artes praedicandi*. It is the 'modern' or 'university' type with which they chiefly concern themselves. This is based not on a long Scriptural passage but on a 'short *thema*'—usually a single verse or part of a verse—and the resulting sermon is remarkably elaborate in structure. The first mention of the *thema* is followed by a transitional section, called the *prothema*, linked to it either by its sense or by repeating some of its words, and leading to a prayer. Then, in a section called the *introductio*, the *thema* is taken up again, and it is divided into a number of parts. This number is most often three, and each part now has to be explained rationally and confirmed by one or more Scriptural authorities, which will also if possible be in verbal concord with the part to which they are attached. This process of *divisio*, *declaratio* (explanation), and *confirmatio* provides the main framework of the sermon, but there may also be further subdivisions, which will again require confirmatory texts, and all these parts will be linked together by an elaborate system of verbal 'correspondences' (*correspondentia*), before finally being brought together again in the *thema* itself.

Clearly, sermons constructed on this plan would be enormously complex in structure, and one might expect that they would be appreciated only by learned, 'clerkly' listeners (such as Peter of

[9] Ed. Th.-M. Charland, *Artes praedicandi* (Paris and Ottawa, 1936), p. 344. All further quotations from Waleys and Basevorn are taken from this edition, from which page-numbers are given as references.

Cornwall). This seems to have been broadly true; the assumption of the *artes praedicandi* is that their readers will wish to preach in Latin. But they insist that the schemes they set out are not to be followed rigidly in every detail. Thomas Waleys remarks: 'I should judge it not only unnecessary but also impossible to deal with all the types and methods of preaching followed by modern preachers, for you will hardly find two, among those who preach sermons composed by themselves, who are identical in all ways in their manner of preaching' (Charland, p. 329). And in fact we can find many surviving sermons written in English which are influenced in their structure by the 'university' method, but which do not follow it in every detail. They were often intended to be preached to a mixed congregation of clergy and layfolk, educated and illiterate people; and we may note that the repetitive patterning of the 'university' method, which would offer aesthetic pleasure to the upper layers of such an audience, would also serve to hammer home the main points of the preacher's message to the lower layers.[10] Such sermons borrow from the *ars praedicandi* not a complete scheme but a general principle of structure: a method of organization by which a sermon, instead of depending on the 'plot' of some Scriptural (or other) extract for its *dispositio*, becomes an independent meditation closely and constantly related to a single *thema*. And within this larger structure there will be an interweaving of sub-themes, involving frequent reappearances of the same sets of words and ideas. The analogy which immediately comes to mind for such a *dispositio* is drawn not from literature but from music: it is there that we find forms of structure based on the recurrence, variation, transposition, and re-creation of certain fundamental thematic material. This analogy was current in the Middle Ages; in the early fourteenth century someone complained that just as plainsong was being superseded by more complex musical forms, so the plain old-fashioned type of sermon was being superseded by preaching whose main appeal was aesthetic.[11] And indeed in the twentieth century it has become a familiar idea that works of literature might have a

[10] For examples of such sermons, see *Three Middle English Sermons*, ed. D. M. Grisdale (Kendal, 1939) and *Middle English Sermons*, ed. W. O. Ross, Early English Text Society 209 (London, 1940).

[11] See Smalley, pp. 42–3.

structure analogous to that of musical compositions. T. S. Eliot, for example, has written that

> The use of recurrent themes is as natural to poetry as to music. There are possibilities for verse which bear some analogy to the development of a theme by different groups of instruments; there are possibilities of transitions in a poem comparable to the different movements of a symphony or a quartet; there are possibilities of contrapuntal arrangement of subject-matter.[12]

And Eliot has explored these possibilities in the group of his poems called *Four Quartets*. It is surely suggestive that a modern scholar, Professor Nevill Coghill, has applied the musical analogy to *Piers Plowman* itself, remarking that the 'foretastes and echoes' in the poem 'resemble the tentative statement of a theme by one group of instruments in an orchestra, taken up and developed later in the symphony by another.' But Coghill goes on to declare that the analogy is imperfect, 'for the musical composer effects it by a conscious technique of musical artifice, by utter skill; there is no reason for thinking that these echoes and foretastes in Langland are placed where they are to suit an exact theory of composition.'[13] We have seen, however, that just such a theory of composition was available to Langland in the *ars praedicandi*. To see what use he made of it, we must now turn back to *Piers Plowman*.

We saw that one thing that particularly struck Peter of Cornwall when he heard a 'university' sermon for the first time was the way in which 'It ran backwards and forwards on its path from its starting-point back to the same starting-point.' A sermon of the 'university' type will begin with a *thema*, and the result of all its elaborate art of variation will be to return us to the same *thema*, but with an enriched understanding of its significance. (In this respect, one might add, the *ars praedicandi* provides a paradigm for any literature based on an immutable revelation. The preacher or poet of Christian orthodoxy cannot leave us with an original message of his own: his aim must be to revitalize for us a commandment whose very familiarity may have deadened it as a motive for action.) Now,

---

[12] T. S. Eliot, 'The Music of Poetry,' in *On Poetry and Poets* (London, 1957), p. 38.
[13] Coghill, *loc. cit.*

like a sermon, *Piers Plowman* returns us at its conclusion to the point at which it began, but this starting-point is seen at the end with a deepened understanding. The poem begins with the field full of folk, a symbol of 'modern life.' This field reappears later as Piers's half-acre, and the poem ends with the same field, but it is now seen as a field of a different kind—a battlefield. The initial innocence of Langland's Dreamer has been superseded by experience, the experience of the poem. The world was displayed at the beginning of the poem as a scene of lively but incomprehensibly confused bustle and activity, full of baffling anomalies:

> Somme putte hem to plow and pleiden ful seylde,
> In settyng and in sowyng swonken ful harde,
> And wonne that thuse wasters with glotenye destroyeth.
> Somme putte hem to pruyde and parailede hem therafter,
> In contenaunce and in clothynge in meny kynne gyse;
> In praiers and in penaunces putten hem manye,
> Al for the love of oure lorde lyveden ful harde,
> In hope to have a gode ende and heven-ryche blysse; . . .
> And somme chosen cheffare; they chevede the betere,
> As hit semeth to oure syght that soche men thryveth.
>
> (C I 22-9, 33-4)

But at the end this field is seen through wiser and sadder eyes as a scene in which the lines of battle between good and evil, between the ploughman and pride, are drawn up all too clearly.[14] Thus the most fundamental sequence of *Piers Plowman*—its movement from the present, through a timeless journey among abstractions and a visit to the historic events of the Incarnation, back to a present which is seen more clearly—can be understood in terms of the *ars praedicandi*. However, the scope of the poem taken as a whole is of course much greater than that of any normal sermon. It has no single occasion, and is developed on the basis of no stated Scriptural text; it is concerned with subjects so wide as to be barely definable—first with 'Truth' and then with the whole problem of how to live. The poem is so fiercely concerned with action rather than doctrine that its theme can hardly be formulated, but only embodied in a living and

[14] Cf. R. W. Frank, *Piers Plowman and the Scheme of Salvation* (New Haven, 1957), p. 96.

acting person—the enigmatic figure of Piers himself, who becomes eventually the human means by which the triumph of the Resurrection is achieved. In all this Langland's work has no connection with the art of preaching. But if we wished to sum up the poem's subject in a *thema breve*, it would not be misleading to choose part of Matthew xix 16: 'What good thing shall I do, that I may have eternal life?' [15] Piers, the ultimate goal, the embodiment of all the Dreamer's longings, is approached through 'What good thing shall I do?'—that is, through enquiry after Do-well. And Do-well, by a process corresponding to the threefold *divisio* of the 'university' sermon, is extended into Do-better and Do-best. There have been many scholarly attempts to identify single and distinct meanings for each member of this triad: it has been argued that the three stand for laymen, clergy, and bishops, or for the active, contemplative, and mixed lives, or for the purgative, illuminative, and unitive ways of mysticism. But the fact is surely that Langland defines the three in different ways at different stages of his poem, and the *divisio* is simply part of the technique of preaching, a device which (to quote a recent critic) 'enables the poet to give twofold or threefold answers about the good life when necessary.' [16] Significantly, the *artes praedicandi* recommend comparison as a means of *declaratio* and also as a means of amplifying a sermon with subdivisions; Basevorn gives, as one example among several, this: ' "Take away the rust from silver, and there shall come forth a most pure vessel" [Proverbs xxv 4, Douai version]. The pure vessels are the laity, the purer the clergy, the purest the bishops' (Charland, p. 293). The 'Do-well' *thema* is stated very early in *Piers Plowman*, in Holy-church's speech in the second passus:

> Alle that worchen that wikkede ys, wenden thei shulle
> After hure deth-day and dwelle ther wrong ys;
> And alle that han wel ywroght, wenden they shulle
> Estwarde to hevene, evere to abyde
> Ther treuthe is, the trone that trinite ynne sitteth.
>
> (C II 130–34)

This is of course the same doctrine as that of the 'pardon' sent to Piers. Do-well itself emerges first as part of a similar antithesis

[15] Cf. R. W. Chambers, *Man's Unconquerable Mind* (London, 1939), p. 124.
[16] Frank, *op. cit.*, p. 42.

between the good and the wicked—the Dreamer supposes that the friars must know 'Dowel and Do-uvele, wher thei dwellen bothe' (C XI 17). It is soon divided into a triad by comparison, when Thought tells the Dreamer that 'Dowel and Dobet . . . and Dobest the thridde / Beth thre fayre vertues' (C XI 76-7). Towards the end of the poem there is a final statement of the original *thema breve* in its original antithetical form, but now modified by the idea of paying one's debts:

> And what persone payeth hit nat, punysshen he thenketh,
> And demen hem at domesday, bothe quyke and dede;
> The gode to the godhede and to grete joye,
> And wyckede to wonye in wo withouten ende.
>
> (C XXII 195-8)

Up to a point, then, *Piers Plowman* considered as a whole can be seen as constructed according to the principles of *ars praedicandi*. But these principles may help us to read the work in detail, as well as to grasp its *dispositio*, for baffling transitions, changes of direction, and a use of recurrent themes are characteristic of the poem's local development as well as of its overall structure. To illustrate this it will as usual be best to take a particular example, a passage of medium length which does not follow an obvious path of development. A suitable passage, as it happens, is one of those explicitly described as sermons in the poem: the sermon preached by Reason, dressed as a pope, to the whole community in passus C VI. The C version of this sermon is rather different from the B version, and on the face of it less coherent, so we may hope that reference to the methods of the sermon will also help us to understand the purpose of the C-revisions. At the beginning of his sermon, Reason (referring to the many outbreaks of plague that occurred in the fourteenth century)

> Prechede, and provede that thuse pestilences
> Was for pure synne, to punyshe the puple.
>
> (C VI 115-16)

He connects these 'pestilences' with another natural disaster sent by God, 'the south-west wynd on Saterday at eve' (117)—probably a particularly memorable storm that occurred in 1362—and then, after bidding 'wastours go worche and wynne here sustinaunce' (127), Reason starts giving more particular advice. He refers to

various typical figures (such as 'Purnele' who ought to give up
expensive trimmings on her clothes), and then finally

> He bad Bette go kutte a bowh other tweye,
> And bete Beton thermyd, bote hue wolde worche.
> He charged chapmen to chasten here children,
> And lete no wynnynge forwene hem the while thei ben yonge;
> For ho so spareth the spring spilleth hus children;
> And so wrot the wise, to wissen us alle,
> > *Qui parcit virge, odit filium.*   (C VI 135–40)

Thus Reason takes up again the theme with which he began—that
of punishment—and this issues in the text from Proverbs xiii 24:
'He that spareth his rod hateth his son.' (The sermon has not begun
with a text, perhaps because its occasion is not a particular day in the
Church year but a particular social situation.) There now follows
in the C-text a section which in B occurs not in Reason's sermon,
but in a quite different part of the poem—a Speech by Learning in
passus B X. This section praises the unworldly life 'in cloistre other
in scole' (154), attacks selfish clerics, and goes on to threaten, in a
passage that mingles political with apocalyptic prophecy,

> Ac yut shal come a kyng and confesse yow alle,
> And bete yow, as the byble telleth, for brekyng of youre reule.
> > (C VI 169–70)

Thus the theme of punishment recurs again, and by paying attention
to the thematic method of the *ars praedicandi* we can begin to see
what Langland was about when he borrowed from B X. The same
theme comes up yet again at the very end of the passage shifted
from B:

> For the abbot of Engelonde and the abbesse hys nece
> Shullen have a knok on here crounes, and incurable the wounde;
> > *Contrivit dominus baculum impiorum, virgam dominanciam, plaga
> > insanabili.*   (C VI 177–8)

The confirming text here is a conflation of Isaiah xiv 5–6: 'The Lord
hath broken the staff of the wicked, and the sceptre of the rulers.
He who smote the people in wrath with a continual stroke, he that
ruled the nations in anger, is persecuted, and none hindereth.' In
the form used by Langland, this text repeats in *virgam* (rod, staff) the
key word of the previous text from Proverbs.

Immediately after this reference to the oppression of the oppressors, the whole direction of the sermon seems to be changed. The line 'And sitthe he consailed the kyng hus comune to lovye' (181) initiates a series of particular exhortations directed to the various members of the community who are supposed to make up Reason's congregation. The 'riche/And comuners' (183–4) are exhorted to hold together in 'unite' (190), and warned against the pride which caused Lucifer to destroy the 'holy comune' (187) of heaven. The Pope is exhorted to 'have pyte of holy-churche' (192) and to see that kings are given 'pees for here penaunce' (196). Finally pilgrims are exhorted to seek 'seint Treuthe' rather than 'seint Jame and seyntes of Rome' (198–9). Here the sermon ends with the conventional *Qui cum patre et filio* (200). This last series of exhortations may appear to be disconnected from the rest of Reason's sermon, though it can easily be seen how the references to 'unite' and 'seint Treuthe' fit it into the greater sermon of the poem as a whole. If we look at it more closely, however, we find that it does have links with what has gone before. Its ideas of community and mutual love can be referred back to the earlier passage on cloisters and schools:

> For in cloistre cometh no man to chide ne to fighte;
> In scole ys love and lownesse and lykyng to lerne.
>
> (C VI 155–6)

And the (as it were, earthly) 'comune' which was in heaven before the rebellion of Lucifer can be connected with the (as it were, heavenly) community of the cloister or school on earth:

> For yf hevene be on thys erthe other eny eyse for saule,
> Hit is in cloistre other in scole, by meny skyles ich fynde.
>
> (C VI 153–4)

Finally, in wishing that kings should have 'pees for her penaunce,' Reason not only prepares the way for the confession of the seven deadly sins (which immediately follows his sermon), but also takes up again the threat to selfish clerics, who have been told earlier that the king will 'putte yow to youre penaunce, *ad pristinum statum ire*' (172). Thus although the sermon may appear on a first reading to be utterly confused (especially in the C Version), we have now seen that it possesses a tenuous but definite thematic organization. It

proceeds with a circling or spiralling motion which constantly
brings it back to the theme of punishment or 'penaunce' as its main
source of continuity. The reader may feel that the last connections
in particular are fine drawn, and that they might be the result of
chance, especially since Langland has taken over a passage from
B X with little alteration; but it must be emphasized that such
connections are exactly what the *artes praedicandi* would lead us to
expect. We have found a sort of organization in Reason's sermon,
but it must be admitted that the sermon also has a sort of disorganization; and this too, I believe, can be traced to the art of
preaching.

It is only in a paradoxical sense that an independent *art* of preaching is possible. Art is a form of display, but the preacher must
preach, as Waleys puts it, 'not in order to show off . . . but for the
praise of God and the edification of his neighbour' (Charland, p.
330). His immediate aim, especially perhaps when he is preaching
to his lay neighbours, will clearly be edification. Horace recommends
a mixture of the *utile* and the *dulce*, the useful and the pleasing, as
the best recipe for literature, but for the *artes praedicandi* the *utile*
comes first, and in fact the very words *utile* and *utilitas* run through
them like a refrain. Basevorn expresses his disapproval of the more
elaborate arrangements of *correspondentia* by saying that one type
is 'more ingenious than useful' and that another is 'useless.' He
commends a method of constructing sermons according to which
the preacher begins by choosing 'three subjects which he supposes
to be greatly useful to the listeners' on the grounds that it is
'extremely useful and efficacious, and intelligible among simple
people in any vernacular language' (Charland, pp. 302, 306, 314).
Waleys tells us that when a sermon is intended for the common
people, the 'ancient' method 'is not only easier for the preacher
himself, but also more useful for the listener.' The *divisio* is not made,
as some suppose, 'only for its ingenuity,' but for its utility: 'it is
useful for the preacher . . . It is very useful indeed for the listener.'
And later Waleys observes that the 'infinite' multiplication of
divisiones, though easy for the preacher, 'deforms the sermon and
renders it insipid and not easily intelligible to the listener' (Charland,
pp. 344, 370, 370–71). Here the aesthetic vocabulary—*deformat*
being, in context, the antonym of *decorat*—is itself employed in the

service of *utilitas*. We find in the *ars praedicandi* the paradox of a utilitarian aesthetic, a literary theory which despises its own techniques.

This theory can be seen at work most clearly in the use of the digression. For the *ars poetica*, it will be remembered, the digression is a purely artistic device; its function is summarized by Geoffroi de Vinsauf's remark that 'Digression at once amplifies and decorates the subject-matter' (Faral, p. 274). *Piers Plowman* contains many digressions, but their function usually seems to be rather different from this. Langland normally digresses in order to clear up some difficulty in argument, or more simply because he has unexpectedly thought of something important to say. Among many examples of this, one might mention the digression on lying in C XXI, which was discussed above, and the 'sermon' of Ymagynatyf (Recollection) in C XV, which is generally concerned with learning, but rambles to take in a description of the Nativity, an explanation that the unlearned thief crucified with Christ is lowest in heaven, and a warning that only Nature knows everything. Now digression of this sort had been defended long before the fourteenth century by St Gregory, as being appropriate to religious discourse. He uses the image of a river to explain his view, and, we may note, also invokes the concept of *utilitas*:

> Anyone who speaks about God should consider it necessary to search out whatever will correct the behaviour of his listeners; and he will be following the proper method of exposition if, when an opportunity for edification occurs, he profitably [*utiliter*] turns away from what he was originally saying. For the commentator on sacred writ should behave like a river. Now if a river, as it is flowing in its bed, runs alongside hollow valleys, the force of its current is turned into them at once; and when it has filled them up sufficiently, it immediately pours back into its bed. There is no doubt that the commentator on holy writ should act just like this: whatever subject he is dealing with, if he happens to find at hand an occasion for appropriate edification, he should as it were turn aside the flood of his eloquence towards that nearby valley; and then, when he has poured enough into it, he should fall back into the channel of his prepared speech.[17]

[17] *Moralium libri*, Epistola cap. II, ed. J.-P. Migne, *Patrologia Latina* LXXV, col. 513.

This river image seems strikingly appropriate to *Piers Plowman*, with its combination of urgent pressure and unforeseen direction. It is borrowed by Basevorn, along with the usual criterion of *utilitas*, to describe *digressio*. He says that digressions should not normally be too long or too remote from the main subject, but that it may be necessary to be prolix where teaching is concerned. 'And thus, as Gregory recommends . . . , as the water of a river flows in wherever it finds low places, so sometimes an authority needs to be turned aside so that things that are useful may be said by the way' (Charland, p. 297). Here, as in the matter of *divisiones*, Waleys shows a fuller realization of the paradoxical nature of this aesthetic. He too argues that if a preacher thinks of something edifying to say, even though it is outside his chosen theme, he should say it, and he continues: 'Nor in that case is it to abandon the art of preaching if one digresses from the theme; indeed it is to keep most strictly to the art of preaching' (Charland, p. 356). A variant manuscript reading sharpens the paradox by substituting *artissime* (most artistically) for *certissime* (most strictly). Waleys goes on to argue that if a poet follows his art most closely by breaking its metrical rules 'so that his meaning may be clearer and fuller,' surely a preacher must act similarly? Langland seems to share this attitude towards his art. Of his skill as a poet there can be no question, and yet when Recollection says accusingly to the Dreamer 'thow medlest the with makynges, and myghtest go sey thi sauter' (B XII 16), the Dreamer accepts the rebuke as true. For Langland perhaps a contempt for 'mere' art was a condition of artistic achievement.

Before we leave the subject of the *dispositio* of *Piers Plowman*, it may be interesting to turn from the theorists of the art of preaching to the practice of a great medieval preacher, perhaps indeed the greatest preacher of the Middle Ages: St Bernard. We find St Bernard treating the *ars praedicandi* in practice as an art of improvisation. In the course of his great series of sermons on the Song of Songs, he will casually remark halfway through an exposition, 'And another sense [of the text] occurs to me; I had not thought of it before, but I cannot pass it by.' Again, in interpreting the text 'Thy name is as ointment poured forth,' he comments: 'Now why is it called ointment? For I have not yet said this. I had begun to say it in a former sermon, but there suddenly came up something that seemed to need preaching about.'[18] The last phrase—*aliud quod praedicandum videbatur*—has a charming simplicity: how often in reading *Piers Plowman* we feel inclined to explain an unexpected transition by the sudden occurrence to the poet of 'something that seemed to need preaching about!' And Bernard begins his very next sermon with a statement in which he defends his methods as a preacher, and which gives us a vivid insight into the whole ethos of preaching in the Middle Ages. He begins by reminding the quick-witted among his listeners, who may be getting impatient at the slowness of his exposition of the Song of Songs, that 'I also have a duty towards slower people, and indeed especially towards them; for I am not concerned nearly so much to explain words as to influence hearts. My duty is both to draw water and to give it to people to drink, and this is not to be done by discussing things hastily and cursorily, but by careful commentary and frequent exhortation.' Here we find the active concern for the needs of the congregation that is characteristic of the *ars praedicandi*. On this occasion the congregation is a mixed one, and so, because the end of preaching (to influence hearts) must always override its method (to explain words), the less intelligent must be provided for. *Piers Plowman* too seems to be directed at an audience of mixed intellectual capacity, and similar provision is made for this. In passus C XX, for example, the doctrine of the Trinity is carefully explained through two separate analogies, one more and the other less difficult. The first and simpler analogy is that of a hand, and its functional purpose as a mnemonic is made clear by the remark with which it is introduced:

And if kynde witt carpe her-agen and other kynne thouhtes,
Other heretikes with argumens, thyn honde thou hem shewe!
(C XX 109–10)

The second analogy, more difficult and more poetic, is that of a taper, composed of an intricately interrelated wax, wick, and flame. It is true, St Bernard continues, that he has not finished in two days an exposition (he calls it 'that shady forest, lurking with allegories') which he had expected to complete in one. But, like a man looking

[18] Sermones IX 9 and XV 5, ed. Migne, *ibid.*, CLXXXIII, cols. 818 and 846.

at a mountainous landscape from a distance, he was not able to see into the valleys and woods before he came to them. Langland's position must have been very similar, as he embarked on his poem, also a shady forest with allegories lurking in it, and involving difficulties he could hardly have foreseen when he confidently introduced the supreme authority of Holychurch to answer all the Dreamer's questions in the very first passus. St Bernard concludes by asking, with admirable panache,

> For example, when we were discussing the calling of the Gentiles and the rejection of the Jews, how could I have foreseen that the miracle of Elisha would suddenly spring out in the middle of them? But now, since we have come upon this subject accidentally, a short delay must not worry us, so long as we return eventually to the subject we interrupted, for that contains just as much spiritual nourishment. After all, hunters and hounds often find that they have to abandon the quarry they had originally started in order to pursue another which appears unexpectedly.

This image of the preacher and his congregation as a hunter and his hounds, who cannot carry out a course of action foreseen in every detail, but must follow whatever quarry they happen to rouse, is again one which it is tempting to apply to *Piers Plowman*. Certainly, in reading the poem, one has the impression that the poet is engaged in a contest against an unpredictable opponent.

In general, what this passage from St Bernard suggests is that his art as a preacher, elaborate and considered as it is, must nevertheless always include an important element of spontaneity. And this will lead him not simply into graces beyond the reach of art, but sometimes into pieces of non-art, produced in response to demands more important than those of literary criticism. This seeming contradiction, of an art that embraces its own negation, is expressed by the preaching theorists, who put forward, along with an intricate formal patterning for the sermon, the warning that this patterning must always be disregarded if necessary. And the contradiction is found embodied in Langland's poem, at once magnificent and impoverished, a work which seems to hang—sometimes uncomfortably and, for the literary critic, disturbingly—at the point of balance between organization and chaos. We have seen, I think, that, so far as the *dispositio* of *Piers Plowman* is concerned, an awareness of the art of preaching as Langland's contemporaries conceived it can usefully suggest to a modern reader what kinds of organization and what kinds of disorganization he is to look for in the poem. It remains to consider briefly the poem's local stylistic detail.

The style of *Piers Plowman*, compared with that of other alliterative poems, such as *Sir Gawain and the Green Knight*, tends to be bare and lacking in any specifically poetic diction. Here too we may find the influence of the *ars praedicandi*, which expresses a traditional Christian suspicion of any kind of ornament. Waleys ridicules sermons full of the rhyming endings typical of medieval Latin artistic prose, because, he says, such heightenings 'obstruct the purpose of a sermon, since, while the external ears are excessively occupied with the sweetness of the voice, the inward ears of the heart gain less from the excellence of the matter and meaning, just as those who take great pleasure in singing attend less to the matter that is being sung' (Charland, p. 373). Basevorn opposes those who say that 'preaching ought not to glitter in the deceptively gorgeous robes of rhetorical colours,' and he cites St Bernard's sermons as examples of the proper use of eloquence. But he insists all the same that edification must come first. Modern preachers, he says, introduce into their sermons 'much that, as it seems to me, belongs more to ingenuity and to vanity than to edification' (Charland, pp. 248, 244). A similar attitude of mind seems to be at work in *Piers Plowman*. One can claim, I think, that Langland usually produces his most impressive poetry at the crucial points in the development of his poem, and that this poetry is all the more convincing for being won out of enquiry and exposition on a deliberately prosaic and unliterary level. Nevertheless, it must be admitted that *Piers Plowman* contains many long passages of sense—excellence of matter and meaning—which only rarely deviate into poetry. The stylistic devices that stand out most prominently in the poem are various kinds of verbal repetition—the simplest type of rhetorical ornament. This is not in the least surprising, of course; such devices, as we have seen, play a large part in the *ars poetica*, and they are commonly used in medieval literature generally. This is what one would expect of a literature largely composed to be read aloud. The use of such devices, however, would seem to be particularly encouraged by

the utilitarian ethos of the *ars praedicandi*, with its strong emphasis
on the preacher's effectiveness in relation to his audience. Repetition
is necessary, on the lowest level, as a means of emphasizing or
clarifying an important point, and so Waleys tells the preacher, 'if
there are any points that are to be strongly emphasized, do not only
say them once with great emphasis, but drum them into the
congregation two or three times' (Charland, p. 335). We often
find in *Piers Plowman* verbal repetitions of the kind that would
result from following such instructions—repetitions serving simply
to underline something that not even a simple listener can be
allowed to miss. For example, when Lady Meed makes her first
appearance, she is described as follows:

> Ich lokid on my lyft half as the lady me tauhte,
> And sauh a womman, as yt were, wonderlich *riche* clothed.
> Hue was purfild with peloure, non purere in erthe,
> And coroned with a corone—the kynge hath no betere.
> On alle hure fyve fyngres *rycheliche* yrynged,
> And theron rede rubies and other *riche* stones.
> Hure robe was *ryccher* than ich rede couthe;
> For to telle of hure atyre no tyme have ich nouth.
> Hure araye with hure *rychesse* ravesshede myn herte.
>
> (C III 8–16)

Here we have a fine example of amplifying *descriptio*, which
includes, in the penultimate line, the typical rhetorical device of
occupatio—a refusal to say what one might say. But the most
prominent feature of the description is the repetition of different
forms of the word 'rich' (a device which the *artes poeticae* recognize
as *adnominatio* or *polyptoton*), and this repetition serves to underline
the most important fact about Lady Meed, that she represents a
form of wealth, attractive and perhaps ostentatious. A little later,
when a closer definition of Meed is necessary, Theology says in her
defence that she is nearly related to Amends, a lawful form of payment, and this point too is underlined by a repetition:

> For Mede is moillere—*Amendes was here dame*.
> Thouh Fals were hure fader and Fykel-tonge hure syre,
> *Amendes was hure moder* by trewe mennes lokyng.
> Withoute *hure moder Amendes* Mede may noght be wedded.
>
> (C III 120–23)

Repetition could hardly be more functional, more obviously a matter of the preacher's need to make things clear to his listeners; but elsewhere in the poem one can find the same device extended from the functional to the poetically creative. For example, in the triumphant speech of Christ to Lucifer as He breaks hell open and lets out the suffering souls, there are thickly clustered repetitions of the word *drynke*:

> The biternesse that thow hast browe, now brouk hit thyself;
> That art doctour of deth, *drynk* that thow madest!
> For ich, that am lord of lyf, love is my *drynke*,
> And for that *drynke* todaye deyede, as hit semede;
> Ac ich wol *drynke* of no dich, ne of no deop cleregie,
> Bote of comune coppes—alle Cristene soules;
> Ac thi *drynke* worth deth, and deop helle thy bolle.
> Ich fauht so, me fursteth yut for mannes soule sake;
> 　　*Sicio.*
> May no pyement, no pomade, ne presiouse *drynkes*
> Moyste me to the fulle, ne my thurst slake,
> Til the vendage valle in the vale of Josaphat,
> And *drynke* ryght rype most—*resurreccio mortuorum.*
> 　　　　　　　　　　　　(C XXI 404–15)

Here the use of words is daringly imaginative, for the image of drinking has grown from a fusion of two different ideas—that of the Devil as a doctor brewing evil medicines, and that of the offering of a bitter drink to the parched Christ on the cross. We cannot say that Langland could have learned to use words thus from the *ars praedicandi*, or from any other source; but he may at least have been encouraged by the repetitive nature of sermon structure and style to allow his powers to develop along this path.

There is a more obvious influence from the art of preaching in a different and more distinctive kind of verbal repetition that Langland uses. We have seen how the texture of ideas and images in a 'modern' sermon, and equally in *Piers Plowman* considered as a whole and in shorter parts of it such as Reason's sermon, is one of thematic interweaving. Now the same pattern is often repeated on a still smaller scale in the style of *Piers Plowman*, where a number of different *words* are interwoven just as ideas and images are interwoven on a larger scale. When the Dreamer asks a character called

'Liberum-Arbitrium' (Free Will) 'What is holychurche, frend?'
the answer is 'Charite,' but this simple reply is then expanded as
follows:

Lyf, and *Love*, and *Leaute* in o *byleyve* and *lawe*,
A *love*-knotte of *leaute* and of *leel byleyve*,
Alle kynne cristene clevynge on on wyl,
Withoute gyle and gabbynge, gyve and selle and lene.
Love lawe withoute *leaute*, lowable was it nevere;
God lereth no lyf to *love* withoute *leel* cause.
Jewes, Gentiles, and Sarrasines jugen hemselve
That *leeliche* thei *byleyven*, and yut here *lawe* dyverseth;
And on god that al bygan with goode herte thei honoureth,
And either *loveth*, and *bilevith* in on lord almyghti.
Ac oure lorde *loveth* no *love* bote *lawe* be the cause;
For lechours *loven* agen the *lawe*, and at the laste beeth
    dampned:
And theeves *loven*, and *leaute* haten, and at the laste beeth
    hanged:
And *leelle* men *loven* as *lawe* techeth, and *love* therof aryseth,
The which is hefd of Charite, and hele of mannes soule.
                                              (C XVIII 126–40)

In this passage of fifteen lines a number of different repetends, all
beginning with the letter *l*, are interlocked: some form of the root
love is repeated eleven times, *lawe* six times, and *leaute*, *byleyve*, and
leel four times each. And the repetition has a special purpose: to
enrich our conception of 'charity' by *re-creating* it from its com-
ponent elements of love, belief, and lawfulness or justice (*leel*,
lawful, giving the noun *leaute*). Liberum-Arbitrium uses words
rather as a juggler uses his balls: several words are tossed so rapidly
from hand to hand that they seem to merge into a single entity—
charity. This really is a distinctive use of a device which in itself is
very common. Comparison with other types of verbal repetition
may make this clear. We have just seen how verbal repetition can
be used simply to underline an important point. It may also be
employed more subtly, as an aid to analysis or definition of whatever it is that is repeated; Chaucer, for instance, sometimes employs
verbal repetition in this analytic way. Thus in *The Wife of Bath's
Tale*, a knight is forced to marry an ugly old woman, whom he

despises for her ignoble birth as much as for her lack of physical attractiveness. But this wife of his lectures him on the subject of *gentillesse* (nobility) in a speech in which the words *gentil*, *gentillesse*, and *genterye* are repeated twenty-one times in sixty-eight lines (*Canterbury Tales*, III 1109–76). The purpose of her speech is to define true *gentillesse* by distinguishing between the nobility of title which men receive from their ancestors and the nobility of behaviour that comes from God alone. This 'analytic' use of verbal repetition contrasts very strongly with that in Liberum-Arbitrium's speech. The latter might rather be called 'synthetic,' for its purpose is to *create* 'A love-knotte of leaute and of leel byleyve'—to fuse a variety of elements into a whole which is felt to be richly meaningful, but which could hardly be defined in conceptual terms.

In this chapter I have not aimed at an 'interpretation' of *Piers Plowman* in any way comparable with the account of *Sir Gawain and the Green Knight* offered in chapter 2. *Piers Plowman* seems to me an immensely more difficult poem, and, despite the great quantity of scholarly work that has been done on it, it appears that we are still at the stage of having to make up our minds what *kind* of poem it is. I have therefore done no more than to try to suggest some ways in which an acquaintance with the medieval art of preaching might usefully affect the expectations brought to *Piers Plowman* by a modern reader. But the remarks in the last paragraph on the 'synthetic' effect of certain examples of verbal repetition suggest some comments on the way in which the local style of the poem reflects the poet's whole purpose. We saw how this was so in the case of *Sir Gawain and the Green Knight*, where the poem's central conception of *cortaysye* was expressed in Gawain's distinctive mode of speech, and also in *The Clerk's Tale*, where tensions within the style were used to express a larger disharmony of attitude. An analogous relation between style and purpose can be seen in *Piers Plowman*. The effect of potent vagueness generated by Liberum-Arbitrium's speech is rather typical of *Piers Plowman* in general: despite the work of various modern scholars, the poem seems to give up very little of itself to attempts at theological analysis or at the separation of its meaning into a variety of allegorical layers. The conceptual vagueness is central to Langland's religious vision, and why this should be so may appear most clearly from

a comparison with a twentieth-century religious poet, T. S. Eliot.
I remarked earlier that the writer whose religious scheme is that
of Christian orthodoxy is in a peculiar position. He cannot offer
any radical novelty of doctrine: his 'originality' must consist not
in the creation of new religious concepts but in the re-creation of
the old so that they may be apprehended with new force. The kind
of re-creation that is necessary will vary from age to age according
to the nature of the most powerful destructive forces at work on
religious language and thought in the immediate past. Eliot has
written religious poetry in a post-Romantic age—an age, that is to
say, when the force of religious terms has been dissipated because
they have been used recklessly in non-religious contexts. Words
such as 'divine' or 'eternal,' for example, have been deprived of all
precision, indeed almost of all meaning, in normal speech and
thought, by having been employed in a loosely emotive sense, as
mere intensifiers, in the common language of nineteenth-century
poetry. Thus Eliot's task has been to avoid too ready an invocation
of familiar concepts, to skirt round them warily, using methods
borrowed from the *via negativa* of mysticism:

> Neither flesh nor fleshless;
> Neither from nor towards; at the still point, there the dance is,
> But neither arrest nor movement. And do not call it fixity,
> Where past and future are gathered. Neither movement from nor
>   towards,
> Neither ascent nor decline.   ('Burnt Norton')

In such poetry, as Dr F. R. Leavis has written,

> Familiar terms and concepts are inevitably in sight, but what is
> distinctive about the poet's method is the subtle and resourceful
> discipline of continence with which, in its exploration of experi-
> ence, it approaches them.[19]

This is the kind of religious poetry that a discriminating mid-
twentieth-century reader has been likely to admire most readily, but
it is not at all the kind he will have come upon in Langland's work. If
in Eliot's age the religious sensibility has been in greatest danger from
Romanticism, in Langland's age the great peril seems to have been
scholasticism. The thirteenth century had been a period in which

[19] *Education and the University*, p. 88.

vast and comprehensive systems of theology and philosophy were built up on a basis of careful definition and minute distinction; the supreme example is the work of St Thomas Aquinas. In the fourteenth century these systems, based on a synthesis of faith and reason, began to give way under the attacks of Ockham and his followers, and the intellectual atmosphere generally was one of criticism and logic-chopping.[20] We can plausibly guess from *Piers Plowman* that for Langland it seemed as though the scholastic impulse in its decay was reducing the method of precise intellectual distinction to a frivolous habit of mind, a sort of uncontrollable mental tic that was obscuring the fundamental motives of Christianity as a way of life. The Dreamer of *Piers Plowman* is presented as a kind of amateur scholastic, searching for *Do*well, without realizing that by satisfying a merely intellectual curiosity he will come no nearer to goodness in action.[21] Thus at the beginning of the *Vita* he is seen in disputation with the friars, parodying the very jargon of scholastic philosophy: ' "*Contra*," quath ich as a clerke, and comsede to dispute' (C XI 20). Later in his quest he is rebuked by Liberum-Arbitrium for a similar wish to distinguish and dispute. Liberum-Arbitrium has explained that he is called by various other names according to his functions—'soul,' 'mind,' 'memory,' 'love,' and so on—and the Dreamer has jokingly said that he is like a bishop who is called *presul, pontifex, metropolitanus,* 'And other names an hepe, *episcopus* and *pastor.*' Liberum-Arbitrium takes up the silly joke with surprising vehemence, and uses it to show what deep roots the wish to know by intellectual distinctions may have, and what grave consequences it may lead to:

'That is soth;' he seide, 'now ich seo thy wil,
How thow woldest know and conne the cause of alle here names,
And of myne, yf thow myghtest, me thynketh by thy speche!'
'Ye, syre,' ich seyde, 'by so that no man were agreved,
Alle the science under sonne and alle sotile craftes
Ich wolde ich knewe and couthe kyndeliche in myn herte.'

[20] See, e.g., Gordon Leff, *Bradwardine and the Pelagians* (Cambridge, 1957).
[21] Cf. John Lawlor, 'The Imaginative Unity of Piers Plowman,' *Review of English Studies* n.s. VII (1957), pp. 113–26.

'Thanne art thow inparfyt,' quath he, 'and on of Prydes
   knyghtes;
For suche a luste and lykynge Lucifer fel fro hevene.'
                                               (C XVII 206–13)

The Dreamer gains his fullest understanding of Do-well by his
vision of the Crucifixion and Harrowing of Hell, where he does not
interrupt but simply observes this supreme example of goodness in
action. Not the '*contra*' of the scholastic but a patient silence is the
means to true philosophy; and indeed the Dreamer has already been
told this by Ymagynatyf when, by thrusting in with a philosophical
question, he has brought one of his visions to a sudden end (C XIV
184–231). It is a paradox perhaps that if the Dreamer were *not* an
amateur scholastic, always demanding reasons and picking arguments, the poem would not exist at all. The tension between
argument and submission is part of the essential nature of *Piers
Plowman*; but the poem's central effort, despite the use it makes
incidentally of scholastic methods, is directed against the making of
intellectual distinctions and towards the building up of large,
theologically undefined ideas which will have the power to stir
men's emotions and move them to action. The supreme example of
the poem's suggestive indefiniteness is of course the ploughman
himself, with his different roles as peasant, secular ruler, Christ's
human nature, and the ideal pope, and with his mysterious appear-
ances and disappearances. We have said that such an imaginative
construction lies beyond the reach of any teaching the *ars praedicandi*
can offer. But Langland's purpose is also expressed in the interweaving and fusing of themes in the whole poem, and of words in
its style; and these are techniques which the medieval art of
preaching can certainly help us to understand.

Chaucer's powers have often been compared to those of a novelist. In making the comparison, people have usually been thinking of certain parts of the *Canterbury Tales*, rather than of Chaucer's earlier poems. Nobody would think of comparing *The Book of the Duchess*, for example, with a novel; but then that poem is usually disregarded as being 'untypical' of Chaucer's true achievement, an achievement which is often thought of as being somehow 'modern.' There is however another of Chaucer's works that also tends to be described as a novel or at least as indicating the transition in Chaucer's development from 'medieval' (and tedious) to 'modern' (and interesting). This is *Troilus and Criseyde*, Chaucer's longest single work. It is described as follows by Mr John Speirs: 'In this poem the modern reader will discover, emerging out of a medieval romance, what is virtually a great novel—the first modern novel.'[1] A description such as this may have its use as an advertising device— a means of attracting to Chaucer readers for whom the novel is the normal form of literature. Beyond this, however, one's immediate reaction is to dismiss the 'novel' label as irrelevant, because to such readers the word 'novel' will probably mean something like what it means to E. M. Forster: a 'fictitious prose work over 50,000 words.'[2] Or, if they thought about the subject a little longer, such readers might come up with an approximation to the definition given in the *Concise Oxford Dictionary*: a 'fictitious prose narrative of sufficient length to fill one or more volumes portraying characters and actions representative of real life in continuous plot.' But there are important respects in which *Troilus and Criseyde* differs from the kind of work that these definitions indicate. Both definitions employ the term 'fictitious.' Now the story of *Troilus and Criseyde* is in fact a fiction, and not even a fiction going back to the legendary history of Homer, but one invented in the Middle Ages. It is first

[1] *The Age of Chaucer*, p. 25.
[2] E. M. Forster, *Aspects of the Novel* (London, 1927), p. 15.

told, so far as we know, in the twelfth century, by the French poet
Benoît de Sainte-Maure. But for Chaucer and his public, the story
of the two lovers was not fiction but history. Chaucer, in his
prologue to Book II, invokes Clio, the muse of history, assures his
audience that he is following his 'auctour,' who wrote in Latin,
and reminds them that methods of conducting a love-affair change
as times pass, so that they cannot expect to find his tale entirely
modern. All this would not seem to matter very much in itself,
since in medieval times the distinction between history and fiction
was often far from clear. But the story of Troilus and Criseyde was
not only thought of as historical, it was also one (like that of the
patient Griselda) with which Chaucer's audience would already
have been familiar. As we shall see, Chaucer makes important use
of this foreknowledge among his audience. In this respect his poem
is very different from what the word 'novel' would suggest to
most modern readers, for one of the main attractions of the novel
has almost always been that it tells a newly invented story. That
is why it is called a 'novel.' This is true even of most historical
novels; even though the events of their setting may be well known,
their main characters tend to be invented people *involved* in historical events, rather than the great figures of history themselves.
The desire to find out 'what happens' may not be very dignified,
and it can certainly be aroused by writers who have no claim to
greatness, but it cannot be doubted that it is a fundamental motive
for most readers of the novel. It cannot have been a motive that
operated for most members of Chaucer's original audience; the
story was well known, and in any case they were warned in the
opening lines of the poem that Chaucer's purpose was

> The double sorwe of Troilus to tellen,
> That was the kyng Priamus sone of Troye,
> In lovynge, how his aventures fellen
> Fro wo to wele, and after out of joie.   (I 1–4)

A second respect in which *Troilus and Criseyde* is different from
the usual conception of the novel is that it is not, as the two definitions demand, written in prose. Again, this fact may not seem very
important in itself, but it is closely connected with something more
important, indicated by the phrase 'representative of real life' in

the dictionary definition. Most people expect of a novel that it will employ a fairly detailed realism in the presentation of human life, and especially perhaps of human motivation. This detailed 'lifelikeness' of the novel helps to distinguish it from the 'romance' (such as Sidney's *Arcadia*) or the 'moral tale' (such as Orwell's *Animal Farm*). Moreover, this 'lifelikeness' is naturally expressed in prose, the least formal kind of writing, since it depends on the impression being given that no patterning has been imposed on the writer's material at any obvious level. Such patterning as it possesses must be felt to be inherent in the material—'real life'—itself. Now *Troilus and Criseyde* is written not simply in verse but in one of the most formal kinds of medieval verse, the seven-line stanzas of rime royal. It is thus elaborately patterned on the surface, and its whole mode of presenting its subject is in accordance with this exterior form. There is much in the poem, it is true, that seems naturalistic— Criseyde's glance in the temple as if to say, 'What! may I nat stonden here?' (I 292), or Pandarus's dash to fetch a cushion for the kneeling Troilus (III 964)—but there is also much that presents the subject-matter in a formalizing or idealizing way. Some examples may make clear what is meant by this. In Book IV Troilus solilo- quizes about predestination and freewill, but his speech does not, and is not supposed to, represent his thoughts on the problem as they pass through his head; it takes the form of a disputation, in which all the arguments on each side are set out with a thoroughness that belongs to philosophy, not to everyday life. Here then the subject matter of the poem has been formalized. The same process occurs in Book V, when the narrator suddenly inserts into his story personal descriptions of Troilus, Criseyde, and Diomede, so that the three are arrested in motion, like figures in a stained glass window. The descriptions form a combination of the devices called by the rhetoricians *effictio* (description of appearance) and *notatio* (description of character), and they bear in their stiffness no relation at all to the intimate acquaintance we have previously been granted with the three characters. Chaucer presents his subject matter in an idealizing way in, for example, his whole treatment of Troilus as a perfect example of the medieval lover—less an individual than a type. C. S. Lewis has shown that it is possible to read the whole poem as a retelling of the story told through personifications in the

Roman de la Rose.[3] This is not, I believe, a complete reading of the poem, but it is certainly a possible reading, and it suggests a degree of idealization far greater than we should expect in a novel.

It is clear enough from all this that, in the way it treats its subject matter, *Troilus and Criseyde* differs in important respects from what most modern readers would understand by a novel. If we call it simply 'the first modern novel,' we shall be inviting those readers to disregard much of what Chaucer was really doing in the poem. But, for all this, in referring it to the novel, Mr Speirs is surely on the right lines. There are many literary works that we should never think of when the word 'novel' is mentioned, but which we should nevertheless be forced to call novels if we had to call them anything. The *Concise Oxford Dictionary's* definition would cover, certainly, *Moll Flanders* and *Emma* and *Middlemarch* and *The Bostonians* and *Sons and Lovers*: but would it also take in *Tristram Shandy* and *The Rainbow* and *Ulysses* and *Lolita*? Probably not; and yet what could we call these works but novels? It seems likely that for the average reader the word 'novel' implies the decorum of a continuous realism, but excludes other resources (such as poetic prose, symbolism, parody, transposition of time sequence, and so on) of which some writers in the past, and many of the greatest in this century, have made use. It might be less misleading to think of *Troilus and Criseyde* as a novel if one had in mind the flexibility of technique of twentieth-century masters such as Lawrence and Joyce. The average reader, giving up in despair any attempt to define 'the novel', would perhaps agree that novels must at least be in some direct sense 'like life,' whatever technical means they use. They must not, for example, be inhabited by personifications: room must be left by the author for our own interpretation of motive and judgment of character to have free play. Most medieval literature is not 'like life,' but *Troilus and Criseyde* is, and in this respect it is also like a novel. Henry James has indicated in an essay on Robert Louis Stevenson in what this 'lifelikeness' may consist. He writes of one quality as being at once 'the most fascinating quality a work of imagination can have' and that in which it resembles

---

[3] See *The Allegory of Love* (Oxford, 1936), chapter IV. For a contrasting view, see Charles Muscatine, *Chaucer and the French Tradition* (Berkeley, 1956), chapter V, to which I am much indebted in this chapter.

'life itself.' This quality is 'a dash of alternative mystery as to its meaning, an air . . . of half inviting, half defying, you to interpret,' so that 'we may take it in different ways.'[4] Much of *Troilus and Criseyde* possesses this quality. Not all of the poem, but important parts of it, are capable of sustaining the same kind of analysis as 'life itself'—an analysis not only of words but also of the human behaviour that the words express. And the analysis is seemingly endless; it leads always to dubieties and ambiguities, for the human story of the poem is so presented that 'we may take it in different ways.' The writer imposes no one interpretation on us. In this sense, *Troilus and Criseyde* really is like a novel, though it may use techniques foreign to the novel as it has traditionally been written. To illustrate this aspect of *Troilus and Criseyde*—and it seems to me one of the poem's most important aspects—I wish to examine two brief episodes from it in some detail. They are not samples chosen at random. Both episodes take place at crucial points in the development of the narrative, and both seem to sum up that development in themselves, in such a way as to have an almost symbolic function.

1. *Criseyde's Dream*

The first episode occurs about halfway through Book II, and it concerns a dream dreamt by Criseyde. Because this dream seems to sum up a whole situation, to mark a watershed in the poem, it will be necessary to look first at the events which lead up to it. It occurs after the first meeting between Pandarus and Criseyde, at which Criseyde has been told that Troilus is in love with her, indeed is dying of love for her. After this, Criseyde sees Troilus from her window, as he rides past from a skirmish against the Greeks. He is a romantic, battle-scarred figure, with his helmet dinted in twenty places, and even his horse wounded and bleeding. And yet he is also described as vulnerable in an almost feminine way. He rides along blushing, with his eyes downcast, as the crowd press forward to catch a glimpse of him; and Criseyde's heart is touched. 'Who yaf me drynke?' (II 651), she murmurs to herself, thinking of those magic love-potions so common in medieval romance. The narrator

---

[4] See *Henry James and Robert Louis Stevenson*, ed. Janet Adam Smith (London, 1948), pp. 146 and 155.

emphasizes that this is a turning-point in his story. Someone in his
audience, he says, might complain, 'This was a sodeyn love . . .'
(667), but, he explains,

> . . . I sey nought that she so sodeynly
> Yaf hym hire love, but that she gan enclyne
> To like hym first. . . .   (673–5)

After Troilus has passed by, Criseyde has a long (and formalized)
debate with herself about what her feelings towards him are, and
what attitude she ought to take up in the future. The debate ends
inconclusively:

> Than slepeth hope, and after drede awaketh;
> Now hoot, now cold; but thus, bitwixen tweye,
> She rist hire up, and wente here for to pleye.
>
>   (810–12)

Now begins the episode with which we are mainly concerned.

Criseyde goes out into the garden with her three nieces, attended
by other women, and they wander up and down talking. One of
the three nieces, Antigone, sings a song in praise of love and of an
ideal lover. Criseyde first enquires who wrote the song, and then
she asks with a sigh,

> Lord, is ther swych blisse among
> Thise loveres, as they konne faire endite? (885–6)

Antigone answers that only those who are themselves in love can
tell of the 'blisse' of lovers:

> Men mosten axe at seyntes if it is
> Aught fair in hevene (why? for they kan telle),
> And axen fendes is it foul in helle.   (894–6)

The state of love is thus left as equivocal as ever—heaven or hell—
and Criseyde does not pursue her question any further:

> Criseyde unto that purpos naught answerde,
> But seyde, 'Ywys, it wol be nyght as faste.'
> But every word which that she of hire herde,
> She gan to prenten in hire herte faste,
> And ay gan love hire lasse for t'agaste
> Than it dide erst, and synken in hire herte,
> That she wex somwhat able to converte.   (897–903)

Criseyde's abrupt change of subject reveals beautifully how difficult she has found it to retain her self-possession during Antigone's song. She has been affected deeply and personally by the subject of 'love,' although this is a subject which in her society (seen by Chaucer as a medieval courtly society, like Camelot in *Sir Gawain and the Green Knight*) forms a normal and rather abstract topic of conversation. Again the subject to which she switches, apparently at random, is revealing. When she says 'it wol be nyght as faste,' she means simply that it is time to go indoors, but the phrase seems to contain a deeper ominousness—a threat held in suspense, and as yet undirected, as she passes into a new phase of experience, which may be heaven or may be hell. Criseyde, then, while she is still awake, is in a state of mind in which she is tending to disclose her hidden motives without being conscious of doing so. Thus we are prepared for her to do the same thing when she is asleep. Chaucer describes the descent of night with an unparticularized but evocative brevity —'And white thynges wexen dymme and donne' (908)—and then Criseyde goes to bed. Once in bed,

> Whan al was hust, than lay she stille and thoughte
> Of al this thing; the manere and the wise
> Reherce it nedeth nought, for ye ben wise.   (915–17)

This enigmatic statement is rather typical of Chaucer's presentation of Criseyde. The responsibility for interpretation is thrown entirely on the audience, and yet we feel that we are far from being wise enough to understand Criseyde's 'real' motives and thoughts. We can reasonably guess, I suppose, that she is thinking of love, and that her thoughts are tinged with anticipation and foreboding. Whatever they are, her thoughts are merged into the song of a nightingale which is singing on a cedar outside her window: singing perhaps, the narrator says, 'in his briddes, wise a lay / Of love' (921–2). Criseyde's love, then, springs from an impulse common to the whole of nature. The idea is similar to that expressed in the opening lines of the General Prologue to the *Canterbury Tales*, where the same impulse makes birds want to sing at night and people want to go on pilgrimages. Now at last Criseyde falls asleep. The actual phrase used is 'the dede slep hire hente' (924); she does not simply fall, she is seized by a sleep which is hovering on the edge of personification, she is drawn into the whole movement of descending night as it completes itself. And there is perhaps a touch of the sinister in this line: the active verb given to sleep has an unusual force, and the effect of the adjective 'dede' is disturbing as well as soothing. Finally, after all this careful preparation, we have the dream itself. In it, these hints from the preceding stanzas of the ominous and the sinister are brought into sharper focus in a symbolic form.

> And as she slep, anonright tho hire mette
> How that an egle, fethered whit as bon,
> Under hire brest his longe clawes sette,
> And out hire herte he rente, and that anon,
> And dide his herte into hire brest to gon,
> Of which she nought agroos, ne nothyng smerte;
> And forth he fleigh, with herte left for herte.   (925–31)

Unquestionably, I think, this has the authentic strangeness of a dream experience. It seems to be saturated with a meaning that demands to be interpreted; but Chaucer offers no interpretation whatever. Having described the dream in the stanza quoted, he leaves the whole subject, and turns to tell us about Troilus instead. The dream has in fact more than one meaning, and in order to make its ambiguity clear we shall have to embark on a short excursion into medieval ideas about dreams.

Dreams were a subject of great interest in the Middle Ages, and there developed around them a large body of theory, with a proliferation of technical terms.[5] They came within the purview of theologians, physicians, astrologers, moralists, and other experts, and almost every writer on the subject had his own bias and his own vagaries of classification. The consensus of medical opinion, however, was that dreams might be caused in three distinct ways, two natural and one supernatural. The type of dream that was thought to have some supernatural cause, whether astrological or theological, may be called the *somnium coeleste*, and was also often thought to be prophetic—to give a genuine insight into the future. A second type of dream, the *somnium animale*, had natural causes of a psychological

---

[5] Much of the following account is based on W. C. Curry, *Chaucer and the Mediaeval Sciences*, 2nd edn. (London, 1960), chapters VIII and IX.

kind: it reflected the preoccupations of the dreamer's waking life, so that, on the simplest level,

> The wery huntere, slepynge in his bed,
> To wode ayeyn his mynde goth anon;
> The juge dremeth how his plees been sped;
> The cartere dremeth how his cartes gon;
> The riche, of golde; the knyght fyght with his fon;
> The syke met he drynketh of the tonne;
> The lovere met he hath his lady wonne.
>
> (*The Parliament of Fowls*, 99–105)

This is how Chaucer puts it in one of his own dream-poems; and in fact in many medieval dream-poems there is a deliberate link between what the narrator has been thinking or reading before falling asleep and what he dreams about afterwards. The third, and lowest, type of dream is the *somnium naturale*, which again has natural causes, but of a merely physical kind. It occurs because the sleeper is hungry, or has indigestion, or is suffering from some disturbance of the 'humours' that in medieval physiology form the body's make-up. Chaucer himself was particularly interested in dreams and dream-theories, and later in *Troilus and Criseyde* he makes Pandarus give a lucid though sceptical summary of the three types mentioned: dreams may be 'revelaciouns,' they may be caused by psychological 'impressiouns,' or they may come from physical 'complexiouns' (V 365–78). Pandarus's scepticism arises from the fact that any dream can be put into any category according to the classifier: priests will say one thing, doctors another, and so on. There is nothing in a dream itself to indicate the type to which it belongs, and thus the meaning of dreams usually remains doubtful despite the elaborate medieval theories of interpretation. Chaucer makes use of this doubtfulness elsewhere in his work. It is a central issue in *The Nun's Priest's Tale*. There, it will be remembered, the cock Chauntecleer has had a terrifying dream about a dog-like creature, coloured 'bitwixe yelow and reed' (*Canterbury Tales*, VII 2902), but with its tail and ears tipped with black. His wife Pertelote is sure that this is a *somnium naturale*, for the very good reason that she is sure that *all* dreams are *somnia naturalia*, occurring 'Whan humours been to habundant in a wight' (2925). A superfluity of the red humour, choler, causes people to dream of red things, and a superfluity of the black humour, melancholy, causes people to dream of black things. Chauntecleer has dreamt of a red and black creature, therefore he is suffering from a superfluity of both humours, and the remedy is to 'taak som laxatyf' (2943). Chauntecleer, on the other hand, is convinced that dreams usually are prophetic, *somnia coelestia*, and he tells a whole string of stories to illustrate this view. So far as his own dream is concerned, he is proved right, for the red and black creature materializes in the form of a fox, who carries him off and nearly succeeds in killing him. But the general question about the nature of dreams is never settled, nor does it seem capable of settlement.

We can now return to Criseyde's dream and its ambiguity. We can exclude, I think, the possibility of its being a *somnium naturale*, for we are told nothing of her physiological state. But it might well be either a *somnium animale* or a *somnium coeleste*. The *somnium animale* view is of particular interest, since clearly more than one psychological explanation is possible for the same dream. Thinking of the dream's symbolism in medieval terms, we can easily see how it reflects Criseyde's mental and emotional state when she is confronted with the possibility of taking Troilus as her lover. The exchange of hearts in the dream obviously reflects Criseyde's preoccupation with love in general. Moreover, the eagle, a royal bird, would seem quite naturally to a medieval writer and his audience to stand for Troilus, who is a king's son. The general outline of the dream's symbolism, then, is fairly obvious; but we have still not accounted for the strange details that give it its peculiarly dream-like quality—in particular, for the lack of pain and fear felt by Criseyde. To account for this, we may turn to speculations of a more modern kind. The medieval view, expressed in *The Parliament of Fowls*, that all dreams are *somnia animalia*, is roughly equivalent to the twentieth-century psycho-analytic view of dreams. For Freud,[6] all dreams have their origins in the individual's psychology, but he distinguishes between a dream's manifest content and its latent content. The manifest content of a dream is the form in which the latent content expresses itself—the form into which it has had to be

[6] The views put forward here are those expressed in Sigmund Freud, *The Interpretation of Dreams*, trans. James Strachey (London, 1954).

changed in order to evade the censorship imposed by the higher layers of the mind. We do not have to accept Freud's suggestion that 'every dream [is] linked in its manifest content with recent experiences and in its latent content with the most ancient experiences' (Freud, p. 218), to see the value of this distinction as a means of explaining the anomalies and contradictions that are so common in dreams. Freud also claims that 'in every dream it is possible to find a point of contact with the experiences of the previous day' (p. 165). Now we may suggest that the latent content of Criseyde's dream is a secret wish to give herself to Troilus—the wish that has caused her to blush as she murmurs 'Who yaf me drynke?' Her wish indeed may have been to be seized by Troilus, to have her mind made up for her, since she is presented elsewhere in the poem as a rather passive creature, always at the mercy of events. This at least is what her passivity before the eagle in the dream suggests. But the form in which her wish-fulfilment expresses itself—the encounter with the eagle—has been moulded by her experience immediately before going to sleep. The nightingale which she had heard singing outside her window reappears in her dream, but it is now transformed into a bird of a different kind. The connection between the nightingale and the thoughts of love that had been preoccupying her is of course traditional, and is in any case made explicit in the narrator's suggestion that the nightingale was singing of love 'in his briddes wise.' This interpretation of Criseyde's dream will also serve to explain the odd fact that she felt no terror or pain when her heart was seized from her breast. Freud points out that 'In a dream I may be in a horrible, dangerous and disgusting situation without feeling any fear or repulsion' (p. 460). He explains this fact by arguing that while the original 'ideational' material of a dream will have been changed so that it may become manifest, the 'affective' shading that goes with it will remain that of the dream's latent content. Thus Troilus (with the help of the nightingale) is transformed into an eagle, of terrifying appearance and savage action; but the desirability to Criseyde of being seized by Troilus is not changed, and so in the dream she feels no fear or pain.

An interpretation of this kind cannot, of course, be more than suggestive. Even if Freud had happened to hit on the one right explanation of how dreams are caused (which seems unlikely), it

would still not be possible to carry out an accurate analysis of
Criseyde's dream without having Criseyde herself present to answer
questions about the associations the various dream-elements had for
her. When one attempts to apply a psycho-analytic interpretation
to a medieval dream, one is probably doing no more than to translate its symbolism into other terms. But these terms seem acceptable
and relevant; and that this should be so is not surprising. Chaucer,
of course, can have known nothing of a psychology that was not
evolved until five hundred years after his death, but his subject was
human nature, and so was Freud's. In so far as Chaucer has success-
fully explored human nature in his poem, we should expect it to
be open to interpretation in terms of the psychology of any age.

So far as Criseyde's dream is concerned, however, a psychological
explanation will be possible only so long as we assume that it is a
somnium animale. In fact, it may, as we said, be a *somnium coeleste*,
and in this case its function in the poem will not be to probe
Criseyde's secret motivation, but to hint in a more impersonal way
at the future course of the poem. Love is the theme of *Troilus and
Criseyde*, but so far we have seen only the more attractive aspects of
love. The dream seems to suggest that it has more sinister and savage
aspects, which will emerge when Criseyde does take Troilus as her
lover. The early effects of *fine amour* are delightful and admirable;
the lover becomes gay and gentle, and is purged even of those faults
of character that Christianity sees as sins:

> Thus wolde Love, yheried be his grace,
> That Pride, Envye, and Ire, and Avarice
> He gan to fle, and everich other vice. (III 1804–6)

But in its ultimate effect this merely human love is bitterly destructive, and by the end of the poem we are prepared emotionally, if
not logically, for a complete change in our attitude towards it. The
narrator, who in Book III can write of the lovers' first going to bed
together,

> O blisful nyght, of hem so longe isought,
> How blithe unto hem bothe two thow weere!
> Why nad I swich oon with my soule ybought,
> Ye, or the leeste joie that was theere? (III 1317–20)

by the end of the poem offers the love of God as a substitute for
earthly love. Human love had seemed to be one with that universal
divine love 'that of erthe and se hath governaunce' (III 1744), but
by the end it is revealed to be the very reverse of an ordering force.
A medieval listener, knowing the story in advance, gets a glimpse
of this ultimate vision of human love in the long-clawed eagle of
Criseyde's dream. But at the time when she has the dream, it is still
possible that it is only a *somnium animale*, revealing her own wishes
rather than the predestined future. The possible and the predestined
are held in balance; or, we may say, they are superimposed one on
the other in this ambiguous dream, with no clue given to the
relationship between them. This is a common effect in *Troilus and
Criseyde*, and the source of much of its power to move us, as we
watch human beings acting for all the world as if their future were
not inevitable. For the moment, offering no gloss on the dream,
Chaucer allows the matter to remain ambiguous.

2. *The Lovers' Parting*

My second example of how *Troilus and Criseyde* is so 'like life'
that 'we may take it in different ways' comes from an even more
crucial stage in the narrative: the interview between the lovers in
Book IV at which (though Troilus speaks a sentence to Criseyde in
Book V) they effectively part for ever. Their parting is caused by the
fact that the Trojan 'parlement' has decided to hold an exchange
of prisoners with the Greeks. Criseyde's father Calchas, a priest and
seer who has fled to the Greeks, persuades them to offer up the
captured Trojan Antenor in exchange for his daughter. The
Trojans decide, despite Hector's opposition, to accept this offer,
and so Criseyde is obliged to leave Troy. We know in advance that
once she has joined the Greeks she will become the mistress of
Diomede. At the end of Book IV Chaucer describes the last meeting
between Criseyde and Troilus. They are in bed together, and
Criseyde tries to console Troilus by assuring him that she will find
some way to return to Troy before long: perhaps the peace talks
will come to a favourable conclusion at last, or if not she will find
some way of deceiving her father. At any rate she will do something;
'And treweliche,' the narrator tells us, 'as writen wel I fynde, / That
al this thyng was seyd of good entente' (1415–16). Troilus however

has misgivings. He fears that, by force or persuasion, Criseyde will
be made to abandon him for some Greek knight, and he begs her
to elope with him in secret at once. In reply, she passionately calls
all the gods to witness that she will never abandon him. She points
out what a loss of reputation elopement would mean for them both
(for, as so often in medieval literature, the intensity of the love-
experience has been heightened by secrecy), and she promises to
return without fail within ten days. Troilus, in a speech only one
stanza long, reluctantly acquiesces in this arrangement, but he adds
a final plea:

> But, for the love of God, if it be may,
> So late us stelen privelich away;
> For evere in oon, as for to lyve in reste,
> Myn herte seyth that it wol be the beste.
>
> (1600-03)

There follows a long speech from Criseyde, in which, as people do
on such occasions, she invokes the concept of trust—if Troilus
really loved her, he would trust her to be true to him—and in
return she begs him not to be unfaithful to her. And Troilus,
completely overcome, replies as before in a single stanza, promising
unbroken faithfulness now and for ever.

A possible reaction to the passage thus summarized would be one
very unfavourable to Criseyde, one that would accuse her of hardly
less than hypocrisy. Thus she would become simply another
version—though unusually fully realized and individualized—of a
traditional medieval figure. She would become the conventional
female betrayer of innumerable medieval poems and tracts, one
with the Biblical betrayers accused by Gawain in that 'discourteous'
speech of his that we discussed in chapter 2. Strong support for this
unfavourable view of Criseyde can be found in the text of the poem.
First of all, as we have seen, the audience already know the end of
the story. They know that what Troilus's heart tells him is the
truth, that once Criseyde leaves him and Troy she will never come
back, and that she will in fact abandon him for a Greek without
even the pressure from her father of which he warns her. And then
the narrator's insistence on her good intentions can surely serve
only to call them in question:

> And treweliche, as writen wel I fynde,
> That al this thyng was seyd of good entente;

And that hire herte trewe was and kynde
Towardes hym, and spak right as she mente,
And that she starf for wo neigh, whan she wente,
And was in purpos evere to be trewe:
Thus writen they that of hire werkes knewe.

(1415–21)

If Criseyde's sincerity were obviously beyond question, we should
not need this assurance. The device of protesting a little too much,
with an appeal for confirmation to the authority of his sources, is
one that Chaucer frequently uses for ironic purposes. 'Thus writen
they that of hire werkes knewe': I agree, the narrator seems to be
saying, that this is not very plausible, but it is what the sources say.
He elsewhere refers to his source in *Troilus and Criseyde* as 'myn
auctour called Lollius' (I 394). His main source is in fact Boccaccio,
and 'Lollius' is probably a myth. There is some doubt as to whether
he was a fiction deliberately invented by Chaucer, but if he was, it
would make even clearer the ironic intention of such references to
authority. Their effect is certainly to sow seeds of doubt;[7] and just
as the Chaucerian narrator is displayed as leaning in this way on
props too weak to support their burden, so Criseyde herself is
displayed as relying on the authority of trite proverbs to support
her case:

Men seyn, 'the suffrant overcomith,' parde;
Ek 'whoso wol han lief, he lief moot lete.'

(1584–5)

And thynketh wel, that somtyme it is wit
To spende a tyme, a tyme for to wynne.   (1611–12)

We saw in chapter 3 how the rhetorical device of *sententia* might be
used critically, and it is surely used so here. Again, there is a sharp
contrast between Criseyde's long elaborate speeches, with their
accumulation of alternative reasonings and various emotional
appeals, and Troilus's two brief stanzas of reply. They are stanzas
which rely not on words but on the promise of deeds:

At shorte wordes, wel ye may me leve:
I kan na more, it shal be founde at preve.

(1658–9)

[7] This case is argued in detail by E. T. Donaldson, 'Criseide and Her
Narrator,' in *Speaking of Chaucer*, pp. 65–83.

It *is* 'founde at preve': Troilus does back up his protestations with deeds, and Criseyde does not. Against his 'shorte wordes' are set Criseyde's long speeches, the product of *amplificatio*, to which, as we have seen, the *ars poetica* is mainly devoted. Indeed, throughout the episode we are considering, Criseyde is presented as an orator, a rhetorician. She makes admirably full use of the whole range of persuasive devices open to her, because, clearly, she badly wants to persuade Troilus to trust her. And yet one may feel that the appeals which persuade him are not intended to persuade us. They are *too* various, *too* glib; moreover, in some places their very language reveals their lack of substance. Take for example this stanza:

> Forthi with al myn herte I yow biseke,
> If that yow list don ought for my preyere,
> And for that love which that I love yow eke,
> That er that I departe fro yow here,
> That of so good a confort and a cheere
> I may yow sen, that ye may brynge at reste
> Myn herte, which that is o poynt to breste.
>
> (1632–8)

The diffuseness here rests on the huddling together of mono-syllables. In a single stanza the utterly colourless word *that* is repeated eight times; but this is not a sign that Chaucer was incompe-tent at writing verse. It serves to express the speaker's embarrassed anxiety to convince, and to expose her lack of material capable of producing rational conviction.

All that has been said in the last paragraph is, I believe, true; but it is not the whole truth. I have remarked on how Chaucer makes use of his audience's foreknowledge of the end of his story as a means of casting an ironic light on the disparity between human intention and human achievement. But this very foreknowledge makes it unnecessary for him to content himself with merely undermining the sincerity of unfulfilled intentions. He does not simply expose unfulfilled and unfulfillable intentions as insincere or hypocritical; on the contrary, intention itself is sometimes allowed a moving strength and sincerity of expression. It is this which gives his poem its radical (and 'lifelike') ambiguity, for we are constantly being invited to regard simultaneously the mutually exclusive

perspectives of intention and deed. *Troilus and Criseyde* is like one
of those diagrams of cubes intended to deceive the eye. It presents
at once the claims of two contradictory but apparently equally
valid points of view.[8] In the poem we are warned that Calchas may
perhaps deceive his listeners with *ambages*,

> That is to seyn, with double wordes slye,
> Swiche as men clepen a word with two visages.
>
> (V 898-9)

Chaucer himself seems to work with a similarly ambiguous
technique. Thus in the stanza discussed above, explaining Criseyde's
good intentions, the ironic vision which juxtaposes the present with
the future also encloses an unironic vision which considers the
present for itself alone. According to this vision, 'al this thyng *was*
seyd of good entente,' and Criseyde *was* 'in purpos evere to be
trewe.' The purpose was only a purpose, but it was real, and it is
given reality by the verse in which it is presented. I want to try to
indicate one or two crucial points at which Criseyde's abortive
purpose is expressed with a depth that commands conviction. One
of these, I would suggest, is the following stanza:

> For if ye wiste how soore it doth me smerte,
> Ye wolde cesse of this; for, God, thow wost,
> The pure spirit wepeth in myn herte
> To se yow wepen that I love most,
> And that I mot gon to the Grekis oost.
> Ye, nere it that I wiste remedie
> To come ayeyn, right here I wolde dye! (1618-24)

The stanza begins with an appeal for sympathy which, by itself,
is no more than selfish, a sort of emotional blackmail. But the next
lines give this an unexpected turn, for it is not Troilus's opposition
by which Criseyde says she is hurt, but his weeping, and her own
pain is convincingly presented in the sudden physiological directness
of The pure spirit wepeth in myn herte.' There is directness here,
though the modern reader may not immediately recognize it. The
words *spirit* and *heart* are not the emotional counters they would
probably be in a more modern work. They are used with scientific

---

[8] Compare the remarks about 'double perspective' in *The Clerk's Tale* in
chapter 4 above. The approach is characteristically Chaucerian, but is used for
different purposes in different places.

exactness, for, according to medieval physiologists, the heart was literally the seat of the 'vital spirit,' one of the three 'virtues' which controlled the processes of life; and one of the functions of this 'vital spirit' was to produce emotions such as anger, joy, or sorrow in the heart. Moreover, the reciprocity of feeling between the two lovers is expressed in the words, in the repetition 'wepeth . . . wepen' (an example of *adnominatio*), and, after the turn of the line on the relative pronoun, by the sudden simplicity of 'that I love most.'

After this Criseyde reverts to speaking, with a confidence for which no justification has been offered, of her powers of practical trickery:

> But certes, I am naught so nyce a wight
> That I ne kan ymaginen a wey
> To come ayeyn that day that I have hight.
>
> (1625–7)

Next comes the monosyllabic stanza which we have already considered. But then the verse gathers itself together with a new power as she makes her final appeal:

> 'And over al this I prey yow,' quod she tho,
> 'Myn owene hertes sothfast suffisaunce. . . .' (1639–40)

The last line seems to gather increasing force as the single phrase of which it consists extends itself with words of an increasing number of syllables (*suffisaunce* being the first word of as many as four syllables for the last fourteen lines), and with a confidently musical alliteration on *s* and *f*. There is of course dramatic irony in the situation as Criseyde reaches the climax of her appeal by begging Troilus not to be unfaithful to *her*, but the possibility that this will be the future retains its imaginative validity despite the audience's foreknowledge. Criseyde's individual fear merges into the condition of human love in general

> For I am evere agast, forwhy men rede
> That love is thyng ay ful of bisy drede   (1644–5)

—and here *sententia* is put to a different purpose, for there is a pathos of uncertainty in her reliance on what 'men rede' for information about love. In the next stanza, the last of her speech, the picture of a reversed situation, in which Troilus should be the betrayer, is developed a little further:

> For in this world ther lyveth lady non,
> If that ye were untrewe (as God defende!),
> That so bitraised were or wo-bigon
> As I, that alle trouthe in yow entende.
> And douteles, if that ich other wende,
> I ner but ded, and er ye cause fynde,
> For Goddes love, so beth me naught unkynde!
>
> (1646–52)

Criseyde's genuine emotion breaks through the controlled surface of her rhetoric as she hurriedly joins three quite separate sentences together with *and*s. There is a real anxiety in her fear of losing Troilus, and she concludes with the simplest possible appeal: 'so beth me naught unkynde!' The practical scheming woman has become a child begging for protection.

We have looked at Troilus's brief reply to this long speech of Criseyde's, but not yet at the stanzas with which this last meeting of the two lovers concludes. It is here, I suggest, that Chaucer supremely, and for the last time, evokes the full power of intention as against fact. The relationship of the Chaucerian narrator to the fixed story he has to tell is a rather peculiar one. As the story brings the two lovers together, they seem to set up a magnetic field of sympathy into which the narrator is drawn, so that when the love affair is at its height he presents their subjective experiences with humane understanding, and indeed seems committed to their un-foreknowing view of things. Hence the culminating point, referred to above, at which he wishes he had achieved such a night as their first together even at the cost of his own soul. But once the lovers part, the force is broken, and the narrator comes more and more to exclude the perspective of what might have been and to concentrate on that of what historically was. Criseyde then becomes a betrayer, and Troilus her pathetic victim. Here, at the end of Book IV, intention—what might have been—is grasped sympathetically for the last time, and the two perspectives are held in equilibrium. After Troilus's words of capitulation there follows a final speech of Criseyde's in which she sets out the qualities of Troilus for which she has loved him. Here there is an interesting and significant divergence by Chaucer from his source: not from 'Lollius' but from Boccaccio. This last speech of Criseyde's is

closely derived from the *Filostrato*, but there Boccaccio had given it
not to Criseyde but to Troilus. Now one can see why Boccaccio
let Troilus have the last word. For a long time most of the talking
has been done by Criseyde, she has at last brought Troilus round to
her point of view, and what better way could there be of bringing
out the full pathos of his situation than to make him end by praising
those not merely external but moral attributes of hers that have
attracted his love? Then, in the light of the betrayal which we know
is going to follow, the praise will turn itself into accusation even as
it is uttered. One can see how tempting it would be to make this
straightforwardly effective dramatic point: women are fickle, you
can't trust them, they easily deceive us poor men. It was a temptation to which Boccaccio succumbed. But Chaucer, a greater and
more humane poet than Boccaccio, resisted the temptation, and,
by transferring the valediction to Criseyde, allowed the great
betrayer a final moment of integrity and dignity. Thus he gave full
value to the faithfulness of intention before going on to record in
the next book the faithlessness of the action ensuing.

To attempt a complete analysis of the speech would be presump-
tuous and unnecessary. I might point however to the richly varied
accumulation mounting gradually to a climax in this stanza:

> For trusteth wel, that youre estat roial,
> Ne veyn delit, nor only worthinesse
> Of yow in werre or torney marcial,
> Ne pompe, array, nobleye, or ek richesse
> Ne made me to rewe on youre destresse;
> But moral vertu, grounded upon trouthe,
> That was the cause I first hadde on yow routhe!
>
> (1667–73)

This stanza is constructed on the basis of the figure which Geoffroi
de Vinsauf calls *oppositio per adjuncta rei* and recommends as a means
of amplification (Faral, p. 218); though as usual Chaucer can get no
help from the rhetoricians as to the *reason* for using the device at this
particular point. Again, I might mention the measured rhythm and
majestically Latinate diction of

> And this may lengthe of yeres naught fordo,
> Ne remuable Fortune deface. . . .   (1681–2)

Here Chaucer displays that 'aureate' language that so bewitched his
followers. (The Scottish poet Dunbar, for example, referring to
Chaucer as 'rose of rethoris all,' praises above all his 'fresch anamalit
termes celicall.'[9]) His imitators did not learn from him, however,
how to make a line of long Latinate words follow one of short
native words (though we find Shakespeare using the same device in
reverse in some beautiful lines from *Hamlet*:

> Absent thee from felicity awhile,
> And in this harsh world draw thy breath in pain.)

Nor did they learn from Chaucer how to use alliteration so delicately
to link the two kinds of diction. In these stanzas a great poet is
deploying some of his greatest poetry, and criticism can barely do
more than to point to it. The two remaining stanzas, with which
the book concludes, seem to me equally successful. Morning has
come, and Troilus reluctantly dresses and takes his last look at
Criseyde, 'As he that felte dethes cares colde' (1692). His feelings
express not only the desolation of the present (and the cold is that of
the early morning as well as that of his sorrow), but also his recurrent
foreboding for the future. And after touching this note of foreboding, Chaucer ends the book with a movingly reticent simplicity:

> For whan he saugh that she ne myghte dwelle,
> Which that his soule out of his herte rente,
> Withouten more, out of the chaumbre he wente.
>
> (1699–1701)

One notices, beneath the bald statement of the penultimate line,
a violence of action (*rente* being what the eagle in Criseyde's dream
did to her heart). One also notices the contrast between this violence
and the outwardly trivial action of the last line, with its unobtrusive
symbolism—the end of the love affair indicated by Troilus's
walking out of Criseyde's bedchamber.

To look in some detail at the techniques Chaucer uses in short
passages from *Troilus and Criseyde*, as we have just been doing, is, I
believe, genuinely illuminating about the work as a whole (and
not, as a purely rhetorical analysis would have been, an exercise

[9] *The Goldyn Targe*, ll. 253 and 257, from *The Poems of William Dunbar*, ed.
W. Mackay Mackenzie (London, 1932).

designed merely to display the ingenuity of the critic). We have
seen how what begins with a novelist's social observation can rise
to the intensity of the highest kind of poetry; we have seen, too,
how in order to understand and appreciate what Chaucer is doing
the modern reader often needs to be put in possession of some scrap
of information about medieval ways of thinking. But in particular
the analysis has brought out Chaucer's use of superimposition to
give the novelist's effect of the complexity and ambiguity of reality
itself: 'we may take it in different ways.' The second episode
discussed contains *both* the Criseyde who is fickle and cowardly *and*
the Criseyde who is worthy of Troilus's love and who truly values
him for his noble qualities. And it allows a genuine, unironic value
to intention, despite the ironic shadow cast by the foreknown
action. (Here we may add that Troilus's discussion of predestination
earlier in Book IV, unassimilated though it is to the 'naturalism'
characteristic of much of the rest of the work, is highly relevant to
the experience of the poem as a whole.) Moreover, these contradictory perspectives are *simply* superimposed. The aim of our
analysis has of course been to establish some relationship between
them, but Chaucer himself makes no attempt at this kind of
articulation. There is not even any attempt in *Troilus and Criseyde*
to push the contradiction to the point at which the sense of contradiction itself becomes a central part of the experience of the poem.
Here *Troilus and Criseyde* contrasts revealingly with Shakespeare's
Troilus and Cressida. Shakespeare's work, like Chaucer's, depends
to a great extent on the audience's foreknowledge of the story,
particularly in the scene where the lovers swear faithfulness to each
other, and Cressida begs that if she is false she may become a
by-word for falseness. But already the irony is more explicit than
Chaucer's, and more bitter; and Shakespeare's play drives towards
an agonized perception of paradox itself, as Troilus oversees
Cressida giving his own love-token to Diomedes, and exclaims,
'This is, and is not, Cressid!' Chaucer keeps the lovers apart once
Criseyde has left for the Greek camp; more charitably than Shakespeare, he allows the opposing perspectives to remain suspended in
a rich ambiguousness, that of 'life itself.' It is thus, in an important
sense, the work of the novel that Chaucer is doing in *Troilus and
Criseyde*.

7   *Conciseness and* The Testament of Cresseid

I have laid a great deal of stress on the diffuseness of medieval literature, noting how it is made necessary by the habit of oral delivery, and is encouraged by the concentration of the *ars poetica* on *amplificatio*. It must not be supposed, however, that *all* medieval poems are diffuse, or that any specific longer poem will be diffuse all through. There is one poem in particular, written in the late Middle Ages, in which conciseness plays a very important part. This is Robert Henryson's *Testament of Cresseid*, and because it seems to me one of the greatest, as well as the most unusual, of all medieval poems, I want to examine at some length its style, the origins of that style, and the *Weltanschauung* that Henryson uses the style to express. But first a few words about the poem in general may be helpful, since it is probably less well known than those discussed in earlier chapters. It dates probably from the late fifteenth century, but this is a question that will be referred to again below. It is unmistakably a 'Chaucerian' work—one that looks back to Chaucer as the great master of English style—but one belonging to the Scottish branch of the Chaucerian tradition. On the whole the works of Chaucer's Scottish followers (who include the author of the *Kingis Quair*, William Dunbar, and Gavin Douglas, as well as Henryson himself) show a far more individual life in their work than is to be found in their English contemporaries. They take much from Chaucer, but what they take undergoes an often radical transformation, since they also draw on a vigorous and non-Chaucerian native tradition. The complex relationship with Chaucer which is characteristic of these poets is exemplified admirably in *The Testament of Cresseid*. The poem opens with a cold winter evening—a Scottish reversal of the May morning on which so many medieval poems begin. The narrator watches the sun going down and Venus rising; it is too cold for him to pray to Venus, and he is too old, and so he pokes up the fire in his study, takes a drink 'my spreitis to comfort' (37),[1] and gets down a book

> Writtin be worthie Chaucer glorious
> Of fair Creisseid and worthie Troylus. (41–2)

He summarizes the later stages of Chaucer's story, and pays tribute to the English poet's 'gudelie termis' and 'joly veirs' (59), but, having in this way invoked the Chaucerian spirit, he now takes down 'ane uther quair' (61), in which he finds the story of Cresseid's end, which Chaucer omits. Whether this 'uther quair' really existed we do not know—it seems most likely to be a fictional source such as the *Gawain*-poet invented to give his work authority —but the attitude it implies towards Chaucer is the significant thing. 'Quha wait gif all that Chauceir wrait was trew?' (64), Henryson's narrator goes on to ask; the work that follows may have a Chaucerian origin, but, in style as well as in story, it will display a sturdy independence of the English master. It will offer not a continuation of Chaucer's story, but an alternative ending to it, one which leaves Criseyde dead and Troilus alive, whereas Chaucer had left Troilus dead and Criseyde alive. Henryson shows his independence, too, in questioning the very necessity for a historical basis for the poem, which Chaucer had seemed to take for granted:

> Quha wait gif all that Chauceir wrait was trew?
> Nor I wait nocht gif this narratioun
> Be authoreist, or fenyeit of the new
> Be sum poeit, throw his inventioun. (64–7)

Here *inventioun*, a technical term from *ars poetica*, appears to have something like its modern sense of 'creation' or 'making up,' rather than its classical and medieval sense of the 'finding' of material (from some source, for instance). And in thus setting what is 'fenyeit of the new' alongside what is 'authoreist' (attested by some *auctour*), as of equal validity, Henryson 'is by way of composing a literary manifesto.'[2] He is aligning himself with a Renaissance conception of the poet as creator rather than reteller or commentator. A century

---

[1] Quotations from *The Testament of Cresseid* are taken from the edition of Denton Fox (London, 1968),

[2] John MacQueen, *Robert Henryson* (Oxford, 1967), p. 55.

later, the road chosen by Henryson here will lead to a position as extreme as that taken by another Scotsman, King James VI:

> ... sen Invention is ane of the cheif vertewis in a Poete, it is best that ye invent your awin subject your self, and not to compose of sene subjectis. Especially translating any thing out of uther language, quhilk doing, ye not onely essay not your awin ingyne of Inventioun, bot be the same meanes ye are bound, as to a staik, to follow that buikis phrasis quhilk ye translate.[3]

Henryson's story is, briefly, of how Cresseid was abandoned by Diomede and, as 'sum men sayis' (77), became a prostitute. She returns to her father's house, where in 'ane secreit orature' (120) she angrily blames Venus and Cupid for her unhappy fate. Immediately she has a vision of the seven planetary gods summoned by Cupid to punish her for this blasphemy. The gods appear in solemn procession, and their decision is for Cresseid

> In all hir lyfe with pane to be opprest,
> And torment sair, with seiknes incurabill,
> And to all lovers be abhominabill.   (306–8)

She awakens from her vision, looks in a mirror, and sees that she has been struck with leprosy. Her father sends her secretly to the leper 'hospitall' (382), and there she speaks a formal 'complaint' upon her fall. While she is out begging with the other lepers, Troilus comes riding by. She does not see him, and he does not recognize her, because of her deformity; but something in her face reminds him of 'fair Cresseid, sumtyme his awin darling' (504), and he throws her a purse of gold. When he has gone, she learns who this generous almsgiver was. She makes her testament, in which she leaves her body to worms and toads, a ring given her by Troilus to Troilus himself, her other possessions to the lepers, and her spirit to the goddess Diana, and then she dies. Troilus is informed of her

[3] 'Ane Schort Treatise' (1584), ed. G. Gregory Smith, *Elizabethan Critical Essays* (Oxford, 1904), p. 221. The reader may care to ponder the implications of the parallel opened up by the coincidence of words between this passage and *The Clerk's Tale*, line 704: just as the medieval poet is 'bound, as to a staik' by the story he gets from his *auctour*, so are his characters 'bounden to a stake' by the impulses which must be predicated to explain their roles in that story.

death, and builds a tomb for her.

So much for the story of *The Testament of Cresseid*. It appears to
be organized around certain crucial moments of recognition or
discovery or realization: the moment when Cresseid, after her
vision of the gods, looks into the mirror for the first time and sees
'hir face sa deformait' (349); the moment when Troilus sees the
leprous beggar,

> And with ane blenk it come into his thocht
> That he sumtime hir face befoir had sene; (499-500)

the moment when Cresseid learns that it was Troilus who gave her
the rich alms. In this respect Henryson's is a poem of a radically
different kind from Chaucer's. Mr John Bayley has written of the
'absence of discovery' which characterizes *Troilus and Criseyde*. 'No
one concerned with the poem,' he remarks, '—neither characters nor
author nor reader—finds anything out in the blinding tragic manner:
there is no *peripeteia*.'[4] One consequence of this difference is that
Henryson, in his poem of clearly defined turning-points, gains, compared with Chaucer, a concentration of effect, a brilliant and overwhelming distinctness. On the other hand he loses some of the
qualities discussed in the last chapter: a spaciousness within which
there is room for uncertainty, alternative meanings, even occasion-
ally irrelevant speculations. Henryson gives us *a* world, uniquely
created by the 'inventioun' of an individual poet; Chaucer, more
simply and yet more confusingly, gives us something more like *the*
world, within which we make observations and judgments exactly
like those of our everyday lives. The style of *The Testament of Cresseid*
is in keeping with its nature, as a work in which crucial moments
concentrate together many strands of action and motive. It has
been described by a twentieth-century Scottish poet, Edwin Muir,
as a 'high concise style,'[5] and indeed in reading the poem one
is constantly struck by lines of an unusual conciseness. Conciseness may be of various kinds: it may for example be achieved
by omission of apparent essentials, or by the use of words which
imply without stating. In both these cases, the reader must supply

---

[4] *The Characters of Love* (London, 1960), p. 67.
[5] Edwin Muir, *Essays on Literature and Society* (London, 1949), p. 18.

something from within himself to complete the sense, but the conciseness of *The Testament of Cresseid* is of a different kind. Henryson's conciseness depends upon precision and completeness; it compresses much explicit meaning into as few words as possible. We may mention for example the last line of those supposed to be engraved by Troilus on Cresseid's tombstone:

> Lo, fair ladyis, Cresseid, of Troy the toun,
> Sumtyme countit the flour of womanheid,
> *Under this stane, lait lipper, lyis deid.*   (607–9)

Or again the description of Cresseid's journey to her father's house after she has been abandoned by Diomede:

> This fair lady, in this wyse destitute
> Of all comfort and consolatioun,
> *Richt privelie, but fellowschip, on fute,*[6]
> *Disagysit,* passit far out of the toun.   (92–5)

In both these examples a series of details is compressed into as little space as possible so as to sum up a whole situation; one is reminded of Milton's magnificent summarizing line about the captive Samson:

> Ask for this great Deliverer now, and find him
> *Eyeless in Gaza at the Mill with slaves.*
> *(Samson Agonistes,* 40–41)

A similar, though not identical, effect of Henryson's may be seen in the lines describing Troilus's recollection of Cresseid when he sees the leper:

> Ane spark of lufe than till his hart culd spring,
> *And kendlit all his bodie in ane fyre.*   (512–13)

Here the effect of compression comes from the tension between two logically precise but contradictory words, *all* and *ane*. And a further type of conciseness in the *Testament* is brought about by omitting all but one or two salient facts, and leaving us to fill in the

---

[6] *on fute* is the reading of the Charteris (1593) and Anderson (1663) editions; the Thynne edition (1532) reads *or refute.* The latter is preferred by Fox as being the *difficilior lectio,* though he uses Charteris as the basis for his edition.

rest for ourselves. One might instance the lines,

> Quhen Diomeid had all his appetyte,
> And mair, fulfillit of this fair ladie. . . .   (71–2)

Here just the two words 'and mair' speak volumes.

Now conciseness as illustrated in these quotations is not what we should normally expect in medieval literature. Such concentration is hardly viable in a literature intended for oral delivery. We saw in chapter 3 that the *artes poeticae*, while recognizing abbreviation as a possible aim of rhetoric, concentrated their attention on the opposite goal of amplification. Indeed, the conciseness of *The Testament of Cresseid* does not seem at first sight to be connected with the medieval view of poetry at all. It appears closer to an approach to literature which we associate with a much later period. This is the revival in the late sixteenth century of the concise prose of Seneca and Tacitus, a revival which was headed on the Continent by scholars such as Muretus and Lipsius, and which did not appear in full strength in England until the fifteen-nineties. In 1591, for example, Anthony Bacon recommended the first English translation of Tacitus in the following terms: 'For Tacitus I may say without partiality, that hee hath writen the most matter with best conceyt in fewest wordes of anie Historiographer ancient or moderne.' And in 1594 Lancelot Andrewes spoke as follows in a sermon on the text 'Remember Lot's wife'—'. . . it fareth with sentences as with coins: In coins, they that in smallest compass contain greatest value, are best esteemed: and in sentences, those that in fewest words comprise most matter, are most praised.'[7] Notions of conciseness such as these continued to influence literary practice, in verse as well as in prose, throughout the seventeenth century and the Augustan period. Dr Johnson effectively summed them up towards the end of their era of predominance under the title of 'strength'—'The "strength of Denham," which Pope so emphatically mentions, is to be found in many lines and couplets, which convey much meaning in few words, and exhibit the sentiment

---

[7] Quotations from George Williamson, 'Senecan Style in the Seventeenth Century,' *Philological Quarterly* XV (1936), p. 327, and F. P. Wilson, *Elizabethan and Jacobean* (Oxford, 1945), p. 44.

with more weight than bulk.'[8] It is surely just this 'strength' that we find in the lines quoted from *The Testament of Cresseid*. Are we to suppose then that Henryson stepped outside the prevalent ideals of the Middle Ages, and into those of a later period, purely by chance? This seems unlikely, because in his poem he does not merely write concisely, but expressly puts forward the idea of conciseness as the goal of rhetoric. When the planet-gods appear to Cresseid in her vision, they choose Mercury as the speaker of their 'parliament' (266). This is an appropriate choice, for Mercury is traditionally the god of eloquence, and he has earlier been described as

> Richt eloquent, and full of rethorie,
> With polite termis and delicious.   (240–41)

The narrator does not report what Mercury says in asking why the session has been convened, but he comments on his speech as follows:

> Quha had bene thair and liken for to heir
> His facound toung and termis exquisite,
> Of rethorick the prettick he micht leir:
> In breif sermone ane pregnant sentence wryte.
>   (267–70)

The orator's 'facound toung' and 'termis exquisite' are predictable ideals for medieval rhetoric, but the concept offered (and exemplified) in the final, summarizing line—weighty meaning in brief speech—seems unmedieval, and is indeed almost identical with the Augustan 'strength.' It appears then that the 'high concise style' of the *Testament* was produced on the basis of a conscious literary theory. In my discussion of the poem I shall first try to decide what relation Henryson's ideal of conciseness bears to medieval thought about literature, and then to define the vision of life which the actual conciseness of his poem expresses.

1. *Conciseness*

The place of brevity in medieval thought about literature has been studied with great learning by E. R. Curtius in an excursus

---

[8] *Life of Denham*, from *Lives of the English Poets*, Everyman's Library (London, 1953), vol. I, p. 52.

to his *European Literature and the Latin Middle Ages*. Curtius shows how, in antique judicial oratory, brevity in stating the facts of the case was recommended on functional grounds, but how 'In the Middle Ages, on the contrary, *brevitas*-formulas were often used only to show that the author was familiar with the precepts of rhetoric—or else as a pretext for ending a poem.' He points out that among the medieval rhetoricians, 'The essence of brevity as of prolixity was seen in the use of particular artifices.'[9] The *artes poeticae*, as we have seen, show some concern with brevity, and give directions, however scanty, for achieving it, but these involve only the minutiae of stylistic detail, and not any aesthetic principles which might lie behind them. Geoffroi de Vinsauf explains that if brevity is desired,

> Everything must be avoided that leads to prolixity—descriptions, circumlocutions, and the other devices mentioned above [in the section on *amplificatio*]. And then, when all this has been cut down, we have to occupy ourselves with what is left, that is, with the plain body of the subject-matter. For we must say only those things that make up the essence of the subject-matter and without which it cannot be understood.   (Faral, p. 277)

We know that the *artes poeticae* show little concern for the effect of a work on its audience, but it is in brevity as a *functional* ideal—a means of avoiding inconvenience to the listeners—that we might expect a continuity from age to age. The *Rhetorica ad Herennium*, after defining *brevitas* (that is, conciseness) as 'the expressing of an idea by the very minimum of essential words,' goes on: 'Conciseness expresses a multitude of things within the limits of but a few words, and is therefore to be used often, either when the facts do not require a long discourse or when time will not permit dwelling upon them.'[10] Among the medieval rhetoricians, Jean de Garlande suggests that the concise style belongs to official rather than purely artistic writing.[11] The twelfth-century historian Gervase of Canterbury proposes brevity as the distinguishing characteristic of the genre of chronicle as opposed to that of history: history expresses

[9] Curtius, *op. cit.* pp. 487 and 491.
[10] *Ed. cit.*, pp. 403 and 405.
[11] *Ed. cit.*, p. 897.

'the deeds, the characters, the very life' of its subject-matter, but chronicle confines itself to a listing of events, and so 'the historian proceeds diffusely and elegantly, while the chronicler writes simply and briefly.'[12] The recommendation of brevity as a quality of the literature of instruction, as opposed to that of delight, goes at least as far back as Horace, who advises: 'When teaching, be brief, since the mind will readily receive and faithfully retain things said quickly, while anything superfluous pours out of the mind again' (*Ars poetica*, 335–7). Horace's advice is taken up by Guillaume de Lorris in the *Roman de la Rose*:

> Or te vueil briement recorder
> Ce que t'ai dit, por remembrer,
> Car la parole moins engrieve
> A retenir quant ele est brieve.[13]

Now I will briefly summarize what I have said to you, so that you can remember it, for a statement is less trouble to keep in mind when it is brief.

It is borrowed in turn by Chaucer in his translation of the *Roman*; and he conveniently illustrates the normal medieval love of amplification by swelling the recommendation of brevity to twice its original length:

> Now. wol I shortly heere reherce,
> Of that I have seid in verce,
> Al the sentence by and by,
> In wordis fewe compendiously,
> That thou the better mayst on hem thynke,
> Whether so it be thou wake or wynke.
> For the wordis litel greve
> A man to kepe, whanne it is breve.   (2343–9)

In the *Canterbury Tales*, Chaucer makes his Squire offer a similarly prolix argument in favour of brevity for the listeners' sake:

---

[12] *The Historical Works of Gervase of Canterbury*, ed. William Stubbs (London, 1879), vol. I, p. 87.
[13] *Roman de la Rose*, ed. E. Langlois (Paris, 1914–24), ll. 2225–28.

> The knotte why that every tale is toold,
> If it be taried til that lust be coold
> Of hem that han it after herkned yoore,
> The savour passeth ever lenger the moore,
> For fulsomnesse of his prolixitee;
> And by the same resoun, thynketh me,
> I sholde to the knotte condescende.
>
> (*Canterbury Tales*, V 401–7)

We have seen how much emphasis the *artes praedicandi* lay on this functional approach, and we can imagine that brevity would have a particular appeal for the preacher. His congregation would be in need of instruction, but it might also be more likely to 'wynke' than to 'wake' through a long sermon. And so Alanus de Insulis advises preachers that 'The sermon must be concise, lest its prolixity should produce aversion.'[14]

These various remarks are all eminently sensible, but they cannot be said to give conciseness the central place among the aims of rhetoric which it has in the lines from Henryson. It is true that Chaucer praises the Clerk in *The Canterbury Tales* by declaring

> Noght o word spak he moore than was neede,
> And that was seyd in forme and reverence,
> And short and quyk and ful of hy sentence.
>
> (*Canterbury Tales*, I 304–6)

Here indeed we seem to be nearer to the praise of conciseness for its own sake, and since a Chaucerian stimulus is so fundamental in the *Testament*, it might be supposed that in his praise of conciseness Henryson was following in the footsteps of his English master. But there still seems to be a crucial difference of emphasis between the two passages. The brevity of Chaucer's Clerk appears in an essentially moral context—it is part of his general abstemiousness, a Christian plainness analogous to the avoidance of rhyming and chiming urged upon the preacher by the *artes praedicandi*. In Mercury's speech, on the other hand, there is no suggestion of any such ethical constraint upon the aesthetic.

---

[14] *Summa de arte praedicatoria*, cap. I, *Patrologia Latina* CCX, col. 114.

It would be an odd rhetoric in which the idea of conciseness played no part at all, and in medieval writings on literary style we have found the seeds of a theory of conciseness. But we have not found in them the idea appearing in Henryson's *Testament*, that the 'prettick' of rhetoric can be summed up as weighty meaning in brief speech. It must be noticed, however, that the medieval works so far quoted derive from the twelfth, thirteenth, and fourteenth centuries, while *The Testament of Cresseid*, though it has not been precisely dated, can probably be assigned to the last quarter of the fifteenth century. We have seen that the earlier *artes poeticae* continued in use as schoolbooks throughout the later Middle Ages. Nevertheless, it seems improbable that men's ideas about literary style remained totally static throughout the medieval period, a time when literary style itself underwent undeniable changes, and when also, as literacy spread and printing developed, the governing habit of oral delivery began to decline. What we really want, in order to see what late medieval people thought about prolixity and conciseness, are some examples of late medieval critical comment. In fact, of course, critical comment upon literature dating from so early a period is very rare, and what examples exist tend to rely upon conventional appreciative phrasing. However, the later Middle Ages in England did produce a certain amount of descriptive criticism. Most of it refers to Chaucer, who was widely recognized by his successors as the supreme English poet. A study of early references to Chaucer does seem to indicate an interesting movement in ideas about literary style towards the end of the fifteenth century—a movement in the direction of a theory of conciseness. Compared with most of his contemporaries and imitators, Chaucer in fact is a concise poet, but this fact is almost irrelevant, since, as Caroline Spurgeon has pointed out, 'the characteristic qualities attributed to Chaucer from 1400 to 1800 are those in which the critics or men of letters of the time were themselves more especially interested.'[15]

As early as the fourteen-thirties we find Lydgate—no devotee of conciseness in his own writing—praising his master Chaucer for

[15] *Five Hundred Years of Chaucer Criticism and Allusion 1357–1900* (Cambridge, 1925), vol. I, p.c.

> Voydyng the chaf, sothly for to seyn:
> Enlumynyng the trewe piked greyn
> By crafty writinge of his sawes swete. . . .

and as one

> Whos makyng was so notable and enteer,
> Ryght compendious and notable in certeyn.

It seems likely enough, however, that Lydgate's praise refers to the selection of material rather than to style. It is not until the last quarter of the fifteenth century that we find clear examples of the praise of Chaucer's writing as stylistically concise. The anonymous author of *The Boke of Curtesye*, published by Caxton about 1477, writes of Chaucer as follows:

> Redith his werkis, ful of plesaunce,
> Clere in sentence, in langage excellent.
> Briefly to wryte, suche was his suffysance:
> Whatever to saye he toke in his entente,
> His langage was so fayr and pertynente,
> It semeth unto mannys heerynge
> Not only the worde, but verely the thynge.

In the same period Caxton himself on two occasions praises Chaucer for avoiding prolixity and pursuing conciseness. In the Epilogue to *The Book of Fame* (dating from about 1483), he claims that Chaucer 'wrytteth no voyde wordes, but alle hys mater is ful of hye and quycke sentence,' while in the 'prohemye' to *The Canterbury Tales* (of the same date), he echoes even more closely Chaucer's own words about the Clerk by writing that 'he comprehended hys maters in short, quyck, and hye sentences, eschewyng prolyxyte, castyng away the chaf of superfluyte, and shewyng the pyked grayn of sentence, uttered by crafty and sugred eloquence.'[16] In this second passage, the praise of Chaucer for his brevity is juxtaposed with a more normal medieval conception of rhetoric as decorative, 'sugred,' ornate. The two ideas are reconcilable, no doubt, but Caxton seems to have made no attempt to reconcile them. A similar juxtaposition is to be found a little later in a poem by Stephen Hawes called *The Pastime of Pleasure*, which was published

[16] The preceding quotations are all taken from Spurgeon, *op. cit.*, vol. I, pp. 28, 42, 57, 61, and 62.

in 1509. There the rhetorical faculty of *elocutio* (style) is described as follows:

> Yet elocucyon, with the power of Mercury,
> The mater exorneth ryght well facundyously,
> In fewe wordes, swete and sentencyous,
> Depaynted with golde, harde in construccyon,
> To the artyke eres swete and dylycyous.[17]

Here conciseness is a means to deliberate obscurity—the aesthetic of the *trobar clus*—and yet the subject-matter is decorated 'facundyously.' Juxtapositions such as these can perhaps most naturally be seen as belonging to an age of transition in literary theory. They are part of the evidence for suggesting that the last quarter of the fifteenth century in England sees a new development in literary ideals, a development which involves making conciseness a primary goal of rhetoric. In this context we can more easily understand the nature of the eloquence which, like Hawes, Henryson attributes to Mercury, and which, unlike Hawes, he displays in his poem.

As we have already seen, the origins of this development in stylistic theory can in part be traced back to the rhetorical treatises of the earlier Middle Ages. In about 1527 Lawrence Andrew printed a third edition of Caxton's translation of *The Mirrour of the World* (first published in 1481), and he added to it a passage on rhetoric as follows:

> And whan a man delatith his matter to long or that he utter the effecte of his sentence, though it be never so well utteryd, it shalbe tedyous unto the herers; for every man naturally that hereth a nother, desyreth moste to know the effecte of his reason that tellyth the tale. . . . Therfor the pryncypall poynt of eloquens restyth ever in the quycke sentence. And therfor the lest poynt belonging to Rethorike is to take hede that the tale be quycke and sentencious.[18]

Here the recommendation of brevity is based on the practical reasoning found in the earlier writers, but the fact that it was added in the early sixteenth century suggests that the desire for brevity

---

[17] *The Pastime of Pleasure*, ed. W. E. Mead, Early English Text Society 173 (London, 1928), ll. 909–13.
[18] Cited by Elizabeth Sweeting, *Early Tudor Criticism* (Oxford, 1940), p. 110.

was gathering new force. Alongside the continuity in thought we seem to be able to trace a connection between the late medieval emphasis on conciseness as an aesthetic quality and the new literary theories of the Italian Renaissance. This may at first appear unlikely, because the reforms in Latin style initiated by the fifteenth-century Italian Humanists were based on a return to Cicero. An imitation of Ciceronian copiousness, whatever other differences it might lead to, could only tend to intensify medieval prolixity. Again, the later sixteenth-century admiration for conciseness in prose, which we referred to earlier, is associated with a reaction *against* Ciceronianism carried to excess. The fact is, however, that the pedantic imitation of Cicero in fashion in the first half of the fifteenth century later began to give way to a more discriminating Ciceronianism; and for this brevity could be a stylistic goal as valid as copiousness. One of the most interesting examples of this reformed Ciceronianism is a work by Erasmus called *De duplici copia verborum ac rerum*. This was not published until 1512, but we know that an earlier version had been written before Erasmus first visited England in 1499. The *De copia* is devoted, as its title suggests, to teaching copiousness, but it also puts forward the argument that a full knowledge of rhetorical devices is necessary as a means of achieving conciseness:

> For, so far as brevity of words is concerned, who could speak more concisely than the man to whom it came easily to select at once out of the huge army of words, out of all the kinds of figures, whatever was most adapted to brevity? Again, with respect to brevity of content, who would be able to despatch the subject-matter in fewest words more readily than the man who knew from thorough consideration which things were most important in the subject—its supports, as it were—which came next, and which were adopted only for the sake of enriching the matter? Surely no-one will see more quickly and certainly what can be omitted without disadvantage than the man who sees what can be added, and how.

Erasmus goes on to put forward a rather more sophisticated concept of conciseness than that of the earlier rhetoricians: 'The lover of brevity should see that he does not pursue it for its own sake, but that he says the best that is possible in the fewest words. . . . For nothing is so conducive to brevity of speech as propriety and elegance of words.[19] Another Humanist, the Spaniard Juan Luis Vives, also discusses conciseness in some detail. In his *De ratione dicendi*, after referring his readers to the *De copia* of Erasmus for information about *dilatatio*, he continues as follows:

> But just as it is artistic to expand one's speech when the matter demands it, and as it were to fill out the sails with a favourable wind, so it is to contract one's speech and compress it, when the occasion suggests. This has much beauty, just like the former method of decorating the speech with copiousness and enriching it; each has its own power, and is effective on its own occasion. What a number of styles there are of this kind! There is the compressed and succinct speech, in which nothing at all is included that could be taken away without loss.... There is another kind of brief speech, where great trouble is taken to bring together much meaning in few words, and as it were to cram or press it together.... There is another concise style, where less is expressed than is necessary for understanding, but familiarity with this way of speaking supports the sense and supplies what is missing.[20]

Here Vives is making a distinction similar to our own between the various kinds of conciseness. Henryson's is the second kind he mentions, in which much meaning is brought together in few words. It will be noticed that Vives returns to expediency—'when the occasion suggests'—as the motive for brevity, but it is on aesthetic grounds that he goes on to praise conciseness—'This has much beauty'—particularly when it is *combined* with copiousness. Vives has succeeded in bringing the concepts of the copious and the concise together within a coherent aesthetic framework, where we have seen Caxton and Hawes merely juxtaposing the two. I shall try to show that Henryson achieves in *The Testament of Cresseid* a practical synthesis comparable to Vives' theoretical synthesis. All that we know of the date of Henryson's death is that it must have occurred before 1508, because in that year was published Dunbar's

[19] Erasmus, *De copia*, lib. I, col. 5 and lib. II, col. 110, in *Opera Omnia* (Leyden, 1703–06), vol. I.
[20] Vives, *Opera Omnia* (Valencia, 1782–90), vol. II, p. 113.

Lament for the Makaris, which mentions him as dead.[21] It is therefore just conceivable that in writing the *Testament* he was influenced by the ideas of the *De copia*. But there is no evidence for any such direct influence. It seems more likely that Henryson, Erasmus, and Vives belong all three to a single movement of thought about literary style, connected with the spread of printing and literacy. On the one hand, Erasmus was not the first Continental Humanist to visit England. He was preceded during the fifteenth century by a variety of others, and though they did not find the prolonged medievalism of Northern Europe very congenial, they no doubt had some opportunity of disseminating new literary ideals. Professor John MacQueen has recently shown that humanism made some progress in fifteenth-century Scotland (he mentions James III's Secretary of State, Archibald Whitelaw, as an example), and has suggested that Henryson himself may have been a student at a continental university, and that he 'must . . . be regarded as in some sense a humanist.'[22] And on the other hand, there is certainly more continuity than has generally been recognized between the ideas about literature which we distinguish under the convenient headings of 'medieval' and 'Renaissance.'

2. *The Testament of Cresseid*

It is now time to return to a critical examination of *The Testament of Cresseid*. The staple of the poem's style is that in which we find 'In breif sermone ane pregnant sentence wryte,' 'much meaning in few words.' 'the best that is possible in the fewest words.' But it also contains one or two rhetorical set-pieces which are copious rather than concise—examples of 'crafty and sugred eloquence'— and these permit us to see the poem as conforming to Vives' scheme of combined conciseness and copiousness, where 'each has its own power and is effective on its own occasion.' However, these more copious passages seem generally to have been felt by critics of the poem to be blemishes. Sir Herbert Grierson has remarked that 'There is a little over-elaboration in the aureate style, especially in

[21] It probably occurred before 1505, the date of death of a writer mentioned as dead 'last of aw' by Dunbar. See Fox, *ed. cit.*, p. 17 and n. 2.

[22] MacQueen, *op. cit.*, p. 22 and chapter 1 *passim*.

the description of the gods,'[23] and Mr John Speirs, referring to this description of the planet-gods and also to the heroine's 'complaint,' has written that

> ... in two passages Henryson does allow himself a certain 'literary' expansiveness. As a consequence they stand out from the rest of the poem as to some extent extraneous. And this must at once be admitted as a fault however justifiably they may claim, as they do, admiration for themselves.[24]

Are these adverse criticisms justified? The crucial case is likely to be that of the description of the gods, which takes up 125 lines—over a fifth of the whole poem. Cresseid's 'complaint' is only half as long, and it has a more obvious function: it 'amplifies' (though in a non-naturalistic way) Cresseid's emotions, and it also serves to clarify the moral pattern exemplified by the action up to that point. So far as the description of the gods is concerned, we must surely agree with Speirs as against Grierson that the passage can claim admiration for itself. The 'aureate' diction is not used particularly thickly in the actual descriptions, and it is usually counterpointed against the solid, unpretentious words of the vernacular. A little later in Cresseid's dream, there is, certainly, an intensification of the aureate language:

> And sen ye ar all sevin deificait,
> Participant of devyne sapience,
> This greit injure done to our hie estait
> Me think with pane we suld make recompence.
>
> (288–91)

The effect of aureation here is very different from what we too often find in fifteenth-century Chaucerian poetry. Compare for example these lines, also by Henryson:

> Esope, that poete, first father of this fabill,
> Wrait this parabole, quhilk is convenient,
> Because the sentence wes fructuous and agreabill,

[23] 'Robert Henryson,' *Aberdeen University Review* XXI (1933–34), p. 208.
[24] *The Scots Literary Tradition* (London, 1940), p. 27. It is fair to add that in a revised edition of this work (London, 1962), Mr Speirs has deleted the second and third sentences quoted.

> In moralitie exemplative prudent,
> Quhais problemes bene verray excellent,
> Throw similitude of figuris, to this day
> Gevis doctrine to the redaris of it ay.[25]

Here the aureate diction is used in an attempt to heighten the tone
and inflate the importance of something trivial in itself—in the
complacent words of Hawes, 'To make of nought reason senten-
cyous'[26]—while in the lines from the *Testament* there is an assured
matching of the tone to the real importance of the subject. Here too
the monosyllabic directness of *pane* (to which I shall return below)
is given startling force by the dignified rhetorical context in which
it is set. There is no reason, I think, to complain of an over-
elaboration of the *style*; Henryson here has the sombre Latinate
magnificence of the aureate style fully at command. Complaint
about the sheer bulk of the passage concerned might seem to be
more justified. One might admit that its copiousness was beautiful,
but still feel that in it Henryson had indulged a characteristically
medieval passion for exhaustiveness at the expense of the balance of
the poem as a whole. It is true that the encyclopaedic list is a
common and, to us, sometimes a tiresome convention of medieval
poetry. It is also true that *effictio* is one of the many descriptive
devices recommended by the *artes poeticae* as means of amplification,
without any suggestion of a purpose beyond simply taking up more
time. But because a convention is found in many different poems,
and was often included by the poets and enjoyed by the audiences
simply *as* a convention, pleasing because of its very expectedness,
it does not follow that it may not have a particular purpose in a
particular poem.

A helpful parallel may perhaps be found in the descriptions of the
temples of the gods in Part III of Chaucer's *Knight's Tale*. At first sight
they, and indeed that whole section of the *Tale*, might seem 'extraneous' and merely decorative—an exercise in rhetorical *descriptio*—
yet a closer examination reveals that they play a crucial part in conveying the meaning of the events of the poem. So it is in the
Testament; and indeed I should wish to suggest that *The Knight's*

[25] *Morall Fabillis*, ll. 2588–94, ed. H. Harvey Wood, *The Poems and Fables of
Robert Henryson*, rev. edn. (Edinburgh and London, 1958).
[26] *The Pastime of Pleasure*, ed. cit., l. 711.

Tale was almost as important an influence on Henryson's poem as was *Troilus and Criseyde*. One sign of this is perhaps to be found in the very genre to which Henryson's poem technically belongs, that of the 'last will and testament.' Chaucerian hints for this are to be found in *Troilus and Criseyde*, both in the testament of Criseyde (IV 785-91) and in that of Troilus (V 298-315), but a closer parallel is in the testament of Arcite in *The Knight's Tale* (I 2769-70). Arcite, like Cresseid, but unlike Troilus or Criseyde, has been struck down by the gods—Arcite by Saturn, Cresseid by Saturn and Cynthia. In both *The Knight's Tale* and the *Testament*, but not in *Troilus and Criseyde*, the maker of the testament is really, not just in imagination, on the point of death and in both cases the physical symptoms of which the victim dies are described in accurate and relentless medical detail. More important, *The Knight's Tale* and the *Testament* are linked in their use of pagan mythology. The setting of *Troilus and Criseyde* is pagan too, of course, but the pagan gods play little part in the action of the poem, and it ends with a glimpse of a heaven which appears to correspond to the Christian heaven. In both *The Knight's Tale* and the *Testament*, however, but not in the *Troilus*, there is a distinct section of the poem which functions as a kind of window opening into the heavenly world of classical paganism (which is also, of course, that of medieval astrology), and which discloses the metaphysical forces which account for the human events of the story. In both poems these forces are terrifying and either vengeful or callous, and there is a striking and pathetic contrast between the planet-gods and the helpless human beings upon and through whom they work their inexorable purposes. In neither poem, as it seems to me, is it possible to interpret the pagan mythology intelligibly in Christian terms—or at least not in terms of a Christianity which emphasizes God's mercy or his providential care for human beings. It is true that it might be seen to correspond to the view of God presented, in the fourteenth century and subsequently, by some of William of Ockham's followers:

> God became involved in the neutrality which the sceptics ex-
> tended to all but fact. Wisdom and mercy lost an intrinsic place
> in His nature, and, as a result, did not necessarily guide and inform
> His actions. God could act irrationally as, for example, in making

a man hate Him, revealing to one in grace his future damnation; or rewarding one for hating Him, while punishing another for loving Him above all. Moreover, he could mislead Christ and cause Christ to mislead the elect; and, most heinous of all, God could . . . sin. It needs no great effort to see how contrary to tradition such notions of Him were: He lost all resemblance to the creator of revelation and tradition and His ordinances became meaningless. [27]

I do not propose to offer here a detailed interpretation of the philosophy of *The Knight's Tale*, but simply to remind the reader that in that poem the supreme deity is Saturn, *Infortuna Major*, the force which makes for disasters, and that Theseus in his final speech, not having himself seen what goes on in the heavens, is simply mistaken in referring Arcite's death to the 'grace' of Jupiter (who was sometimes identified with Christ or the benevolent God of traditional Christianity). [28] Nor do I wish to suggest that Henryson's descriptions of the seven planetary gods are verbally derived from the descriptions in *The Knight's Tale*. But I do believe that a reading of *The Knight's Tale* as well as of *Troilus and Criseyde* is extremely helpful as an aid to recognition of what Henryson is doing with the gods in the *Testament*. He gives the description of the gods a purpose which owes nothing to the *artes poeticae*, and we shall only complain that the description stands out from the rest of the *Testament* as extraneous if we fail to take account of this purpose.

The general intention behind the procession of the seven planet-gods is to display their irresistible power, and to impress on us, sometimes by means of which we may not be directly conscious in reading or listening to the poem, that this power is largely destructive and malicious. In order to show how this intention is carried out, it will be worth examining the successive descriptions of the gods in some detail. Saturn, the oldest god, coming first, gives us

[27] Gordon Leff, *Bradwardine and the Pelagians*, p. 160.

[28] I have suggested an interpretation of *The Knight's Tale* in my edition of the poem (Cambridge, 1966). Theseus mentions Jupiter as first cause in line 3035, and Jupiter's grace in line 3069. For Jupiter as equivalent to Christ or to the Christian God, see Jean Seznec, *The Survival of the Pagan Gods* (New York' 1953), p. 99, n. 72, and p. 200; Dante, *Purgatorio* VI 118–19; and *Everyman* (ed. A. C. Cawley [Manchester, 1961],) line 407.

our earliest impression of the powers whom Cresseid has offended.
Henryson employs his harsh and vivid native vocabulary to build
up a brilliant grotesque: a type, and yet fully realized in its undigni-
fied particularity:

> His face fronsit, his lyre was lyke the leid.
> His teith chatterit, and cheverit with the chin,
> His ene drowpit, how sonkin in his heid,
> Out of his nois the meldrop fast can rin,
> With lippis bla, and cheikis leine and thin.
>
> (155–9)

He goes on to describe Saturn's weapons, the symbols of his cruel
destructive power:

> Ane busteous bow within his hand he boir,
> Under his girdill ane flasche of felloun flanis
> Fedderit with ice and heidit with hailstanis.
>
> (166–8)

And this destructive power has penetrated even his physical appearance:

> The ice schoklis that fra his hair doun hang
> Was wonder greit, and *as ane speir als lang.* (160–61)

The second god, Jupiter, is 'Fra his father Saturne far different' (172),
and he is presented as an idealized type parallelling the grotesque
type whom he succeeds:

> His garmound and his gyte full gay of grene
> With goldin listis gilt on everie gair.   (178–9)

But through the calm surface of this description can be felt the pull
of a more sinister undercurrent. Weapons are again used symbolically to hint at a destructive power latent in the 'amiabill' outward
form:

> Ane burelie brand about his middill bair,
> In his richt hand he had ane groundin speir,
> Of his father the wraith fra us to weir.   (180–82)

The implications here are contradictory. On the one hand 'there is a
strong hint in this line [182] of the equation between Jupiter

and Christ which was sometimes made';[29] on the other hand, the
spear corresponds to the vengeful or punitive thunderbolt which was
one of Jupiter's traditional attributes, and it is not normally a defensive weapon; which goes some way towards undermining the pro-
tective effect of the last line. Jupiter may be potentially a merciful
intercessor, but in this case he is not so in practice. Third comes Mars,
and here of course we should expect what we in fact find—an
emphasis on ferocity and warlike weapons:

> In hard harnes, hewmound, and habirgeoun,
> And on his hanche ane roustie fell fachioun,
> And in his hand he had ane roustie sword,
> Wrything his face with mony angrie word.
>
> (186–9)

He is 'Lyke to ane bair quhetting his tuskis kene' (193). After these
three portraits which repeatedly thrust upon us images of war and
terror, comes that of Phoebus, on the whole attractive, and
mentioning no weapons. In the astrology of the *Testament*, Phoebus
is propitious and life-giving: significantly, both at the beginning of
the poem and on Cresseid's entrance into the lepers' house, he is
mentioned as descending, giving way to less propitious forces. But
even he, when described here, is connected with power by a
reference to the intolerable brightness of his face and by a description
of the sun's four horses, and this power's destructive potential is
glanced at with a reference to Phaeton. The fifth planet in the
procession is Venus. She is conventionally fickle, but here the malice
of her disfavour is presented with unusual vigour:

> Under smyling scho was dissimulait,
> Provocative with blenkis amorous,
> And suddanely changit and alterait,
> Angrie as ony serpent vennemous,
> Richt pungitive with wordis odious.   (225–9)

The image of the poisonous snake is particularly striking. Next,
presented first as a poet and then as a doctor, is Mercury, towards

---

[29] Fox, *ed. cit.*, note on 1.182, p. 101. MacQueen sees an 'obvious' phallic
symbolism in Jupiter's weapons (*op. cit.*, p. 75), but it seems to me no more
obvious than in any other pointed object.

whom, on the face of it, Henryson's attitude appears entirely favourable. But beneath his praise, one is right, I think, to detect the presence of a cold Chaucerian irony, especially in the concluding lines of the description:

> Doctour in phisick, cled in ane skarlot goun,
> And furrit weill, as sic ane aucht to be,
> Honest and gude, and not ane word culd lie.
>
> (250–52)

A connection with Chaucer has in fact been suggested by several commentators on the poem. Henryson's description of Mercury is influenced by Chaucer's portrait of the Doctor of Physic in the General Prologue to the *Canterbury Tales*, and one scholar comments: 'The parallel to Henryson is close, from the general attitude of approval to the phrase "Doctour in Phisick."'[30] But the 'general attitude of approval' attributed to Chaucer is not easily found in the closing lines of his portrait—

> His studie was but litel on the Bible. . . .
> He kepte that he wan in pestilence.
> For gold in phisik is a cordial,
> Therefore he lovede gold in special.
>
> (*Canterbury Tales*, I 438, 442–4)

—and there seems to be a Chaucerian protesting too much in Henryson's 'as sic ane aucht to be' and 'not ane word.' We have seen that in matters of tone such as this it is unwise to be dogmatic: a twentieth-century reader may be liable to unearth ironies that a fifteenth-century poet would not have intended. Still, prosperous doctors are a favourite subject for satire in medieval poetry, including Henryson's—in another of his poems, called *Sum Practysis of Medecyne*, he parodies the pretensions of medical jargon. In any case, whether or not it is ironic, the praise of Mercury as a doctor is likely to look somewhat pallid in the cold light of the incurable disease with which he and his fellow deities are about to afflict Cresseid. This disease is alluded to in the last of the seven portraits, that of Cynthia. Her appearance is sinister:

[30] M .W. Stearns, *Robert Henryson* (New York, 1949), p. 94.

Of colour blak, buskit with hornis twa,
And in the nicht scho listis best appeir,
Haw as the leid, of colour nathing cleir.

Hir gyte was gray and full of spottis blak.

(255–7, 260)

The 'spottis blak' are intended to suggest those of leprosy.

It will be clear from this detailed examination that the description
of the gods in *The Testament of Cresseid* is by no means merely
decorative or 'literary,' in the presumably abusive sense in which
Mr Speirs uses the word. The very length of the description will
impress us with a sense of the gods' overwhelming power, obtruded
forcibly upon the helpless Cresseid's consciousness, while in its
details there are continual hints from beneath the surface magnificence of the threatening, the destructive, and the malicious.

If we return to consider the poem as a whole, we can now see that
the conciseness of Henryson's staple style—a conciseness which can
include an *appropriate* copiousness—exists as a reflection of the
compression of his story. We have seen something of the reasons
for amplification in the description of the gods and in Cresseid's
'complaint,' and we shall consider in a moment the expansive
introduction to the poem. Outside these passages, the tale is told
with remarkable brevity. We are quickly informed of what has
happened before the beginning of the poem: Cresseid has betrayed
Troilus, been betrayed by Diomede, and turned prostitute. She
joins her father in the temple, and there makes her reproachful
invocation of Venus and Cupid—an event which occurs at once so
far as Henryson's narrative is concerned, though apparently after
some time ('at the last' [112]) in the plot's 'real' sequence of events.
Immediately, the vision of the gods begins, without any of the
common medieval preliminaries to a poetic dream (as in *The Book
of the Duchess*):

Quhen this was said, doun in ane extasie,
Ravischit in spreit, intill ane dreame scho fell.

(141–2)

Henryson was evidently bound by convention only so far as he
chose. Then comes the procession, and this is followed by the

'parliament,' which is dealt with a great deal more briefly than we should expect in an age which loved exhaustive disputations in literature. It has been suggested that this part of the *Testament* is based on Lydgate's poem, *The Assembly of Gods*;[31] if so, Henryson has made considerable use of *abbreviatio*. Cupid's statement of the case is followed in quick and callous succession by the appointment of assessors and the passing of the sentence. At once Cresseid awakens, and, taking a mirror, realizes what has happened to her; and so on. There would be little point in extending this summary of the story, which continues, except for the 'complaint,' to be narrated in the same rapid manner. What must be noticed is that its presentation is an example of true conciseness, not mere simplicity; as with the poem's style, much is compressed into little.

If we ask how this compression is possible, and possible without any loss of clarity, we shall begin to approach the heart of the poem. We know that Henryson's starting-point is Chaucer's *Troilus and Criseyde*, which is perhaps the most diffuse poem of the least diffuse of Middle English poets. Since Henryson's conciseness seems the very opposite of Chaucer's prolixity, a further comparison may be helpful. The diffuseness of *Troilus and Criseyde* is not a fortuitous stylistic quality, but is closely related to the action presented and the poet's attitude towards it. We have seen how Chaucer presents parts of his story with a 'lifelike' ambiguity; he writes diffusely in order to maintain until the last moment a balance between a wide variety of possible attitudes towards Criseyde and Troilus's love for her. He builds up an iridescent structure, showing a different light at every movement, and his story enables him to do this, for it is not until the end of the fifth book that Criseyde's treachery is made certain. After this, Troilus is slain in battle, and his spirit ascends 'to the holughnesse of the eighthe spere' (V 1809). It is not until, in the last few stanzas of the poem, he looks down on the earth from this withdrawn distance that he realizes how absolutely he has been betrayed. Only then is there a reduction in the variety of possible attitudes towards the situation. In Henryson's poem, on the other hand, the coldly objective vision of things from the eighth sphere is transferred to the earth, and the reduction is present from the

[31] Stearns, *op. cit.*, pp. 70–72.

beginning. Henryson's narrator has, like Chaucer's, Troilus undergone the experience of human love and its decay—

> To help be phisike quhair that nature faillit
> I am expert, for baith I have assaillit,   (34–5)

—and then, by withdrawing from involvement in it, has been able
to see it in clearer perspective. Troilus withdraws to the eighth
sphere, the narrator of the *Testament* to the comfort of a private
room. And it is made clear that this narrator's withdrawal is only
part of a more general withdrawal from youth into age, and that
the cold of the winter night corresponds to the cold of an old man's
blood:

> Thocht lufe be hait, yit in ane man of age
> It kendillis nocht sa sone as in youtheid.   (29–30)

The *Testament* is presented as the poem of an old man, free from
the magnificently idealizing illusions of the young Troilus, and
seeing in his story no complication of issues and attitudes, for

> The northin wind had purifyit the air
> And sched the mistie cloudis fra the sky.
>
>   (17–18)

The 'mistie cloudis' of Chaucer's diffuseness have been swept away,
and with them what they express: the variety of contradictory
perspectives suspended in the mind of a garrulous and enigmatic
narrator. Though Henryson's narrator is not necessarily to be identified with Henryson in every respect, I believe he is much closer to
the poet than Chaucer's narrator is. The Chaucerian method, with
its teasing uncertainties and disclaimers of responsibility, probably
depended for its effect, and indeed for its initial development, on an
intimate rapport between the poet and his normal listening audience.
In the fifteenth century that rapport was broken, and I doubt
whether any later medieval poet, with the possible exception of
Skelton, fully understood Chaucer's subtle use of a narrative *persona*.
In the case of Henryson, there are in the early lines of the *Testament*
a few fossilized remains of Chaucer's technique in the *Troilus*: for
example, the thrusting of responsibility for statements injurious to
the heroine upon 'some men'—

> Than desolait scho walkit up and doun,
> And sum men sayis, into the court, commoun   (76-7)

—and the expression of a wish to excuse conduct of hers that might seem beyond excuse—

> Yit nevertheles, quhat ever men deme or say
> In scornefull langage of thy brukkilnes,
> I sall excuse als far furth as I may
> Thy womanheid, thy wisdome and fairnes.   (85-8)[32]

But as the poem gets under way devices of this kind are soon abandoned, because they can have no purpose in the world of the *Testament*, a 'fenyeit' world, and therefore one which leaves little room for uncertainties. Professor Denton Fox has described Henryson's narrator as 'stupid and passionately involved' and as 'an unintelligent, low-minded and agreeable old man,' who could be seen as 'St Paul's *vetus homo*, the "Old Man" which represents unredeemed man, corrupt and concupiscent';[33] but this seems to me a highly melodramatic response to the narrator's wry acceptance at the beginning of the poem that, in the winter of his life, the time has come for him to turn from love to a drink and a book by the fire. One of the many ways in which he differs from the Januarie of Chaucer's *Merchant's Tale*, with whom Professor Fox compares him, is precisely that Januarie does *not* accept that he is too old for love. There is no evidence for any consistent dramatic projection of the narrator as the *Testament* proceeds, and it is perhaps significant that, as one reads on, one becomes less and less aware of the presence of any narrator at all—the very opposite of what happens in *Troilus and Criseyde*.

At the very beginning of Henryson's poem Cresseid has already betrayed Troilus, been betrayed by Diomede, and become a prostitute, and thus the idealized *Weltanschauung* to be seen through the eyes of Chaucer's Troilus is no longer possible. Or rather, it is possible only in looking back on a past which stands in ironic

---

[32] Compare in *Troilus and Criseyde* 'Men seyn—I not—that she yaf hym hire herte' (V 1050) and 'And if I myghte excuse hire any wise,/For she so sory was for hire untrouthe,/Iwis, I wolde excuse hire yet for routhe' (V 1097-9).

[33] *Ed. cit.*, pp. 23, 53, and 55.

contrast with the present—that is to say, in Cresseid's 'complaint'
and again briefly in the moment when Troilus, looking at the real
Cresseid of the present, sees the Cresseid of the past. It is this
exclusion of any idealizing vision that enables a comprehensive
description of the situation to be brief. Thus Cresseid can tell her
father, with curt accuracy,

> Fra Diomeid had gottin his desyre,
> He wox werie and wald of me no moir.   (101–2)

The Testament of Cresseid is a 'tragedie' in the medieval sense
explained by Chaucer's Monk:

> Tragedie is to seyn a certeyn storie,
> As olde bookes maken us memorie,
> Of hym that stood in greet prosperitee,
> And is yfallen out of heigh degree
> Into myserie, and endeth wrecchedly.
> > (*Canterbury Tales*, VII 1973–7)

Such a story represents the downward turn of Fortune's wheel. In
substance, Henryson's tale consists of a relentless accumulation of
misfortunes for Cresseid: betrayal, prostitution, disease, bitter self-
knowledge, death. And the aspect of these misfortunes which is
stressed is not their purifying or redemptive power, but simply their
factual quality. They possess the inescapable factuality of physical
and mental anguish. I have mentioned how the word *pane* in
Cupid's speech stands out threateningly against its aureate background, and it is not by accident that this one word is several times
echoed in that section of the poem. The word, in a legal context,
may mean 'penalty,' but it has also the same sense as the modern
'pain.' Cupid has earlier said that

> . . . quha will blaspheme the name
> Of his awin god, outher in word or deid,
> To all goddis he dois baith lak and schame,
> And suld have bitter *panis* to his meid.   (274–7)

Mercury proposes that Saturn and Cynthia should be chosen as
assessors, 'The *pane* of Cresseid for to modifie' (299). Their immediate decision is for Cresseid

> In all hir lyfe with *pane* to be opprest,
> And torment sair with seiknes incurabill,
> And to all lovers be abhominabill.   (306–8)

It is important that this 'seiknes incurabill' should be not only
painful but also physically disgusting, and that its ugliness should be
emphasized constantly and in detail. Thus Cynthia dwells lovingly
on the physical effects of leprosy:

> Thy cristall ene minglit with blude I mak,
> Thy voice sa cleir unplesand hoir and hace,
> Thy lustie lyre ouirspred with spottis blak,
> And lumpis haw appeirand in thy face.   (337–40)

We are never allowed to forget these physical facts:

> ... scho was sa deformait,
> With bylis blak ouirspred in her visage,
> And hir fair colour faidit and alterait.   (394–6)

> My cleir voice and courtlie carrolling,
> Quhair I was wont with ladyis for to sing,
> Is rawk as ruik, full hiddeous, hoir and hace;
> My plesand port, all utheris precelling,
> Of lustines I was hald maist conding—
> Now is deformit the figour of my face;
> To luik on it na leid now lyking hes.   (443–9)

There is, too, a constant reversion to the squalid details of the
leper's existence—the cup and clapper—and a reiteration of the very
word 'lipper.' It is this insistence on the facts of physical suffering
that makes possible the concise treatment of mental suffering—

> And quhen scho saw hir face sa deformait,
> Gif scho in hart was wa aneuch, God wait.
>
> (349–50)

It also makes possible the concise summary of Cresseid's epitaph.

Such is the pattern which the poem presents: a closed pattern of facts, which does not point to significances beyond itself.

This is not the view taken by other critics, who have preferred to give a symbolic interpretation of the facts of the poem. Professor Denton Fox has argued convincingly that the disease of leprosy with which Cresseid is smitten was widely thought in the Middle Ages to be sexually transmitted; and it would follow from this that it might be seen as a natural or even inevitable consequence of the promiscuous way of life upon which she entered when she deserted Troilus. Hence, he argues, 'Her verbal blasphemy is itself a symbol: Henryson makes her swear at Venus and Cupid in order to show that her life has been a blasphemous sin against the laws of love, of nature, and of God.'[34] Against this, is must be said that Cupid and Venus, as presented in the poem, cannot easily be translated into 'the laws of love, of nature, and of God.' As in so many medieval poems, from the *Roman de la Rose* onwards, it seems clear that they represent sexual love only: Cupid claims that it is he who made Cresseid 'sum tyme flour of lufe' (279), and, as we have seen, Venus is described as 'Provocative with blenkis amorous' (226). There is no allusion here to the

> Love, that of erthe and se hath governaunce,
> Love, that his hestes hath in hevenes hye,

invoked in *Troilus and Criseyde* (III 1744–5), still less to the 'love that moves the sun and the other stars' with which Dante concludes his *Paradiso*. A somewhat similar position is held by Professor John MacQueen, who believes that Cresseid was already suffering from a 'venereal affliction' when she returned to Calchas's house, and that her subsequent blasphemy and its punishment are to be understood in a purely symbolic sense: 'given the conduct of Cresseid, her leprosy was inevitable; at this stage of the poem, however, she regards it as the blind blow of an essentially malignant fate. This attitude of mind, and the conduct which it entails, Henryson regards as blasphemy.'[35] Against this, I would say no more than that, if this

[34] *Ed. cit.*, pp. 26–8 and 37.
[35] *Op. cit.*, pp. 62 and 64–5. MacQueen goes further, and interprets the whole poem as an allegory, in which Troilus represents moral virtue,

was what Henryson had meant, he would surely have said so. What plainly happens in the poem is that Cresseid brings punishment upon herself by blaming the gods for her miseries, and that this punishment is seen both by Cupid and by the narrator as vengeful. The spots of leprosy correspond appropriately to the 'spots' of sin—she is already 'maculait' with 'fleschelie lust' (81)—but they are not the *same* as moral blemishes, and there is no sign that Cresseid would have become physically leprous if she had not blamed Venus and Cupid for her woes. Cresseid, after all, is a pagan, and her world (like the world of *The Knight's Tale*) is conceived in terms of a pagan theology, of gods who are vengeful and malicious. The gods correspond, no doubt, to the general conditions of human existence, but we should utterly distort the experience of the poem if we saw it as presenting those conditions as, in themselves, 'indifferent.'[36] I have already suggested that the theology of the *Testament* can be translated into a Christian theology only of an extreme and controversial late-medieval kind; whether Henryson himself held such a view of life, or whether he is only making use of it for imaginative purposes, I do not know, and, for the purposes of the poem, it does not matter.[37] Do we need to know whether Shakespeare really believed that life 'is a tale/Told by an idiot, full of sound and fury,/Signifying nothing'?

It is true that medieval writers normally use 'tragedie' as a means of pointing out some moral lesson, and *The Testament of Cresseid* is no exception. Cresseid, in her 'complaint,' after she has established the tragic pattern of ironic reversal, goes on to address the 'ladyis fair of Troy and Grece' (452), and to introduce two of the commonest medieval moralizing devices. They are to use her as a *speculum*,

Cresseid appetite, Saturn time, and so on. If Henryson had meant his poem to be read in this way, he would surely have supplied it with an explicit 'Moralitas', as he does *Orpheus and Eurydice* and the *Moral Fables*. The presence of a 'Moralitas' in these two works, and its absence from the *Testament*, is an argument against allegorical interpretation of the *Testament* rather than, as MacQueen seems to suppose, for it.

[36] MacQueen, *op. cit.*, p. 70.

[37] For this reason, I cannot accept Douglas Duncan's assertion that the *Testament* 'questions the divine order quite peremptorily' ('Henryson's *Testament of Cresseid*,' *Essays in Criticism* XI [1961], 128–35; p. 129). The poem is a Christian poet's fiction about a pagan world. Mr Duncan's study of the poem is otherwise extremely penetrating.

a means of seeing their own true state—'in your mynd ane mirrour mak of me' (457)—and as an *exemplum*—'Exempill mak of me in your memour' (465). But it must be noticed that this moralizing does not propose any possible remedy for the whole situation, comparable with the turning from earthly to heavenly love at the end of *Troilus and Criseyde*. Indeed, a 'lipper lady' who overhears the 'complaint' points out its uselessness. Her own advice is severely practical: to descend from the high rhetoric of tragedy, to submit to what cannot be remedied:

> I counsall the mak vertew of ane neid;
> Go leir to clap thy clapper to and fro,
> And leif efter the law of lipper leid.   (478–80)

It is not a mere coincidence, I think, that the advice to make a virtue of necessity is precisely that given by Theseus in the second 'movement' of his closing speech in *The Knight's Tale*, after he has turned away from the attempt to show that all is for the best in the world of that poem. Whatever the condition of man, under the rule of the planetary gods, the best he can do is no more than to put up with it:

> Thanne is it wysdom, as it thynketh me,
> To maken vertue of necessitee,
> And take it weel that we may nat eschue.
>
> (3041–3)

At the end of *Troilus and Criseyde*, Chaucer is able to make the transition from earthly to heavenly love acceptable on at least an emotional level, because the love of Troilus and Criseyde has been presented as sharing the universal qualities of the love of God. But in Henryson's poem, by the very nature of his story, earthly love has no such qualities, and no positive alternative can be proposed. There is simply the grim warning—'Your roising reid to rotting sall retour' (464)—and the casting off of illusion—'Be war thairfoir, approchis neir your hour' (468). The pattern disclosed by the poem is in fact meaningless so far as any future action is concerned. From it can be deduced only that 'Fortoun is fikkil quhen scho beginnis and steiris' (469). The poem echoes with the phrase 'no moir.' We have already noticed Cresseid's

> Fra Diomeid had gottin his desyre
> He wox werie and wald of me no moir,   (101–2)

and there is also Troilus's comment,

> I can no moir;
> Scho was untrew and wo is me thairfoir,   (601–2)

and Henryson's last line: 'Sen scho is deid I speik of hir no moir.' The stylistic compression of these sentences results from the very nature of the fictional world that Henryson has opened to us. On such a view of reality, however strong the will to moralize, Cresseid's treachery and her death, once they have themselves been recounted, do leave nothing more to say.

It may appear from what has been said so far that the view of life presented in *The Testament of Cresseid* is merely cruel, and that the conciseness of style that it renders possible would be better described as low than high. It is true that the view is pessimistic, but its pessimism is not felt as a simplification. The gods are malicious, and their punishment of Cresseid is presented not as justice but as an arbitrary vengeance. Cupid asks the other gods, 'Thairfoir ga help to revenge, I yow pray' (294), and later the narrator refers to

> . . . the vengeance and the wraik
> For hir trespas Cupide on hir culd tak.   (370–71)

While not attempting to extenuate Cresseid's evil actions, Henryson invites us to offer her a compassion which will include those actions. We may see this invitation given on a small scale in the movement of a single stanza:

> O fair Cresseid, the flour and A per se
> Of Troy and Grece, how was thow fortunait
> To change in filth all thy feminitie,
> And be with fleschelie lust sa maculait,
> And go amang the Greikis air and lait,
> Sa giglotlike takand thy foull plesance!
> I have pietie thow suld fall sic mischance!   (78–84)

The first two lines seem to offer Cresseid an unqualified pity, which runs the risk of existing only in the mode of sentimentalizing rhetoric. The next four, however, move in a different direction, away from the idea of misfortune and towards that of moral culpability, which is felt particularly strongly in the relentlessness taken on by the conventional tag 'air and lait,' and in the direct accusation of 'takand thy foull plesance.' The stanza's last line reverts to the attitude of its first two, but adds a new depth of meaning: the compassion remains, but it can now be seen that, if we are to use the concept of misfortune, it must include the sins men *choose* to commit. Even the prostitute's 'foull plesance' is a 'mischance' which has befallen her. Again, the gods, for all their malice, are supremely powerful, and to offend them is foolish: thus in Cresseid's own comment on her punishment,

> ... Lo, quhat it is...
> With fraward langage for to mufe and steir
> Our craibit goddis,   (351–3)

blame and justification are nicely balanced in 'fraward' and 'craibit.' The situation is rather like that in some of Euripides' plays—the *Hippolytus*, for example. Gods who are powerful and cruel are set against human beings who are impotent, foolish, and wicked, but who demand our emotional involvement, our compassion, because they are capable of suffering and the gods are not. The *Testament of Cresseid* is a compassionate poem as well as a harsh one. Alongside Cresseid's

> Fra Diomeid had gottin his desyre
> He wox werie and wald of me no moir,

there is the fine humanity of Calchas's greeting to his daughter when she returns to him with her reputation lost: 'Welcum to me; thow art full deir ane gest' (105). Nevertheless, the compassion of the narrator does not blur the harshness of the universe as he sees it:

> O cruell Saturne, fraward and angrie,
> Hard is thy dome and to malitious!
> On fair Cresseid quhy hes thow na mercie,
> Quhilk was sa sweit, gentill and amorous?
> Withdraw thy sentence and be gracious—
> As thow was never; sa schawis through thy deid,
> Ane wraikfull sentence gevin on fair Cresseid.
>   (323–9)

'As thow was never': the human protest is not allowed to interfere with the malice of the gods.

For this reason it is difficult to agree with what seems to be the usual view of the *Testament* as a humane work, in which we see Cresseid 'healed and repentant by the way of suffering, and we are left in mind at peace with her as with Troilus.' This was the view stated forty years ago by Grierson, and it has been repeated more recently by Professor Fox, who writes that 'she has come through her purgatory to purification and wisdom.'[38] It is true that the encounter with Troilus enables Cresseid to look behind her disproportionately severe punishment for blasphemy against Cupid and Venus, and to recognize in herself a deeper guilt—a sin which a Christian audience would recognize as such. She is repentant, certainly, but there is no suggestion of healing or purification. It may be that 'a medieval reader would have been ready to regard Cresseid's leprosy ambivalently, as an affliction, yet one which set her above other human beings';[39] but *in the poem* there is no hint that it sets her above other human beings or leads her to redemption. There are grave dangers involved in importing into a poem written centuries ago our own preconceptions as to what its readers would have looked for in it.[40] It will be safer to follow the poem itself; and what we actually find in the *Testament* is an uncomforting moral application:

> Lovers be war, and tak gude heid about
> Quhome that ye lufe, for quhome ye suffer paine.
> I lat yow wit, thair is richt few thairout
> Quhome ye may traist to have trew lufe agane.
>
> (561–4)

Against this dark background, the beautiful lines of the testament itself, in which the prostitute bequeathes her spirit to the goddess of chastity—

---

[35] Grierson, p. 211, Fox, p. 48. A similar view is expressed by Kurt Wittig, *The Scottish Tradition in Literature* (Edinburgh and London, 1958), p. 49.

[39] Fox, p. 41.

[40] Cf. Fox, p. 58: 'modern readers do not have what Henryson took for granted in his audience: an unquestioned belief in the culpability of sexual love, in the efficacy of penance, and in the existence of an afterlife.'

> My spreit I leif to Diane, quhair scho dwellis,
> To walk with hir in waist woddis and wellis

(587–8)

—can communicate only a pathetic helplessness. Henryson's poem is compassionate, but it is consolatory only in the sense in which any great work of art is so, by its very existence.

Index

(Technical terms used in the *artes poeticae* and *artes praedicandi* are grouped together under the heading 'Rhetorical terms'.)